The Ethics of
HOMICIDE

The Ethics of
HOMICIDE

WITH A NEW PREFACE BY THE AUTHOR

PHILIP E. DEVINE

University of Notre Dame Press
NOTRE DAME AND LONDON

Copyright © 1978 by Cornell University
Cornell University Press
124 Roberts Place
Ithaca, New York 14850

First Published 1978 by Cornell University Press
Published in the United Kingdom by Cornell University Press, Ltd.,
2–4 Brook Street, London W I Y IAA.

Paperback edition 1990
University of Notre Dame Press
Notre Dame, Indiana 46556

Printed in the United States of America

Library of Congress Cataloging-in-Publication Data

Devine, Philip E., 1944–
    The ethics of homicide / Philip E. Devine.
        p.   cm.
    Reprint, with new pref. Originally published: Ithaca : Cornell
University Press, 1978.
    Includes bibliographical references.
    ISBN 0-268-00924-4
    1. Homicide. 2. Ethics. I. Title.
HV6515.D49 1990
179'.7—dc20   89-29098

TO RACHEL

who wept for her children

What should we all most earnestly pray against, and

in all the laws what end is the most eagerly sought?

THAT PEOPLE MAY NOT KILL ONE ANOTHER.

Demosthenes

Contents

Contents

Preface

I HERE ATTEMPT two distinct but overlapping tasks. I examine the moral rule against homicide, its logic, its structure, the arguments that support exceptions to it, its relationship to various traditions of normative ethics, and the relationship of the word "homicide" to such words as "murder." I also present and attempt to defend what I hope is a coherent set of views concerning controversial questions in the ethics of homicide—under which I include abortion, capital punishment, euthanasia, suicide, and war—as well as more recondite questions such as those involving the killing of fat men who block the exits to caves. Perhaps my treatment of these questions will be of interest to theologians, legal scholars, and other citizens as well as to philosophers. The central assumption of both these discussions is that homicide is prima facie wrong in itself, apart from the bad side effects it is also likely to have.

In discussing particular situations, I attempt to take into account the diversity of human problems without lapsing into that pragmatism which, as Bertrand Russell said, "is like a warm bath that heats up so imperceptibly that you don't know when to scream." Expressions of doubt and hesitancy are meant, and no discussion of a case carries with it a claim that I would act as I should even in less difficult situations. About euthanasia, for instance (and I think this remark applies to all sides of the debate), the issues are bound to look very different when the sick person is oneself or someone one cares for. This changed appearance may be a source of moral insight, but then again it may be a source of moral confusion.

I assume throughout that we do have moral obligations (in the sense of acts or abstentions required by morality), in particular obligations to other people, and that it is in principle possible on dispassionate reflection to discover what these obligations are. I make no attempt to refute egoism, subjectivism, immoralism, or moral nihilism. And I am concerned with relativism only in so far as the practice of other cultures might be thought to undercut moral judgments reached here and now.

I gratefully acknowledge the influence of the Christian tradition in the formation of my moral consciousness. And I draw upon classical moral theology both for conceptual equipment and for discussions which, while originally pursued within a particular theological context, are also of wider interest. At the same time, I scrupulously attempt to remove from my argument any religious overtones or assumptions. Incidents from Scripture, and practices such as baptism, are cited as part of our common cultural tradition, not as data possessing theological authority.

This feature is, I believe, one of the strengths of my argument—that I present the grounds for some widely held views without depending upon religious or theological doctrines. Responsible, thinking persons, whether they are of one religious persuasion or another, or none, may perhaps gain insight, or possible reinforcement of their own moral intuitions, by considering a strictly philosophical presentation of arguments for and against some important current practices and ideas.

The problem of how to engage with those who—while they may have objections to deceit or the infliction of pain—have no scruples about homicide as such is complex. The counterargument depends on the contours of the position adopted by such persons. If they claim that the fear aroused by approaching death is an evil, but not the death itself, one can question their underlying concept of the self, insisting, for instance, that we have arms and legs as well as sensations, and that there is a conceptual connection between pain and damage to the body of the sufferer. But if someone insists that only psychic states have ground-level moral significance, there is no knock-down, drag-out argument against him. As far as I can see, hedonism can be maintained as a philosophy of life without the aid of any philosophical errors about pleasure, even though most of its plausibility derives from such errors.

My choice of opponents has been dictated in part by the needs of the present debate rather than by any abstractly philosophical consideration. I make no attempt, for instance, to consider in detail challenges to the commonly held belief that contraception is an acceptable way of avoiding unwanted parenthood, beyond making the obvious point that there is *some* moral difference between contraception and abortion or infanticide. I do, on the other hand, give extensive attention to claims that infanticide is acceptable. From a philosophical standpoint all views of reflective persons, however unmodish, are entitled to attention, and it is hard for me to see how one might justify the exclusion from the intellectual community of the foes of contraception and not the defenders of infanticide. I do not, however, attempt to answer every conceivable opponent, even when there are some reasons to believe that his views may gain ground. While I have something to say, I hope, to those who would painlessly put defective infants to death, I have nothing to say to those who would be prepared to subject babies to vivisection.

The examination of cases and disputed questions is not only interesting and important in its own right. It also contributes to the defense of one of my central theses: that acts of homicide are prima facie seriously wrong because they are acts of homicide, and not for any supposedly more fundamental reason, such as that they tend to produce disutility or are unjust or unkind, and that this prima facie wrongness cannot be overridden by merely utilitarian considerations. A second thesis, which is important in discussions of suicide and euthanasia, is that it is not possible to determine by calculation whether a given life is worth living or not. This means not only that the "rational suicide" defended by many utilitarians is impossible, but also that our ordinary desire to go on living cannot be explained as based on a calculation that we are on the whole better off alive than dead.

A rough guide to the structure of my argument may now prove useful. The Introduction is devoted to a preliminary statement of themes, and to the justification of an ethics of homicide developed as a branch of morality in its own right rather than as a part of a theory of justice or as a set of corollaries to a utilitarian or other comprehensive moral theory. This chapter is somewhat technical and abstract, and its conclusions are largely commonsensical. The chapters on the scope of the prohibition against homicide are concerned with the question: the killing of what creatures is morally speaking homicide? My most controversial conclusion here is that the normal (and at least in most cases the defective) human fetus is a person with a right not to be killed from at least the sixth week of gestation, and that the case for holding that younger fetuses and embryos are persons is by no means weak. Chapter IV is devoted to a defense, rather technical, of two distinctions whose importance for the casuistry of homicide is very great—between direct and indirect killing and between killing and letting die. In the following two chapters, these distinctions are applied in a discussion of the two kinds of justification for homicide which are characteristically offered: that it is required for the sake of others; and that it is in the interests of, or consented to by, the decedent himself. The Conclusion sums up the argument and deals with some radical objections to my entire approach.

Thanks are due to the following, among others, whose comments, encouragement, and criticisms entitle them to share the praise for this book's merits but not the blame for its defects: Peter Garber, Germain Grisez, James Hanink, John Koller, Wallace Matson, Joseph Ryshpan, Charles Sanford, and David Wieck. Thanks are also due to the Inter-Library Loan Departments at North Adams State College and Rensselaer Polytechnic Institute for securing needed materials; to Frances Anderson, Dotti Flores, JoAnne Howley, Linda Switzler, and Marie Waitekus for their typing; to Roger Guttentag and Jim Pullaro for help in proofreading the manuscript; and to the editors of the *American Journal of Jurisprudence*, 19 (1974), 44–60, for permission to use as the basis for Chapter IV an article previously published in their journal.

PHILIP E. DEVINE

Troy, New York

Preface to the
Paperback Edition

SINCE *The Ethics of Homicide* was published in 1978, the necessity of a rational perspective on issues of life and death has become, if possible, even more evident. I offer here some revisions suggested by subsequent reflection and discussion as well as by the experience of using *The Ethics of Homicide* in the classroom.

Religion and Philosophical Ethics

THE FIRST ISSUE is the relationship between religion and philosophical ethics. As I attempted to make clear in the original book, there is no good reason to regard the contribution of religious perspectives to our understanding of issues of life and death as either intellectually or sociopolitically illegitimate. But a need exists for a more narrowly grounded inquiry addressed to persons of all religious beliefs and none, in order to advance public discussion in a society with a constitutional principle requiring the coexistence of a variety of religious and non-religious modes of life.

Hence I assume, for the purpose of argument only, that human existence begins and ends as does the life span of the human organism. I have no philosophical argument against the possibility of an afterlife, nor are my remarks to be understood as a confession of unfaith. But I

1

think it well to explore the implications of a widely shared view against which I have no decisive argument, that death is the unequivocal termination of human existence, especially since these implications are in my view widely misunderstood. For analogous reasons, my discussion of abortion proceeds on the assumption that contraception is legitimate; an examination of this premise would require a significantly different inquiry.

Still, there are limits to how far the intellectual world can be partitioned. Philosophical ethics, in every form with which I am familiar, implicitly or explicitly refers to intuitions shared by author and reader. These intuitions reflect a shared cultural background, including the religious beliefs that have shaped our common culture. My argument therefore leads to—but does not pursue—the issue whether the faith that in some way has molded each of us is tenable or compelling in any form.

Moreover, the possibility remains that my conclusions, however strongly supported in their own terms, might be modified or overridden by distinctly religious considerations, among them the pronouncements of contemporary religious authority. I mention theological issues only to make clear what lies outside the scope of this book; at the same time I wish to affirm that I advance none of my conclusions with such confidence that not even a voice from heaven can disturb them.

In *The Ethics of Homicide* I finessed the question of relativism. Insofar as a relativist accepts a moral code—say as an element in the way of life to which he is committed—he can accept both my premises and my conclusions. But I have since—in my book, *Relativism, Nihilism, and God*—developed a further argument on this issue. Very briefly, relativism is false (and indeed self-destructive), but the arguments for this conclusion do not yield principles of sufficient richness to overcome the de facto relativism characteristic of our culture. Hence we need to keep arguing with one another and hope that our differences will lead neither to civil war nor to the coercive imposition of the point of view of some militant group.

I have also become more aware of the need for a wider perspective in ethical theory, linking questions of killing to other moral issues such as deceit and sexual behavior. Since 1978, John Finnis and Germain

Grisez, with the assistance of Joseph Boyle, have greatly developed their version of natural law ethics in philosophical, theological, and practical contexts. But I remain unconvinced that proportionalist methods of moral reasoning, unsatisfying though they may be, can be wholly unavoided. I hope to publish soon my own version of natural law ethics; it acknowledges that human nature, at least as we know it, is a source both of rational norms and of persistent conflicts that philosophical ethics and practical morals can manage, perhaps, but not resolve.

Conclusions Amplified, Modified

THESE WIDER REFLECTIONS have led me to amplify and modify the conclusions of *The Ethics of Homicide* in some respects.

ABORTION

THE ARGUMENTS in the "masculine voice" that I have developed, while necessary, are not sufficient to an adequate pro-life perspective on the abortion issue. It is also necessary to confront the reasons that have led many writers to conclude that access to abortion *must* be permitted. Chief among these is an entrenched ideological commitment to the availability of abortion as essential to the liberation of women, to which considerations of abstract morality must somehow be made to bend. The relevance of my arguments is somewhat limited because I concentrate almost entirely on the status of the fetus killed in an abortion rather than on the nature and interests of women—as viewed both by women themselves and by men—that also inform the abortion dispute; however decisive the question of fetal rights may be, the situation and needs of pregnant women also require attention. Celia Wolf-Devine has made an indispensable contribution to the discussion by examining the implications of the feminine voice for the abortion debate (see below, Additional Bibliography).

I would go further. What is wrong with the feminist contention that abortion is a "woman's issue" about which men had best be silent, is that women themselves are in deep disagreement about it, as they are about all issues in the ethics of sex and reproduction. Under the circumstances, a male cannot simply defer to the opinions of women.

3

Hence a commentary on the more abstract issues might still be in order, even if the deepest issues about sex, reproduction, and womanhood are left to women to resolve among themselves.

The discussion of abortion in *The Ethics of Homicide* now seems to me in error on one point. There I took very seriously the suggestion that "a necessary criterion of personhood is the possibility that the creature regarded as a person be the object of at least a modicum of sympathy" (p. 84). Thus I concluded that a rational reconstruction of conventional morality would "ascribe a right to live to the fetus or embryo from the sixth week of gestation at the very latest, since this is the latest point at which the possibility of arousing sympathy may be said to begin" (p. 90). My present view, however, is that sympathy is too fickle an emotion to provide a usable criterion of personhood. In particular, the enormous variety of modes of life pursued by human beings, and the difficulty I might feel in sympathizing with those whose mode of life I am disposed to regard as defective or degraded, convinces me that where the right not to be killed is in question, sympathy is not a reliable guide. There remains the question whether, in view of the possibility of the splitting or merging of human zygotes, the appropriate cutoff is not two weeks after conception. It is sobering that so narrow an issue should turn on metaphysical issues of bewildering intricacy. (I here use the postscript added to the selections from *The Ethics of Homicide* reprinted in the second edition of Feinberg's *Problem of Abortion*; see Additional Bibliography).

The most difficult issue is how a notion of human dignity that does not admit of degrees can be placed in a world that contains no sharp edges. The most difficult case is those forms of fetal defect that preclude the development of human capacity, and thus place the embryo outside the scope of the potentiality principle. But the prospect of describing some members of our species as subhuman remains as unattractive as it was when I wrote *The Ethics of Homicide*. Nor do those (animal rights advocates, for example) who place the line between persons and things somewhere other than at the boundaries of the human species escape this problem.

As for the law, it now seems probable that the judiciary can be brought to accept, and public opinion (at least in many jurisdictions) to support, legislation restricting abortion in significant ways, though usually not the sorts of abortion laws that prevailed before the pro-choice movement began. It appears that the *Webster* decision has mortally wounded *Roe*, though it has fallen well short of a decent burial.

An example of more restrictive legislation is the proposal of the American Law Institute: abortion should be permitted only when pregnancy endangers a woman's life or health; in cases of severe fetal defect; or when the child was conceived by rape or incest. Other, more innovative, approaches would work with such notions as parental consent and notification, informed consent, the attempt to eliminate the profit-oriented abortion industry (perhaps by limiting the places where abortions could be performed), and the use of civil rather than criminal penalties. The widely shared perception that abortion becomes worse as pregnancy proceeds should also be reflected in the law, however difficult it may be to provide that perception with a philosophical rationale.

From a moral point of view, such laws might be less than ideal; even jurisprudentially, they would have to be protected against loopholes that would render them meaningless. But the alternative may be a continuation of a situation in which abortion is virtually unregulated, with the result that it can be used to weed out female (or male) offspring. In politics an all-or-nothing attitude is self-defeating. Further discussion belongs to the realm of political strategy and tactics rather than to philosophical analysis. In any event, the prospects of what I would consider an unduly restrictive abortion law being enacted and enforced seem utterly unreal.

A broader political point needs to be made. It is important that pro-life attitudes about abortion be separated from hawkish approaches to foreign policy, vindictive attitudes toward criminals, hostility toward welfare, and indifference toward environmental concerns. Neither logically nor in any other way do such conclusions follow, and confusion on this point can have very bad political effects, both within and outside the sphere of abortion policy. Lest they be forced into the hands of an abortionist by our indifference, women suffering from crisis pregnancies need our help, and they also need help in avoiding such pregnancies in the future. These remarks are not intended to replace detailed discussion of moral and political issues other than abortion: the principle of the seamless garment only provides an orientation with which to approach complex problems.

CAPITAL PUNISHMENT

CAPITAL PUNISHMENT also requires further attention. I assume in the text that punishment for retribution alone is not legitimate, though retributive considerations may be invoked to limit the imposition of punishment. But this assumption at least requires defense. The desire for retribution is deeply ingrained in human nature and is connected with traits we would not want to see disappear, such as disposition to uphold standards of justice even when the forces of injustice appear to have all the cards. Theological questions are difficult to avoid here: one cannot leave vengeance to the Lord unless one believes that there is a Lord to whom vengeance can be left.

OTHER MORAL ANALYSES

SOME DETAILED POINTS of moral analysis also require attention.

Infanticide. In section 11 (pp. 69–73), I examine the view that infants should be treated as "courtesy persons." Under that assumption, I point out that "assuming that at least some value is placed upon nascent life, it would be wasteful to perform a eugenic abortion where there is some doubt that the fetus is defective, if the defect can be diagnosed at birth and the infant then killed without violating anyone's rights" (p. 72). I emphasize that the judgment here is comparative— under some circumstances infanticide might be less wasteful, and for that reason a lesser evil, than abortion. In addition, these remarks are part of a larger argument to the effect that both infants and fetuses are persons in their own right.

Self-execution. I have had difficulty with the case of Socrates, who (in the *Phaedo*) condemns suicide and then takes poison. As a further complication, he believes that the sentence of death imposed on him is unjust, so that his position is similar to that of an executioner with private knowledge of the condemned person's innocence. It now seems to me that his intentions can be construed as follows: I will do what the

6

law requires of me and drink the hemlock, even though I foresee that it will bring about my death; what happens if the hemlock fails to have the expected effect is not my present concern.

The situation of a Japanese warrior ordered to commit *seppuku*, or of a Roman of Nero's court commanded to open his veins, is significantly different in that both are required to wound their own bodies. The situation is that of an executioner, who may act as such as long as he is not convinced that the execution he is asked to perform is unjust.

Nuclear Deterrence. Nuclear deterrence is not, as I argue in the text (section 22 [3d], pp. 164–65), a problem in the ethics of deceit. Rather, we are dealing with a particular sort of conditional intention—one entertained for the express purpose of preventing the situation on which one would act from arising. (Compare the situation of someone who manages to avoid suicide by telling himself that he will be able to kill himself later if things become intolerable.) By both consequentialist and deontological criteria, there seem to be important differences between this form of conditional intention and a straightforward intention to kill. This sort of distinction does not preclude opponents of nuclear deterrence from arguing that the dangers of the policy outweigh its benefits.

Cessation of Artificial Feeding. Another difficult case is the cessation of artificial feeding, even with liquids, of the comatose incurably ill. This case is difficult because our perceptions of normality are divided. Food and liquids taken by mouth are the usual way human beings maintain themselves in being, so the cessation of the availability of food and liquids looks very much like killing (by starvation). On the other hand, it is normal for human beings to be able to chew (or at least swallow their food); while in many circumstances we are obliged to make up for deficiencies here, sometimes artificial feeding might well seem to be unnecessary meddling with the course of nature.

In the absence of a decisive argument of which I am unaware, the question is a matter of prudence, including the important prudential principle that one does not—at least when another person's interests are at stake—go to the limits of the permissible without compelling reason.

7

I his principle has a wide application both within and outside the ethics of homicide.

Prudence. The mention of prudence leads to a more general point. My somewhat schematic discussion conceals the fact that moral principles are guides to prudence rather than substitutes for it. Prudence may generate constraints on its own exercise, as Ulysses did when he instructed his crew to bind him so that he could hear the Sirens with impunity. Still, the selection of these constraints and their application to concrete cases is a matter of virtue using its head rather than of the quasi-mechanical application of rules.

Suicide

THE LARGEST CHANGE in my views concerns suicide. The discussion in *The Ethics of Homicide* suffers from a double deficiency: it focuses too much on self-killing at the expense of other forms of self-injury; it is unduly concerned with morality as a form of social control rather than as an ethics of self-perfection. Since there are important limits to the extent suicide can be prevented by social control, emphasis on that aspect of morality will tend to place suicide outside the moral realm.

Consider moral suicide—the decision to rid oneself of the burdens of moral reasoning and choice, for example by joining a cult in which every decision, even the most intimate and detailed, is made by the cult's authorities, who employ psychological manipulation to extinguish the members' capacity to evaluate or resist their dictates. While libertarian concerns might restrain us from active interference, at least when no children are involved, few of my readers will, I hope, regard such a way of life as a good one. And if moral suicide is excluded from our conception of an admirable way of life, the same will be true of physical suicide. Questions of justification and excuse remain, however.

I remain convinced, however, of the truth of the central doctrine that informs my discussion of suicide and euthanasia, namely that death is opaque and thus incommensurate with life. (I am replying here

8

to the critical discussions of David Mayo and Michael Wreen, listed in the Additional Bibliography.)

In *The Ethics of Homicide*, I argue: 1) In order to choose rationally to bring about a certain state of affairs, one must know what one is choosing. 2) But we do not know what death is. Hence, 3) we cannot rationally choose to die.

First, my argument implies that the decision to continue living is not, in a certain sense, rational: it does not rest upon the weighing of alternatives. To say this is not to "condemn the choice *not* to suicide," as Mayo would have it, but to make a conceptual point about our ordinary desire to go on living. We are self-continuing beings, who, before any consideration of alternatives, naturally desire to preserve ourselves in being, at least until something takes place that throws this desire into question. It is no more necessary to defend our habitual desire to go on living against skeptical attack than it is necessary to defend the habitual trust we place in our senses. That skepticism, once admitted in principle, turns out to be unanswerable in either case is no cause for alarm.

Second, the opaqueness of death is not merely a matter of imperfect information. Once we grant, for the sake of argument, that death is annihilation, then there is nothing further to know. Our ignorance of death so conceived is a fact of metaphysics: the annihilation of the self is radically incomparable with any of the possible futures, pleasant or otherwise, that we may imagine for ourselves. It is this incomparability of death with its alternatives that defeats the attempts to choose death rationally.

Third, we may ask, Why not make the decision to live or die on the basis of the information available to us? The decision to live or die would then seem to be in a rationally privileged position, since one side of the balance is logically complete.

The inadequacy of this criticism can be seen by imagining a case in which a person, despite the logically complete information he is supposed to possess, is nonetheless undecided about suicide. Such a person can, to be sure, further examine his life prospects, but further information about them may not be available. The issue, moreover, is frequently not the lack of information about one's life prospects, but the strength and persistence of one's desire to die. One possibility is that he gives himself another day; sometimes the desire for death then prevails and sometimes not. But the further information by which he could rationally regulate his desire to live or die is not available and cannot become available. The "logical completeness" of one side of this balance conceals the lack of criteria by which a decision can be made and evaluated.

It remains only to explain how a generally rational person whose reason is not openly incoherent might reach a different conclusion. It is easy to take literally one's imaginative representations, say the portrayal of death as perpetual or even as prolonged sleep, and to prefer death represented in this way to the sort of continued life that lies before one.

Fourth, Wreen suggests that my argument precludes not only a rational decision to choose death, but also a rational decision to risk death, or to accept it as an unintended consequence of one's actions. But it seems to me that the distinction between intention and foresight continues to be relevant in prudential contexts—or, more deeply, that the sort of prudence that takes into account only consequences is out of place when death is at issue (if indeed it is in place anywhere). What someone does when he decides to take a pain reliever that may shorten his life is to compare the relative attractiveness of two lives—one highly painful (but perhaps containing some possibility of knowledge or friendship), and one lived in or near complete unconsciousness. The fact that the second life is shorter than the first enters deliberation only obliquely.

Finally, I deny that it is necessary to know death in order to regard it as an evil. Our avoidance of death, like our repugnance to damage to our bodies, is an instinctive reaction before it enters reflective judgment. Further, the sort of knowledge that (I am supposing for the sake of argument) is all we have—that death is the annihilation of the self—does not make it possible for us to choose death rationally. For it does not permit us to understand what death is like and to compare it with other alternatives.

But the issue can be put more sharply. I may, looking back on a particularly bad day, think that I would have preferred to have spent the entire day in deep, dreamless sleep. And if I know that tomorrow will be just as bad as today, I might prefer to spend tomorrow in deep, dreamless sleep. Hence if I know that all the remaining days of my life are going to be just as bad as today, I might prefer to spend the rest of my life in deep, dreamless sleep, not waking before I die. And if I know that death, from a subjective point of view, is identical to a deep, dreamless sleep from which I do not wake, I might rationally prefer to die right now. Such would be the case, for example, if my entire prospective future were one of torture.

This argument appears to depend on an assumption made only by utilitarians: the value of my life depends wholly on my states of consciousness. Usually, though not inevitably, those who think this way will identify good states of consciousness with pleasure and bad states of consciousness with pain. But a person may experience all the states of consciousness associated with friendship and not enjoy the good of friendship itself. Such will be the case if his supposed friend secretly despises him and is using their relationship for monetary or other ulterior purposes.

Once we grant that the value of my life does not depend wholly on the states of consciousness that comprise it, there will be an important difference between death and a deep, dreamless sleep from which waking is at least possible. Even from the subjective point of view, deep, dreamless sleep differs from death, for a preference for deep, dreamless sleep over some alternative derives importantly from the experience of waking rested.

True, when I opt for an anaesthetic before having my appendix taken out, I do not want the experience of feeling rested but the absence of pain. What I want is to exist in a painless state rather than in a painful one; that this is a state of unconsciousness does not matter unless the value of my life is wholly a matter of consciousness. In addition, my desire for deep, dreamless sleep is not a desire to wake feeling rested; rather it is in the light of the possibility of a rested waking that I may come to regard deep, dreamless sleep as desirable.

A more moderate reading is that the negative value of my states of consciousness can *in some circumstances* override the other values my life may hold. When we ask what these circumstances are, however, we need to compare our present situation—bad states of consciousness and all—with death. And it is this sort of comparison whose possibility is at issue here. That comparing some other future to death is not the same as comparing it to dreamless sleep follows immediately from the premise that death is not dreamless sleep.

But there are kinds of suicide not touched at all by my argument against "balance sheet" suicide. Suicide as a substitute for destroying the universe is, considered in terms of the agent's intentions, the worst thing a person can do (or very nearly so). Suicide to protect others against oneself is analogous to killing another person to protect third parties, as long as the harmful behavior one is trying to prevent (say giving information under the influence of a drug) is beyond one's control.

But there is another kind of suicide, whose possible justification at least requires further discussion. I refer to what may be called, in a broad sense, suicides of honor. These include not only the suicide of an aristocratic warrior acting in accordance with the code of his caste, but also that of a patient at the Mayo clinic who kills himself to prevent the use of his comatose body for experiments he finds degrading. As this last example shows, dishonor need not involve pain, though people are usually pained to believe that they have incurred dishonor.

A suicide of honor implies a judgment that, viewed from outside— whether from a "God's eye point of view," or from the standpoint of the *mores* of a given society—a life is better ended than continued. The Christian teaching that any situation, however degrading, can be a source of spiritual goods excludes the possibility of justified suicides of honor, but this premise is not available for strictly philosophical arguments.

An adolescent contemplating the world within and outside himself could easily conclude that his prospects of living a life worthy of human dignity are negligible, and for that reason kill himself. Most of us would do everything we can to dissuade such adolescents from suicide. It is not at all evident, however, what principles distinguish such adolescent suicides from other suicides of honor with which we may be in greater sympathy.

* * *

This preface concludes with a question of terminology and my acknowledgments. The expression *present enjoyment principle* has proved misleading, especially to students. I now prefer the expression *present possession principle.*

Finally, I wish to thank all those persons whose belief in the value of my work has helped me continue it through the academic depression, especially those who do not accept my conclusions; persons and institutions from which one might have expected support have not always been so helpful. I wish to thank Father Lockary for giving me access to and providing for my instruction in the use of Stonehill College's excellent computer, and Dr. Ray Pepin for continuing my account. Special thanks are due to Michael Wreen, whose reading of *The Ethics of Homicide* was the start of a fruitful intellectual friendship; and, as always, to Celia Wolf-Devine.

Additional Bibliography

GENERAL

Devine, Philip E. *Relativism, Nihilism, and God.* Notre Dame, Ind.: University of Notre Dame Press, 1989.
Donagan, Alan. *The Theory of Morality.* Chicago: University of Chicago Press, 1977.
Finnis, John. *Foundations of Morality.* Washington, D.C.: Georgetown University Press, 1983.
———. *Natural Law and Natural Rights.* Oxford: Clarendon Press, 1988.
Grisez, Germain. *The Way of the Lord Jesus.* Vol. 1: *Christian Moral Principles.* Chicago: Franciscan Herald Press, 1983.

LIFE, DEATH, AND KILLING

Wreen, Michael. "The Logical Opaqueness of Death." *Bioethics* 1 (1987): 366–71.

ABORTION

Campbell, Courtney S., et al. "Abortion: Searching for Common Ground." *Hastings Center Report* 19 (July/August 1989): 22–37.
Feinberg, Joel. *The Problem of Abortion.* 2nd ed. Belmont, Cal.: Wadsworth, 1984.

Glendon, Mary Ann. *Abortion and Divorce in Western Law*. Cambridge, Mass.: Harvard University Press, 1987.

Sumner, L. W. *Abortion and Moral Theory*. Princeton: Princeton University Press, 1981.

Wolf-Devine, Celia. "Abortion and the 'Feminine Voice.'" *Public Affairs Quarterly*, July 1989.

CASE: *Webster v. Reproductive Health Services*, United States Supreme Court, decided 3 July 1989.

STATUS OF NONHUMANS

Regan, Tom. *The Case for Animal Rights*. Berkeley: University of California Press, 1983.

WAR, CAPITAL PUNISHMENT, AND POLITICAL VIOLENCE

Finnis, John, Joseph Boyle, and Germain Grisez. *Nuclear Deterrence, Morality and Realism*. Oxford: Clarendon Press, 1988.

SUICIDE AND EUTHANASIA

Battin, M. P., and D. J. Mayo, eds. *Suicide*. New York: St. Martin's Press, 1980.

Grisez, Germain, and Joseph Boyle. *Life and Death with Liberty and Justice: A Contribution to the Euthanasia Debate*. Notre Dame, Ind.: University of Notre Dame Press, 1979.

Lynn, Joanne, ed. *By No Extraordinary Means*. Bloomington: Indiana University Press, 1986.

Mayo, David. "The Concept of Rational Suicide." *Journal of Medical Ethics* 11 (1986): 143–155.

I /

INTRODUCTION

I BEGIN by defending the claim that what makes homicide presumptively wrong is, centrally, that it produces the death of the victim. I use conceptual analysis to establish the evaluations implicit in our ordinary ways of talking and then defend these evaluations. I then argue that death is an evil incommensurable with other evils such as the suffering of pain, and that unjustified killing is a wrong not reducible to injustice or cruelty. Then I examine three traditions of moral theory—utilitarianism, social contract, and natural law—and conclude that none of them is adequate to the ethics of homicide.

1. Murder

THE TERM "MALICE," which occurs in the traditional legal definition of murder, is misleading both from a moral and from a legal standpoint. It is of course not necessary that a murderer act with malicious glee—he need not even feel hatred for his victim. What is more, there is no requirement that a murderer act from a bad motive. If I kill my rich uncle in order to benefit a charity to which he is leaving his money (let us suppose that he is about to change his will in favor of his cat), my motives may be excellent but I am a murderer nonetheless.

The somewhat more plausible definition of murder (in the moral sense) as "wrongful killing [of humans]" is wrong in two ways. First, not every intentional killing of a human being which is morally wrong is murderous. In law, provocation may reduce a charge of murder to manslaughter. And though it is morally speaking wrong to kill even combatants in an unjust war, most moralists would find it harsh to call an ordinary German soldier's killing of Polish soldiers in the invasion of 1939 "murder." (Legally speaking it was no offense at all.)[1]

The second difficulty arises because not all wrongful homicides are wrong because they are homicide. Suppose a man ensconced in a tower at a university and shooting the crowds below also is in possession of the key to a cure for cancer, which he will disclose if captured. It might be wrong, but hardly murder, for the police, knowing this to be the case, to kill him to stop his escapade, even though the alternative ways of stopping him involve some greater risk to them and to third parties.

Consider by contrast wrongful assertion. An assertion may be morally objectionable for a number of reasons: it may be a falsehood; it may be the disclosure of information given in confidence; it may be unnecessarily wounding to the hearer, whether true or false. In no case is a wrongful assertion wrong because it is an assertion (although one would still want to distinguish assertions that are wrong because of their content from otherwise innocuous assertions that cause avalanches by their sound).

Equally, one ought not to define murder as (say) the direct killing of an innocent person, however innocence is specified. Defenders of mercy-killing should not be foreclosed from arguing that the killing of the innocent is not always murder, nor should pacifists and opponents of capital punishment be foreclosed from arguing that killing of the guilty and of those threatening harm is murder nonetheless. Such moralists might be in error, of course, but their claims should be refuted in substance rather than by definition.

The word "murder" stands to "homicide" much as the word "lie" stands to "falsehood." A lie is not just a wrongful falsehood, but wrong because it is a falsehood, even though not all falsehoods are lies. Although not all homicides are murders, still that an act is homicide states a reason for regarding it as murder and hence as wrong. The conclusion that an intentional homicide is murder can be refuted, but unless a refutation is provided, the conclusion need not be defended.

It follows that it is quite acceptable to say, in explaining why a given act is wrong, that the act is murder. If murder simply meant "wrongful homicide" (as a similar word might mean "wrongful assertion"), the

16

statement "Act A is wrong because it is a murder" would be a trivial remark, like "Act A is wrong because it is wrong." But to say that an act is wrong because it is murder is to say that the act is wrong because it is homicide, and to indicate further that none of the possible justifications or mitigation of homicide obtain.

Calling an act murder presupposes that, since the act is homicide, that is a reason why the act is wrong. At a minimum, a rule of thumb to the effect that acts of homicide usually satisfy some more fundamental criterion of wrongfulness is a requirement for employing the concept of murder, and there is a strong suggestion in the concept's structure that there is a prima facie obligation to abstain from homicide not reducible to anything more basic. Someone who believes that homicide is morally neutral would be forced to say of "murder," as Oscar Wilde once did of "blasphemy," that it is not one of his words. The evaluation of the view that homicide is morally neutral is a matter of substantive morality, not of conceptual analysis, but our possession of a concept of murder testifies to the existence of a contrary intuition that deserves respect. I will in any case want to argue that the concept of murder should be retained, and that the fully deliberate killing of a human being, if it is not to be murder, will have to be justified in some way other than its being best on the whole (discussed in section 20).[2]

2. *Why Killing Is Bad*

ONE DISTINCTION between irreducible moral rules and moral rules that obtain because experience has shown that violating them tends to produce bad results is that in the one case the harm done by violation is specified in the rule itself (the act as described is inherently wrong), whereas the harm feared from violation of the latter kind of rule is extrinsic to its violation. Thus, for an act-utilitarian, the infliction of pain is inherently wrong, whereas lying is not; for many other moralists, lying is inherently wrong, for the evil that issues from a lie is deceit. (It is necessary to distinguish kinds of acts that are inherently wrong [wrong because they are that kind of act] from kinds of acts that are necessarily wrong [every instance of that kind of act is wrong, regardless of circumstances]. Inflicting pain is of course not necessarily wrong for the act-utilitarian.) As part of an argument for the autonomous status of the moral rule against homicide, I argue that the principal or central, although not necessarily the worst, harm inflicted by homicide is the death of the victim.[3] To avoid question-begging, I shall call the victim the "decedent" in the course of my argument.

Harms produced by an act of homicide are of four sorts: harms to the killer, harms to the decedent's friends,[4] harms to the society in which killer, decedent, and others live, and harms to the decedent. I argue first, that harm to the decedent is central to our condemnation of homicide, and that other harms, while important, are distinctly subsidiary to this harm. I then examine the nature of the harm to the decedent.

A killer may be harmed by being made a worse person by having done something which is wrong or which he thinks is wrong. He may also be harmed by being rendered more likely to do wrong in the future, and he may suffer social (including criminal) penalities as well as remorse. The harm inherent in being the perpetrator of a wrongful act cannot, of course, explain why the act was wrong in the first place, for assessment of such harm is not independent of judgment as to the character of the act. If the act is not wrong, but the agent thinks it is, he will be harmed, but in this case we will want, if possible, to change his moral beliefs rather than get him to abandon that kind of act. That killing in one context may lead to killing in others may be of use in arguing from the wrongfulness of one kind of killing to the wrongfulness of others, but it does not explain why these original cases of homicide are wrong. Nor is the harm involved in the punishment or remorse suffered by the killer essential to the wrongfulness of homicide. It would neither justify nor mitigate a killing that the killer suffered no remorse and escaped all penalties. Rather, it is the wrongfulness of the killing which—in one way or another—justifies both penalties and remorse.

The decedent's friends will lose his companionship, and his family also may suffer financial loss. To a limited extent these harms can be made up by replacing the decedent with someone else having roughly similar qualities. Moreover, when a friend leaves the country, almost all the losses of this sort which one experiences when someone dies may be experienced, and yet such a parting is not death. To be sure, if someone were to undergo a period of suspended animation from which he was to be roused only when all his friends were dead, the emotions he and his friends would feel at parting would draw on grief for one dead, as well as on the regret one feels before a permanent separation resulting from a journey. But the very reason that such a parting is not death—that both sides will continue to live and have experiences afterward—makes possible the kind of attenuated companionship which is possible between friends who will never see one another again (and which accounts in part for attempts to mitigate death by such expressions as "He is just away").

There is also a kind of loss which cannot be lessened by replacing the decedent with someone like him—the loss of that unique human being, expressed in what we call (in the fullest sense) "grief." It would be a mistake to treat grief merely as a kind of mental pain, conceptually unconnected with the death that both explains and justifies it. While grief or something like it without death is possible, because it lacks the intelligibility of ordinary grief, it also lacks clear moral weight. Hence when Margaret mourns for fallen foliage, it remains for Hopkins to make her grief intelligible to us: she is grieving for herself, and for all mankind.

Harm to society is not, I think, a distinct consideration. Society is made worse by wrongdoing within it, both directly and through the weakening of the force of its moral norms, and will suffer from loss of the services of at least some of its members. Again, there is something like collective grief, arising from the rupture of what may be called social friendship when one member of a society is lost by death. There is finally the anxiety that spreads within a group of people when lives are in danger. But these harms are the consequences of the kinds of harm suffered by wrongful killers, their victims and prospective victims, and their victims' friends and families. Materially, a society might be better off if one fifth (say) of its members were killed.

Someone who is killed is, or may be, harmed in three ways: (1) by being put in fear of being killed, (2) by suffering pain, and (3) by losing his life. Harms (1) and (2) may be suffered when homicide is only threatened or attempted, and harm (3) can be suffered without the decedent's suffering harms (1) and (2). I shall argue that, just as the grief felt by the family and friends of the decedent and the brutalization of the killer are derivative harms, so the other aspects of the harm suffered by the decedent are derivative from the loss (or threatened loss) of his life.

19

That human beings normally fear death and seek to avoid it is not an accident. The connection between death on the one hand and fear and avoidance behavior on the other does not invariably obtain, but the connection is not thereby rendered merely contingent, any more than the fact that human beings do not always try to get what they want means that the connection between wanting and trying to get is merely contingent. Fear and avoidance of death are connected to and continuous with the fact that human beings are, among other things, organisms: self-maintaining systems that, often without any explicit consciousness of what they are doing, seek what will maintain them in existence and ward off what threatens to destroy them. Indeed, even the case of someone attempting to kill himself confirms this remark: the suicide must defeat both his body's mechanisms of defense (e.g., the vomiting of poison) and his own "animal" horror of annihilation if he is to be successful. And these phenomena are as intimately connected as are the pain of burnt flesh and the reflex movement of a burnt member away from the fire.

Likewise it is not a mere contingency that death is often painful. There is a conceptual connection between pain and damage to the body; in attempting to determine whether ambiguous expressions, including words in an unknown tongue, are in fact expressions of pain, and not for instance sexual pleasure, we would look for correlations between these expressions and bodily damage. (Damage to the body is of course not the only criterion of pain, else we would be unable to recognize expressions of pleasure in a sexual masochist.) And death and bodily damage are also conceptually linked: death, as opposed to suspended animation, is damage to, or deterioration of, the body so severe as to prevent the continued functioning of the organism.

Although I am not now arguing from the biological concept of a self-maintaining system to that of a moral wrong, but only to that of harm or injury, is-ought problems are beginning to surface. Suffice it for the moment to say that the notion of a self-maintaining system is as much, or as little, ethically neutral, as that of a desire, and that the needs of self-maintaining systems argue that some of our desires can be viewed as reflection of our structure as self-maintaining beings.

Loss of life, then, is the central harm inflicted by an act of homicide. This is a harm that can be inflicted on any organism; plants,

20

nonhuman animals, and human organisms of every stage of development including the embryonic can all suffer loss of life. A consequence is that plants (and consequently animals and all members of the human species without exception) have interests, so that, if the sole logically necessary condition of ascription of rights is having interests, it makes sense (although nearly everyone would consider it mistaken as a matter of normative ethics) to say that plants have rights, whereas the ascription of rights to rocks, oceans, or swamps makes no sense whatever.

Joel Feinberg denies that plants have interests, but his discussion contains concessions sufficient for his refutation.[5] Plants have needs (e.g., for light and water); some things are good for them and some bad; and plants, even weeds, can be said to thrive or flourish quite independently of human interests. (That such flourishing is often defined in a human-centered way is true also of animals, who clearly have interests.) Furthermore, that plants are not conscious does not mean that they cannot be harmed. It is possible to harm an unconscious person; indeed to harm him in such a way that he will never become aware that he has been harmed (not only by killing him, but also by reducing him to idiocy). I do not want to argue that there is *no* sense of "interest" in which "plants cannot have interests" is true (it is clear, for instance, that plants cannot make prudential decisions). My point is simply that there is a sense of "interests" in which plants can and do have interests, and thus can be harmed.

It follows that one cannot defend the killing of any living being whatever on the grounds that it is incapable of suffering loss, though one might still argue that the loss is of negligible moral importance. Sissela Bok objects to this proposition in the case of the embryo: "I find that I cannot use words like 'deprived,' 'deny,' 'take away,' and 'harm' when it comes to the group of cells [developing into a human infant], whereas I have no difficulty using them for the hermit. Do these words require, if not a person conscious of his loss, at least someone who at a prior time has developed enough to be or have been conscious thereof?"[6] But loss comprises two elements: that one no longer possesses a certain good, when one has had it in possession or clear prospect of possession; and the sense of loss arising from the knowledge or belief that the first element of loss is present.[7] Let us call the first element of loss the "objective" and the second the "subjective" element of loss. In any instantaneous killing the subjective element of loss is absent; in any killing whatever the subjective element can only take the form of expectation, since the dead are never conscious of having lost their lives (supposing death to be annihilation). Hence it is hard to see why any subjective element should be required at all for it to be possible to speak of loss of life, or to regard it as an evil. A being that is now alive and has a prospect of continued life can lose its life whatever its state of consciousness, past or present. (One can never be deprived of one's past consciousness in any case.)

Moreover, the death of the victim alone is sufficient to render homicide wrongful. Consider the case of someone—about to die of a fatal blood disease—whose final act is painlessly to kill a sleeping hermit. [8] It is clear that, absent unlikely justifications, such an act would be murder, although the hermit suffers neither fear nor pain, has no friends to mourn him (or at least no friends who learn of his death), and the killer by his timely dying removes himself as a social danger. Likewise, it would be (at least) murder for a human being to annihilate the universe, although the annihilation would destroy the agent along with his victims, leave no one behind to mourn the dead, and happen so quickly that there would be no time for fear or pain. [9] So also the killing of an embryo might be considered murder, even though those who might mourn its death are parties to the act, though the embryo itself suffers neither fear nor pain, and though the act is socially isolated from all other possible cases of killing.

I conclude that the death of the person killed is the central wrong inflicted by an unjustified killing. It does not follow that all such killings are equally bad, even apart from the possible existence of mitigations. The loss of an irreplaceable human being is a serious one, even apart from that person's death. It would not be much consolation to parents whose children were stolen (and raised, let us say, in at least as good circumstances as they would be able to provide), that they can always have other children. And this kind of loss is not produced, of course, by the killing of a friendless orphan.

What is more: if one gauges the harm done by killing in terms of what the person killed loses by being killed, then not all killings would be equally damaging to their victims. In particular it would be in general worse to kill young people than old ones. This last point has a disturbing corollary: to the extent that the length and richness of future life is the measure of the badness of a killing, it is worse to destroy a burdensome embryo than it is to destroy a burdensome aged person. In other words, geronticide is a less objectionable way of dealing with social (e.g., demographic) problems than is abortion. Against this kind of argument must be set the egalitarian intuition that all people are essentially equal, and that one homicide is therefore just as bad as any other.

If the foregoing arguments are sound, we now have grounds to reject the distinction, upon which Glanville Williams founds his treatment of homicide, between aspects of the law and ethics of homicide which rest on "pragmatic considerations of the most obvious kind" and those which are "the expression of a philosophical attitude rather than the outcome of a social necessity,"[10] or at least to insist that it cannot be pressed in the way Williams wants to press it. To be sure, some forms of homicide are more socially disruptive than others, and the desire to spare those who could be done away with without undue scandal does reflect something like a philosophical attitude. But, if the principal harm done by homicide is the death of the victim, social disruption is a subsidiary matter. Moreover, the value attached to social stability and solidarity is philosophically disputable, particularly if society itself is an instrument of homicide on a large scale, or if social stability is maintained by lynching or the like. To argue in this way is not, of itself, to determine how serious a loss the loss of a given individual's life is, nor is it to settle the conditions (if any) under which an individual's life can be rightfully taken. The point is that the taking of the life of any organism is a harm to that organism, and that this harm is at least sometimes the decisive and central reason for regarding an act of killing as seriously wrong.

3. Why Death Is an Evil

I SHALL NOW ATTEMPT to define with greater precision why death is an evil. In so doing, I shall assume that death is the unequivocal termination of human existence. Even such expressions as "death is eternal sleep" will be, on this assumption, euphemistic evasions of the reality of annihilation, or else a kind of subdued mythology. In the same spirit, I shall bar any appeal to certain kinds of extreme materialist contentions, for instance that I am my body in the sense that I will also be my corpse, so that what happens to my corpse will also happen to me (although I will not feel it). A human person, I shall be assuming, is something which normally has arms, legs, thoughts, and intentions, and which comes to be at birth, conception, or some time in between (precisely when will be discussed in section 12) and ceases to be at death.

A celebrated Epicurean argument runs as follows: since death is annihilation, since (in Aristotle's phrase) "nothing is thought to be any longer good or bad for the dead,"[11] it follows not that death is the greatest of all evils but that death is no evil at all. Fear of death is irrational, because there is nothing of the appropriate sort—no state or condition of ourselves as conscious beings—to be afraid of in death.[12] I shall consider two major replies to this argument found in the current literature, reaching my own—already suggested in section 2—by a process of elimination.

Before doing this, however, I wish to discuss critically the common contention that death may sometimes be an object of rational choice, and to attempt to support the claim (for which the testimony of sensitive persons is overwhelming) that there is something uncanny about death, especially one's own, without falling into the logical errors criticized by someone like Paul Edwards.[13] I do not want to deny that a suicide can be calmly and deliberately, and in that sense rationally, carried out. But then someone might calmly and deliberately do something blatantly foolish or even pointless, and it is sometimes rational to act quickly and with passionate fervor. But if, as seems plausible, a precondition of rational choice is that one know *what* one is choosing, either by experience or by the testimony of others who have experienced it or something very like it, then it is not possible to choose death rationally. Nor is any degree of knowledge of what one desires to escape by death helpful, since rational choice between two alternatives requires knowledge of both. The issue is not whether pain (say) is bad, but whether a certain degree of pain is worse than death. It might seem at least that progressively more intense misery gives progressively stronger reasons for killing oneself, but the situation is rather like this. If one is heating a metal whose melting point one does not know at all, one knows that the more heat one applies, the closer one gets to melting the metal. But it does not follow that it is possible to know—before the metal actually starts melting—that one has even approached the melting point.

It is necessary, however, seriously to consider the contention that there are experiences—being flayed and kept alive by ingenious means afterwards for instance—in preference to which it is clearly rational to choose death. At this point in the argument it is necessary to separate the claim that such a choice would be rationally required (that it would not be rational to decide to continue to live under such circumstances) from the claim that it is rationally permitted (that it might be rational both to decide to live and to decide to die). As far as the first of these possibilities is concerned, I do not see how someone could be considered irrational if he decides to show what a human being is capable of enduring. As for the second, while it is true that suicide under such circumstances has a powerful appeal, so does suicide in many other circumstances as well, such as when one will otherwise be exposed to disgrace and dishonor of an extreme sort, or when one is convinced that one's unbearable emotional difficulties will never be resolved. Perhaps all these kinds of suicide are rational too (although contemporary defenders of the possibility of rational suicide do not commonly think so), but if so their rationality is not of the calculative sort. We are dealing, that is, not with a situation concerning which rational men will exhibit a range of estimates, but with a situation in which one man's estimate is as good as another, because what is being done is a comparison with an unknown quality.

I do not mean to imply that we can have no knowledge of what death is, that we cannot for instance teach a child the meaning of "death." But consider what we can do. We can show the child a corpse, but a corpse is not a dead person (that is, not in the required sense of something which is dead and a person, something one of *us*—except in a stretched sense—could be), but only what a person leaves behind when he dies. We can make the child a witness at a deathbed, but to do that is simply to show a living person becoming a corpse. We can tell the child that death is not seeing friends any more (and so on), but somehow he will have to learn how to take these negatives properly, since otherwise death will be confused with all one's friends' leaving town. Finally, we can tell him a myth, even a subdued one such as

25

"death is everlasting sleep," or that death is the absence of life, much as nakedness is the absence of clothing. (In nakedness, of course, the person who existed clothed continues to exist unclothed.) And that such mythology is logically appropriate is part of what I shall call the opaqueness of death.

The opaqueness of death does not result from uncertainty as to our condition afterward, although what I am getting at is sometimes expressed in such terms. My point is rather that it is folly to think that one can housebreak death by representing it as annihilation. One might—considering that the opaqueness of death is a *logical* opaqueness—be tempted to compare the qualms I have expressed about rationally choosing death with skeptical qualms about our right to believe that the sun will rise tomorrow, which rest on the logical difference between inductive and deductive reasoning. To press this comparison would be a mistake, however, for two reasons. First, we routinely have to make choices based on inductive evidence, whereas we do not routinely choose to die or to go on living. Second, the myths cited indicate that the opaqueness of death is a real element in human motivation and self-understanding, an element that cannot be neglected even, or especially, if one considers these myths all to be false.

Human beings characteristically find themselves in profound imaginative and intellectual difficulty when they attempt to envisage the end of their existence. This difficulty is not lessened by the experience of sleep, since sleep, even when dreamless, presupposes the continuation of the self in being and the possibility of an awakening. (I say the possibility, since someone might die before he wakes, and Sleeping Beauty remains alive though asleep even if Prince Charming never arrives.) Nor is the difficulty lessened by interviewing those whose hearts have stopped and who have revived, since what one would learn about in that way is not death but apparent dying.

The difficulty does not lie, at least not centrally, in imagining a world without me, but rather in connecting this world with my (self-regarding) concerns. (Altruistic and disinterested concerns are not at issue at this particular point, since they do not bear on the question of why death can be an evil for the dead person himself. In any case, an altruistic suicide can be rational or irrational in a straightforward way: I might be rational in believing that my suicide will protect my comrades

26

from the secret police, whereas if I lived I would talk and they would be captured and tortured to death, and I might be quite unrealistic in my calculation of the effect my self-immolation will have on public opinion.) Even my aversions, my desires not to experience certain things, do not connect easily with such a world, since there is for instance a logical gap between "freedom from pain" resulting from the nonexistence of the subject of pain and ordinary painless existence. To put the same point another way, if I am contemplating suicide, I am not trying to choose (not centrally, that is) "between future world-courses: the world-course which contains my demise, say, an hour from now, and several possible ones which contain my demise at a later point."[14] What I am contemplating is much more intimate than a world-course. It is my own (self-chosen) death, and such a choice presents itself inevitably as a leap in the dark.

But the decision to kill oneself—it might be argued—need not reflect a preference of death over life, but rather of one (shorter) life over another, or of one (speedier) death over another. The clearest cases of preferences of this sort are choices it would be odd to call suicide. I might take a remedy that makes my present life more tolerable, while somewhat shortening its length, or I might, being tied up and about to be hanged, decide to jump rather than wait to be pushed. Self-execution is in a class apart from ordinary suicide in any case, as any reader of the *Phaedo* might confirm, and it may be possible to speak of self-execution even in cases where the person convicted does what the executioner ought to do, and commutes, with his own hand, a painful and degrading death to one that is relatively painless. The distinction between choosing death rather than life and choosing one kind of life or death rather than another does not turn, in any case, on the nearness of the death in question. A remedy that makes present life more tolerable may shorten a life expectancy of forty years to thirty-five, or of a week to a day. And if a twenty-year-old should choose irrevocably to be killed at seventy, it would, I think, be fair to say that he had chosen death (at seventy) in preference to old age. (The distinction between suicide strictly speaking [choice of death] and choice resulting in death will be further clarified in Chapter VI, and the various kinds of suicide will be further discussed in section 26.)

One can perhaps get a better grip on what is involved here by comparing the choice of death with other radical and irreversible choices. (Some first-time choices, e.g., to visit London, present no problem, since one knows that one can always cut one's losses if things do not turn out as desired.) In many of these choices one can be guided, in part at any rate, by the experience of those who have gone before, but this will not always work, since there had to be a first person to undergo a sex-change operation, take LSD, and so on. Choices of this sort are not necessarily irrational, but if rational (they may be neither rational nor irrational on the theory of prudence with which I am working), their rationality must be explained in terms of the general rationality of risk-taking (which is supported to a degree by experience). This notion does not seem to apply in the case of choosing death. The difference between these choices and that of death is a logical one. While it is logically possible (even if not possible in this particular case) to get an idea of what it is like to have taken LSD, from someone who has done so, death is of necessity that from which no one returns to give tidings.

One might, indeed, attempt to explain our fear of death in precisely these terms: fear of death is fear of the unknown. Of course this is a metaphor, since the opaqueness of death is logical rather than epistemological. But the unknown is attractive as well as fearful, and death has in fact, alongside its fearfulness, the attractiveness which is a feature of the limits of human experience. It does not seem possible, on these premises alone, to resolve the tension between death's fearfulness and its attractiveness.

Bernard Williams's reply to Lucretius involves the notion of a categorical desire.[15] In contrast with desires conditional on continued life (desire to live in a certain way if one lives at all), categorical desires (desires not so conditioned) provide us with reasons to desire to continue living. If I categorically desire to see the sunlight tomorrow morning, I have a reason not to want to die, and thus to regard killing me as an injury to me.

One can, I think, make fair sense of Bernard Williams's distinction. An example of a conditional desire would be the following: I would rather not work at all, but if I have to work, I would prefer to work (say) as a college teacher. This is of course an example of a desire conditional on my working, not my living, but if there can be conditional desire of the one sort, it seems that there can be conditional desires of the other. An example of a categorical desire is the desire to see some specific

28

event (a holiday, the birth of one's grandchildren, the death of one's enemy) which is either fixed in time or beyond one's control. And if there is something special about tomorrow's sunlight, so that a desire to see it is not a desire not to live underground for as long as one has to live, then a desire to see it will be a categorical desire, while otherwise it might be conditional. Not everyone who wants to live has such explicit categorical desires, however, and when such desires are present they are often generated, even consciously, to serve a more fundamental desire to go on living. Hence we remain confronted with the possibility that—but for the desire to live itself and occasional exceptional other desires—all our desires are at root conditional on our continued living. Nor can one refute this suggestion by pointing to our desire to continue living, for the precise question at issue is whether our desire requires or can get support in categorical desires at all.

Bernard Williams replies to the suggestion that all our desires but the desire to live are conditional in the following way:

> Consider the idea of a rational forward-looking calculation of suicide: there can be such a thing, even if many suicides are not rational, and even though with some that are, it may be unclear to what extent they are forward-looking. . . . In such a calculation, a man might consider what lay before him, and decide whether he did or did not want to undergo it. If he does decide to undergo it, then some desire propels him on into the future, and *that* desire at least is not one that operates conditionally on his being alive, since it resolves the question of whether he is going to be alive.

But, as I have argued, the notion of a rational decision to kill oneself is too questionable to bear the weight proposed for it here. It is not possible to explain why death is an evil by appealing to the notion of a categorical desire, nor to support the claim that it would be bad for me (now) to die by appeal to other circumstances where it would be rational for me to kill myself.

Thomas Nagel presents a reply to Lucretius that does not use any of the premises of Bernard Williams's account, to which I have objected. His premise is that the suffering of an evil need not consist in the experience of it.

> A man's life includes much that does not take place within the boundaries of his body and his mind, and what happens to him can include much that does not take place within the boundaries of his life. These boundaries are

commonly crossed by the misfortunes of being deceived, or despised or betrayed. . . . The case of mental degeneration shows us an evil that depends on a contrast between the reality and the possible alternatives. A man is the subject of good and evil as much because he has hopes which may or may not be fulfilled, or possibilities which may or may not be realized, as because of this capacity to suffer and enjoy. If death is an evil, it must be accounted for in these terms, and the impossibility of locating it within life would not trouble us.

When a man dies we are left with his corpse, and while a corpse can suffer the kind of mishap that may occur to an article of furniture, it is not a suitable object for pity. The man, however, is. He has lost his life, and if he had not died, he would have continued to live it and to possess whatever good there is in living. [16]

Nagel's formulation is very nearly adequate—but not quite. There is, as Mary Mothersill has pointed out, something distinctly odd (although natural, too) about pitying (or envying) the dead, given that death is the unequivocal end of our existence. [17] We may pity Galois for having died at twenty, since Galois was conscious that he was dying. But the death of a young person suddenly and without warning provokes not so much pity as a shudder. What seems to need explanation is not a sense that the dead are badly off but the desire experienced by the living to stay alive, the horror they frequently experience when they witness death, and the moral significance of that desire and that horror.

The desire human beings have to continue living, and the aversion to annihilation that goes along with it, are, I think, as primitive a feature of human life and as little in need of explanation as the fact that human beings normally do things which they expect will produce the states of affairs they want. A human being is, among other things, an animal—a thinking animal, to be sure, but an animal nonetheless. And an animal is a system that maintains itself in existence in a certain complex way. Although special reasons can sometimes be adduced for someone's striving to continue to be (just as they can for his doing what he enjoys), and in some circumstances he may not try to continue living (and indeed may seek his own death), still no special reasons are *required* to explain why he wants to continue to be, and special reasons are always required if suicide is to be intelligible.

It follows that death as such, not just untimely death, is an evil. Old people like young people spontaneously keep themselves going, and there is no criterion by which one can determine, apart from the fact of dying itself, that death at a certain age is timely. True, we expect and resign ourselves to the death of the aged (and of ourselves when aged) but where infant mortality is high parents expect and resign themselves to the death of many of their infant children. That death can seem a good because life is attended by so much suffering (or even boredom) is true of people at any age: not just the old but also the young sometimes find continued existence too much to bear.

It also follows that the desire to live is not primordially a desire to live one way rather than another, or to have any particular experiences. (It seems likely that being alive at all entails at least the possibility—which might be quite tenuous—of some experience or other, although I think I can understand how someone might be comforted by thinking of his death as permanent and irreversible unconsciousness rather than annihilation—thus indicating that he regards the former as a kind of survival.) We do not go on living, not centrally that is, for the sake of any of the experiences that compose our life. Unamuno's preference for hell-fire rather than annihilation may be extreme, but it is neither unintelligible nor (necessarily) irrational. Others may strike a different balance between their desire to live and their desire to avoid pain, but their balance, like Unamuno's, is between two motives, each having independent force and intelligibility.

4. Compassion and Justice

THE PRESENT SECTION is concerned with the relationship between the moral rule against homicide and the precepts of compassion and justice which for some seem to constitute the whole of morality.[18]

I find the common definition of murder—"unjust killing of humans"[19]—questionable. It is odd to call the killing of another without semblance of justification injustice, not of course because it is justice, but because the norm violated is of a very different sort from those involved in the distribution of goods and burdens, the fairness of legal procedures and judgments, and so on.[20] Such killing is better described as wanton than as unjust. Indeed, even when the killing is done under color of state authority, the expression "unjust killing" seems to imply something more than slaughter pure and simple. The Nazis killed their political opponents unjustly, perhaps: the Jews, Gypsies, and others they called "subhumans" they simply murdered, although they no doubt treated them unjustly in calling them subhumans. One implication of these remarks is that the relevance to the moral problem of suicide of Aristotle's discussion whether one can treat oneself unjustly[21] is very sharply limited. Another is that our inclination to call the killing of babies inhuman rather than unjust does not argue for a lesser moral status for babies than for adults.

On the other hand, it does seem correct to treat murder as the violation of the decedent's right to live. True, it is extremely pretentious to speak of the Boston Strangler as violating the rights of his victims, and prosecutions for murder under the guise of violation of civil rights are rather strained. Still, "the right to life" is a perfectly natural bit of eighteenth-century rights-talk (cf. the Declaration of Independence), and the usage is confirmed by the most natural analysis of the concept of a moral right: an interest protected against the assaults of others by a moral rule, or a moral rule of a peculiarly important and emphatic sort.

For all living beings have an interest in continuing to live (although this interest may conflict with other interests of theirs such as the avoidance of pain). Where the creature in question is a human being or person,[22] this interest is a prima facie right (i.e., an interest protected against violation on the part of others by a moral rule—in this case that against homicide). Where no conditions which would defeat the claim that a given homicide would be murder are present, the right to life is a right absolute. Hence it makes sense to ask what creatures have a prima facie right to live, and under what conditions this prima facie right could in some way be overridden or otherwise defeated. So that, if "injustice" is given the somewhat stretched sense of any violation of another's rights, then the murder of another can be described as the worst sort of unjust killing. And since this is what those who call murder "unjust killing" usually mean, they are not wrong. It is still useful, however, to insist that this is a somewhat stretched sense of injustice, since it helps us to see the vast difference between wrongly killing a person and taxing him unfairly.

It is also, I think, as unsatisfactory to regard wrongful homicide as

32

principally cruel, as it is to regard it as principally unjust. Homicide is often cruel, of course, but to say that it is, is usually to pick out some additional feature of the act over and above its being an act of homicide, say that it is performed in a manner particularly painful to the victim, or particularly insensitive to the sensibilities of the onlookers or the needs of the decedent's family. It is as odd to call the painless killing of a hermit in his sleep "cruel" as it is to call it "unjust"; yet it is certainly murder.

Finally, it is not plausible to regard the rule against killing either as want-regarding or as ideal-regarding.[23] For some of the creatures the rule protects—unconscious people for instance—do not, except in an extended sense, "want" to live at all, although it is natural and rational to treat them as so wanting. On the other hand, to treat so socially central a norm as that against killing—in its conventional scope, I mean, not in its pacifist and vegetarian extensions—as embodying an ideal is highly implausible. The wrongness of killing people stands on its own basis, not reducible to any other.

5. *Some Moral Theories*

I NOW TURN to the contributions of some of the various traditions of normative ethics to the ethics of homicide.

1. *Utilitarianism.* Utilitarian ethics may be divided in two rough halves: one part affirming that right action consists in maximizing pleasure or happiness, as experienced by sentient beings at the time of the particular consequence in question; the other affirming that what counts is the satisfaction of desires or preferences existing at the time of action. (A third variant—according to which what matters is what someone is glad to have done to him—will be briefly discussed in section 6.) For the first sort of utilitarianism, it is hard to see why we should not be plugged into happiness machines if such things existed; for the other it suffices that we do not *want* to be plugged into such machines.

The obstacles to a credible utilitarian ethics of homicide of the first sort are very great.[24] If the end of utilitarian action is the greatest possible balance of happiness over unhappiness obtaining in the universe, the result as to homicide—that, *ceteris paribus*, all and only those whose expectation of happiness is negative should be killed—has a tolerable claim to be the correct position, given appropriate stipulations concerning the secondary bad effects of killing (pain and grief), a high estimate of the average person's expectation for happiness, and a willingness to give the case for euthanasia a substantial run. And given natalist inclinations and an appropriate estimate of secondary effects, the result concerning reproduction—that (ceteris paribus) all and only those possible children should be begotten whose expectation of happiness (judged from their heredity and probable environment) is positive—might also be acceptable. But the two positions taken together are quite incredible, for they imply that there is no essential moral difference between killing someone already in being, and failure to bring him into existence. It is for instance hard to see, on such utilitarian premises, why it should matter whether we view a fetus, infant, small child, or human being at any other stage of life as a person, or as something out of which a person might arise. On such a view many moral disputes, such as that over abortion, become unintelligible.

A similar difficulty requires the rejection of a utilitarian ethics of homicide founded on the precept of maximizing the average utility obtaining within the population. That only those possible children who will be more happy than half of the present population should be begotten is a possible moral position, but the results of such an approach to the ethics of homicide are wild in the extreme. As Richard G. Henson observes, the killing of the hedonically deprived to increase the average utility of the population tends to general extermination:

> Note first that in being below average, hedonically—"hedonically deprived," as we might say—the fellow in question is probably like about half the population: if it is right to kill him, it is right to kill about half the population. But note second that as you kill those who are in the lower half of the population, hedonically speaking, you are steadily raising the average, so that some who used to be just above average will now be below it. Eventually, the conscientious utilitarian will be playing "Ten Little Indians" with the last ten people alive (if he is happy enough himself to have lasted so long).

Henson's argument of course neglects effects of killing other than the death of the victim, but it is not plausible that what is wrong with killing

34

of this sort is that it produces distress and inconvenience for people other than the victims.

An example of utilitarianism of the second sort is formulated by Jan Narveson. [25] According to Narveson, what is decisive is not pleasure or happiness but utility however the subject conceives it. This formulation has two advantages over textbook utilitarianism that are of relevance to the present discussion. (1) Since the unconceived have no concept of their own happiness, even if we impute to the unconscious concepts of their own happiness on one ground or another, troublesome obligations to beget disappear. Since we have obligations only to those in being, the asymmetry between not producing a person and killing him is restored. (2) Both the ordinary desire to go on living and the extraordinary desire to die can be allowed moral weight without inquiry into their rationality. A man's continued life if he wants to live it, and his death if he wants to die it, will just be part of his good, and thus part of the good at which utilitarian action is aimed.

But Narveson's theory, too, faces considerable objections. One difficulty is to what extent we are allowed to define our own utility to include things outside our own experiences. If such definition is left unrestrained, a desire that one's enemies suffer extreme torment (even when one is not around to witness it) is entitled to as much moral importance as more respectable human desires of the same strength. If my definition of my own good is limited to my own experience, death will no longer be contrary to my good, since once dead I will experience nothing whatever. If my definition of my own good is limited by ethical considerations—if I refuse to regard satisfactions objectionable on moral grounds as being good—then Narveson's utilitarianism will not represent a sufficient basis for morality, since he starts with the assumption that all desires are equally worthy of satisfaction. And the problematical character of the desire to be killed (section 3) re-enters the argument.

A problem that raises this issue clearly is the status of the desires of the dead. Shall we count the wishes entertained by our dead ancestors (before they died), concerning the way their descendants should live, as strongly as we count the (equally strong) wishes of the living to live in possibly contrary ways, or shall the wishes of the dead be dismissed as ethically unimportant, since the dead will not suffer if their wishes are frustrated? Was anything of ethical significance achieved when the right to hold public office was restored to Robert E. Lee long after his death? Unable to reach a satisfactory resolution of this sort of question, Narveson settles on what is at best a vaguely plausible compromise: that the satisfactions "enjoyed" by the dead are "the pale ghosts of satisfactions, and not to be counted for very much." While this society would probably accept Narveson's compromise without difficulty, not all societies would, and Narveson has no theoretical argument against those who do not. A more adequate view would distinguish what the dead might reasonably claim of us from what they might not. Such an account cannot be constructed on Narveson's utilitarian basis, however, since utilitarianism for Narveson holds as a central assumption that all desires are equal in their moral relevance.

The other side of the difficulty lies in the status of those who have no present desires or preferences. Thus while it is clear that utilitarians such as Narveson wish to treat the normal unconscious as desiring to awake in due course, it is not at all clear why, as a matter of utilitarian ethics, this conclusion should hold. And the point may be sharpened by considering a consequence of Narveson's account, which is at least remarkable (although difficult to avoid on any premises): that procreation is always a morally neutral act as it affects the person produced. Since a person has no concept of his own happiness until he is in being, we could not have deprived him of happiness as he conceives it by begetting him, no matter how miserable his life might be. (Future persons that will exist apart from our actions might be treated as existing and having the concepts of happiness they will have for purposes of present action affecting them, but this assumption is obviously not possible when the existence or nonexistence of a possible future person is at issue.)

I am here assuming that the crucial question is always the affected person's concept of his own happiness *prior to the action*, not subsequent to it. Such an assumption is necessary for an ethics of killing, since the dead have no concept of their own happiness. I have cast the foregoing argument concerning procreation in terms of Narveson's system, where the individual's concept of his good is what is crucial. My own preferred formulation—in which the evil of death is explained in terms of the objective loss—does not escape my argument either, since the unbegot cannot be thought of as gaining or losing anything.

36

I do not mean to imply that Narveson takes the position on the ethics of procreation I have suggested he should. [26] On the contrary, not only does he muster the traditional problem of evil against the existence of a creator God: he holds that a utilitarian God, if He were for some reason unable to create perfectly happy creatures, ought to create no creatures at all. [27] But this view is so extreme—one would hardly hold that it is wrong to have children who would not be *perfectly* happy—that it is best set to one side in trying to understand Narveson's system. What Narveson ought to hold is that the creation of a universe in accordance with the Creator's desires is a morally neutral act, since there is no one existing prior to the act whose concept of his happiness can be consulted.

In any case—whatever the final verdict may be on the status of the interests ascribed to the dead or the unconceived—Narveson's utilitarianism succeeds neither in evading nor in answering the question of membership in the moral community, a question that is vital for both the ethics of homicide and ethics as a whole. In this it differs from textbook utilitarianism, which evades the point by—most implausibly—treating pains and pleasures in abstraction from the subjects whose experiences they are.

I have limited my consideration of utilitarianism to versions close to hedonistic act-utilitarianism. Rule-utilitarian arguments—arguments that proceed from the consequences of our moral rules rather than of our individual acts—are casuistically very powerful. But since rule-utilitarian arguments concerning homicide largely rely on the tendency for the permission of killing in one context to produce killing in another, they are not useful in remedying failure of utilitarianism to take adequately into account the kind of evil death is. [28] Ideal utilitarianism can remedy this defect by positing a high nonhedonic value for the continuation of life once begun (as well as an appropriately lower nonhedonic value for the fulfillment of mere possibilities of human existence), but this kind of solution—providing as it does a mechanical way of resolving all conflicts between utilitarian ethics and the common moral consciousness (or any other set of moral views)—is not very illuminating. [29]

2. *The social contract.* A moral theory that takes as central the model of a contract among the members of society not to injure one another (at

least)[30] is in several ways more helpful than utilitarianism. First, the model of a nonaggression pact makes it clear that what is crucial in our moral judgments concerning homicide is the harm done to the victim, not, as R. E. Ewin puts it, to "his mother or his maiden aunt." Second, the contractarian need not worry about the reasons death is an evil. Since the preservation of our lives is one of the motives for our entering into the social contract, the contractarian can treat continued life as a basic good[31] and proceed with his discussion.

There are, however, two decisive difficulties with the contractarian approach. One has to do with the grounds on which a claim of murder can be defeated given the act of homicide. The other has to do with the question whether a given act is a homicide at all as opposed to (say) the killing of a nonhuman.

A plausible contractarian account of the justifiability of killing in self-defense runs as follows: "One condition releasing me from the obligation not to kill somebody else . . . is that he is trying to kill me; he is then failing to keep his side of the bargain and thus releases me from mine. I promised not to kill him provided I was given security for my life, and that condition is not being met."[32] A violation of the social nonaggression pact releases the other members from adherence to it.

But this account raises considerable problems. In the first place, culpable violation on the part of another is neither a necessary nor a sufficient condition for the exercise of my right of self-defense against him. I am not justified in killing someone who is trying to kill me by voodoo, since though his intent is lethal, his means are inefficacious against a skeptic, and I stand in no danger of my life. And I may kill a madman who is attacking me, although he is not a culpable violator of the social contract, only an unfortunate. Nor does danger to my life release me from all my obligations to others (although Hobbes probably was committed to the conclusion that it did). Otherwise there would be no moral limits on what I might do to others in order to save my own life. Finally, it will not do to treat a deadly assault not as a default from the social contract but as a waiver of one's rights under it, since few advocates of euthanasia will want to honor a healthy person's wish to die, expressed in a moment of despair, but I may, on most views, kill if necessary to save myself from someone acting on a momentary fit of passion. Hence there does not seem to be any way of satisfactorily explaining our right of self-defense in contractarian terms.

Of course one might appeal to the specific terms of the social contract to explain the precise shape of the right of self-defense claimed by members of our society. Such an analysis could also explain our views on homicide with consent, since there is nothing absurd in my contracting (or thinking of myself as having contracted), to be protected from myself, as Ulysses did with his crew when he wished to hear the Sirens. One can indeed imagine a social contract that bars killing of the parties under any circumstances whatever. But to rest one's case on the details of the social contract we are to think of ourselves as having signed is to make the ethics of homicide a matter of convention in a way that cannot help but be extremely disturbing. Alternatively, one particular possible social contract might be thought of as normative, but a contractual argument is then necessary showing why this is so.

The difficulty becomes more intense when we confront the question: who are the signatories to the social contract—the people we are to think of ourselves as having promised not to kill? The contract tradition points out the features of humanity, that mankind is both rational and social, which make it reasonable to treat human beings as persons, but it does not tell us whether the class of persons would include (*a*) only those in present enjoyment of rationality and a capacity for social life, (*b*) all those, whether or not in present enjoyment of such qualities, who have the capacity to acquire them in due course, (*c*) all members of a *species* characterized by rationality and social life, or finally (*d*) all those who share with human beings such traits as a self-preservation instinct and a capacity for pain.

At this point contract doctrine branches into two forms which I shall call realistic and ideal. According to realistic contract doctrine, the parties to the social contract are those with whom I would find it in my interest to establish a pact of nonaggression and mutual assistance.[33] As one writer in the contractual tradition rather brutally puts it, "Any being with the capacity to pull the trigger of a gun, and to refrain from doing so out of obedience to moral rules, deserves our equal moral respect."[34] Such a doctrine implies that rights under the social contract do not accrue to those, such as small children,[35] with whom I have no such motive to sign a pact. On the other hand, if the social contract is read in its ideal form, as negotiated under conditions of ignorance as to my social position, talents, and powers, everything will turn on what I am allowed to know. A person in the moral sense will be a creature who shares with me those traits of whose existence I continue to be aware while negotiating.

But, someone will reply, certainly there must be some features of myself of which I have to be aware if I am going to sign the social contract. I have to know that I am conscious and capable of rational thought if I am going to engage in negotiating contracts at all. But those who are at the moment unconscious at least need to be brought within the social contract; moreover, if ability to work out the implications of the original position is required in the contractors, Rawls's social contract will protect philosophers only. The ignorance involved in the initial position is fictional only, restraining the contractors from using certain things that they know in a certain way. There is thus no reason why the contractors should not be enjoined from using the knowledge that they are conscious to discriminate against the comatose, or the knowledge that they are grown humans to discriminate against children, infants, and fetuses. Of course these kinds of cases are not quite the same, since one normally does not know that he will not be comatose for a long period some time in the future, whereas one does know that he will not be a fetus or a child below the age of reason. One might, however, still be tempted to discriminate against the comatose, for instance if one systematically discounts the future.

There is, that is to say, nothing in Rawls's social-contract model to eliminate from consideration the position urged by James Childress, according to which the veil of ignorance prevents the contractors from knowing at what stage of life they are, specifically whether or not they are in the womb.[36] Indeed, this may be the position adopted by Rawls himself, or so his rather unclear remarks about those who will attain a sense of justice "in due course" would seem to indicate.[37] But neither this position nor any other will emerge from the social-contract theory taken alone, unsupplemented by some theory of what constitutes a person.

3. *Natural law.* By "natural law" I do not mean the minimum content of the natural law as H. L. A. Hart defines it.[38] If human beings

were not vulnerable to one another, approximately equal in power, and limited in altruism, resources, understanding, and strength of will, morality and law would have a very different shape from the one they now have. But it would be foolish to think that these considerations combined with a desire to preserve social life uniquely determine even an ethics of homicide. Human beings could be much more murderous than we would consider minimally acceptable without making social life of any sort impossible, although the resulting society would not be considered a good one. Nor do I mean the notion that the best life is the most natural one, in the sense of most free of technology, convention, artifice, or restraint upon instinct. Some murders are in this sense extremely natural. Still less do I mean the notion that we should take nonhuman animals as our moral models, eating our young like hamsters or throwing ourselves into the sea en masse as lemmings are said to do.[39] I mean by "natural law" a tradition of moral philosophy which reaches back at least to Aristotle and whose best-known later representative is St. Thomas Aquinas.[40]

The natural-law tradition in this sense has three elements. One is the premise that the world is organized in a morally significant way, so human beings can learn what they ought to do by attending to the kinds of creatures they are. One way of explaining how this is so is to say that we are the work of a creator God to Whom we owe obedience, but so strong a premise is not required. The minimum requirement for a natural-law ethic is only that there be a "normic"[41] sense of "human," in which someone who is not at least reluctant to perform certain kinds of action (or, more broadly, who is not responsive to certain kinds of moral consideration) is defectively human. Examples of such defective humans are those who see nothing wrong with killing other people. In other words, what the natural-law tradition requires is that an immoral person be not merely bad (to have around) and a human being, but also a bad human being, in a sense like that in which one speaks of a bad poem or a bad automobile. (This is not to say that human beings are in an ordinary sense artifacts.)

The second stage in the development of natural law ethics is identifying man as a certain sort of creature, and specifying the good for man in terms of the kind of creature he is. Since man is an organism—St. Thomas says a substance—his good includes the preservation of himself in being. Since man is a creature that reproduces sexually, his good includes the procreation of offspring by sexual union. Man's good as a social being includes friendship in the widest sense. Finally, since man is an intellectual being, his good includes knowledge of himself, the world, and (if there is one) God.

It is already clear that the natural-law moralist need have no difficulty with the objection formulated by Richard Robinson: "Once we have explicitly asked ourselves why we should do anything just because nature does it, or why we should aid nature in her purposes, we see that there is no reason why we should. Let nature look to her own purposes, if she has any. We will look to ours."[42] The answer is that nature's purposes *are* our purposes, purposes built into us by virtue of the kinds of creatures we are—organisms, animals, and rational, social beings. Only by observing these purposes, the natural-law moralist will argue, can we lead the sort of life that is suitable for human beings. Moreover, since these purposes are part of our structure, our reason will be practical from the start, so that no radical is-ought problem is to be expected.

The third stage in the development of natural-law ethics is the correlation of these kinds of human goods with particular moral rules. Since man's good includes his preservation in being, suicide is at least prima facie wrong. Since man's good includes sexual reproduction, various conclusions (which need not be examined here) have been drawn concerning the ethics of sex and reproduction. The bulk of the ethics of social relations follows from the social nature of man, and man's good as an intellectual creature imposes duties of loyalty to truth. A further assumption of natural-law ethics, or at least of its most distinctive presentations, is that, while prudent allocation of both personal and social resources is necessary in deciding to what extent to pursue the various human goods, none of these goods is in any event to be attacked or repudiated.

An objection commonly raised to the natural-law tradition is that it draws normative conclusions from merely descriptive premises, thereby breaching the wall of separation between fact and value which empiricist philosophers are pledged to defend. But there are two powerful counterarguments to this objection. (1) The natural-law moralist need not assert an entailment between his premises and his conclusion: like a moralist of any other school, he can be content with arguing that his premises provide adequate reasons for asserting his conclusions. No philosopher, no matter what he may say, wants to regard facts about human beings as morally irrelevant. [43] (2) The sharp dichotomy between normative and non-normative discourse maintained by the empiricist does not obtain in fact: there are many propositions, such that tuberculosis is a disease, or that a human child ought to be able to talk before reaching the age of five years, which do not fit comfortably on either side of the dichotomy. If there is a way of ascertaining that some modes of human life are defective in the way tuberculosis is a disease and a five-year-old child who cannot talk is retarded, then the characterization of these modes as defective will legitimately partake of both factual and normative elements. [44]

One area where the natural-law tradition is vulnerable as to homicide, and not only as to homicide, is its assumption that no basic human good is ever to be directly sacrificed for another. One can, of course, treat the concept of a direct sacrifice or repudiation of such a good as a conclusory claim that the action in question is illegitimate, but one would then be faced with having to justify this conclusion in each case. Such notorious results as that a vow of celibacy, and thus a permanent renunciation of one's procreative capacities, is a legitimate (and laudable) sacrifice of the animal to the spiritual, whereas the employment of contraceptive devices to avoid procreation at one time in order to procreate better at another is forbidden, suggest that what counts as a direct attack will vary according to the natural-law moralists' larger social assumptions rather than resting on an analysis of the acts themselves. On the other hand, if workable ways of distinguishing direct from indirect attacks on human goods are available, we still need to know why such attacks are always wrong, however great the good to be gained (or the evil to be avoided) by them.

The most plausible ground for such an assertion is that basic human values are incommensurable, so that there is no rational ground upon which one might be sacrificed to others. But even if no calculus of values is possible, it still might—except the contrary be proved—be perfectly clear in particular cases that a relatively small sacrifice of one value in order to gain a very great deal of another was warranted. On the other hand, if the prohibition on direct attack is dropped, we are left with an ideal utilitarianism of a rather shapeless sort.

43

There are also problems for the tradition special to homicide. On one interpretation, any killing of a human being (or perhaps, though natural-law moralists of course do not so hold, of any living creature), even to save the lives of others, is an attack on the value of life and hence forbidden by natural-law principles. This result is more stringent than is commonly reached.[45] On the other hand, if to attack or repudiate a human good is to act in such a way as to declare that good not valuable, then only suicide is such an attack. One who kills another, even wantonly, is not indicating that he regards life as not valuable: he may care intensely about preserving his own life while selfishly not caring whether others enjoy this value or not. Once we have established the wrongfulness of suicide, we might, to be sure, argue—by way of some version of "do as you would be done by"—that the killing of others except under stringent conditions was a violation of a man's good as a social being. But to argue in this way would be to rest the wrongfulness of killing others on that of suicide, a rather odd result at least. On this view, the problem of making out the moral community is the same as for the social-contract tradition, so the discussion of this point need not be repeated here.

These considerations do not make the natural-law tradition irrelevant to the ethics of homicide any more than the objections raised to utilitarianism and the social-contract tradition render irrelevant these traditions. The various traditions of normative ethics are supple and capable of taking on a variety of forms. But these considerations do mean that it will not be possible to deduce an ethics of homicide from natural-law (or from utilitarian or from social-contract) premises. What we have, in short, is a set of intuitions and problems in search of a theory. The examination of these intuitions and problems in some detail will occupy the bulk of this book. Perhaps my efforts will provide a stimulus for a more satisfactory reconstruction of one of the moral traditions discussed.

The time has come to sum up the rather tangled arguments of this chapter.

First, the word "murder" means neither "wrongful homicide" nor "killing of the innocent." The first of these definitions suggests that the morality of a particular killing could be worked out without special emphasis on the fact that it is a killing; the second begs many serious moral questions, for instance that of euthanasia. Rather, the proper definition of "murder" is homicide that is neither (*a*) justified, nor (*b*) excused or mitigated. The kinds of justifications that have been offered for homicide will occupy us at length (in Chapters V and VI), but the important point here is that there is a bias or presumption against killing, so that a form of intentional killing which is not in some way justified or excused will be murder and thus gravely wrong.

Second, the reason homicide is prima facie wrong—the central harm that an act of homicide inflicts—is that it kills the victim. That death is an evil follows from the nature of man as a self-continuing being, but the moral importance of this evil and the relative unimportance of the deaths of animals and plants are points requiring separate discussion (in Chapters II and III). There is no rational way of concluding, in a balance-sheet fashion, that death is under some circumstances not an evil, but a benefit. People kill themselves because their sufferings exceed their capacity for endurance, not because they have weighed the respective merits of death and life.

Third, none of the major traditions of moral philosophy is altogether adequate to the ethics of homicide. Utilitarianism treats human beings as means to a universe full of happiness (or happiness per capita) and thus breaks down where we have not a population which we are trying to make as happy as possible but the prospect of decreasing (or increasing) the membership of that population. Social-contract theory and natural-law ethics both start (correctly) with the assumption that the continuance in being of a human person is a basic good for that person, but neither is quite adequate to the question of when that basic good might be sacrificed. The social contract requires either very brutal conclusions, such as that, since small children are not parties to the contract, their parents may kill them at pleasure; or else stipulations external to the contract, such that all human beings within its boundaries are to be thought of as parties, which mean that the social contract itself does not decide our ethics of homicide. The natural-law tradition is unclear on the following point: whether the rejection of the basic good of life consists only in intending one's own death, or whether the killing of others may be a breach of this natural good as well. In the first case, the problem of defining the moral community is the same for the natural-law tradition as for the social-contract tradition; in the second, one needs to ask why only human life is protected, and how the line between human and subhuman is to be drawn. [46]

45

II /

SCOPE OF THE
PROHIBITION:

Nonhumans, Robots, and Infants

THIS CHAPTER and the next are concerned with the question: the killing of what kinds of beings constitutes homicide? Three principles specifying the scope of the moral rule against homicide are considered: the species principle, the potentiality principle, and the present-enjoyment principle. In this chapter, the species and present-enjoyment principles are expounded, and the latter rejected on the grounds that it fails to comport with our considered judgments concerning the morality of infanticide. Michael Tooley's arguments in defense of infanticide are considered, and the legitimacy of appeals to intuition of the sort I rely on are defended.

6. Persons and Nonpersons

SOME HAVE ARGUED that questions such as that of abortion can be resolved without attempting to determine who or what is a person, or who or what has a right to live. According to R. M. Hare, for instance, an adequate set of moral views regarding abortion is to be reached by applying the Golden Rule (or one of its philosophical progeny) directly to the data without asking first who the "others" are to whom we are obliged to do as we would have them do to us.[1] The result of this reasoning is that there turns out to be no essential moral difference between abortion and contraception or failure to procreate, but that this conclusion is not so favorable to the defenders of abortion as it sounds. For just as we should do to presently existing others as we would have them do to us, so we should do to potential others as we were glad was done to us (Hare assumes his audience is glad to have been brought into the world) and procreate unless there is a good moral reason not to (as there often is). Likewise, although abortion is prima facie wrong, since it prevents the coming-into-being of a person, it is not very difficult to justify in hardship cases. Thus Hare aligns himself with that form of utilitarianism which holds that what is to be sought is the greatest possible total utility, and that the world can be made better by increasing the number of happy people in it.

But even for Hare there is a class of persons—normal adults—who are entitled not to be killed in their own right, and not because to do so would be to prevent the coming-into-being of their future selves. Hence he has not evaded, but has taken sides in, the dispute between the typical defender of abortion, who holds that a fetus is not a person, and the typical opponent who holds that it is. And the same will be found to be the case, I think, of attempts to evade the question of whether the "others" we are exhorted to treat as we would ourselves include animals, robots, Martians, or computing machines.

This and the following chapter will accordingly be concerned with the scope of the prohibition against homicide and other moral rules protecting the interests of human beings or persons. What kinds of creatures, I shall be asking, are comprised within the class whose members the moral rule against homicide protects? What is the status of normal human fetuses and infants? of human defectives? of robots and androids? of dolphins and chimpanzees? Is it even prima facie wrong to kill such creatures, and if so, need the justifications for killing them be as compelling as those required to warrant killing a normal adult human? These questions are important not only for the ethics of homicide, but for ethics generally, since if a creature has no right not to be killed, it cannot have any other serious rights in contexts where its interests and those of persons are in conflict. Such a conflict could always be resolved by killing the troublesome creature.

The first task is to defend the enterprise of marking out the morally privileged class against attempts to undermine it in the name of an ecological ethic. Sissela Bok for instance writes:

> One or both of two fundamental assumptions are made by those who base the protection of life upon the possession of 'humanity.' The first is that all

human beings are not only different from, but *superior* to, all other living matter. . . . The second assumption holds that the superiority of human beings somehow justifies their using what is non-human as they wish to. . . . Neither of these assumptions is self-evident. And the results of acting upon them, upon the bidding to subdue the earth, to subordinate its many forms of life to human needs, are no longer seen by all to be beneficial. The very enterprise of *basing* normative conclusions on such assumptions can no longer be taken for granted. [2]

Thus those who oppose abortion on the ground that it is the taking of a human life are frequently charged with an arbitrary narrowing of the scope of their moral concern to human beings; so also on the same day that it deplored the conviction of Dr. Edelin for manslaughter in the death of a baby resulting from an abortion, the *New York Times* vehemently condemned the killing of large numbers of blackbirds.

But to argue for, to even raise the issue of, vegetarianism or concern for the rights of trees in the course of a defense of abortion [3] is on its face a very odd procedure, as odd as the converse procedure of assuming the moral acceptability of abortion in the course of a defense of vegetarianism. [4] Nonhuman animals and human embryos are not in this sense rivals for status as persons: it does not follow from the premise that we ought to cease eating animals that we are justified in taking the lives of fetuses. Indeed even supposing that the wrongfulness of killing fetuses entails the wrongfulness of animal slaughter, the opponent of abortion could accept the conclusion as to animals and still put more effort into the attempt to protect fetuses than into the attempt to protect sheep and cattle, quite simply because his chances of success are greater. Difficult as it may be in the present cultural context to reverse pro-abortion trends, it would be much more difficult to get people to abandon meat-eating on moral grounds. [5]

Moreover, while it is clearly not possible to defend everything that human beings do to animals, [6] good reasons can be supplied for regarding the lives and interests of nonhumans as of less moral importance than those of humans. If the killing of nonhumans is murder, then we no doubt ought to stop animals from killing each other, not, to be sure, because they are guilty of murder in so doing (they are not moral agents) but on the same grounds on which we stop the activities of homicidal maniacs. This endeavor would involve a restraint of the characteristic modes of activity of many animal species. But such behavior would fit oddly with the kinship with animals which the defender of vegetarianism asserts. (The case of the human killer is different, since it is possible to live in a characteristically human way without killing people, but not in a characteristically tigerish way without killing gazelles, or at least eating flesh.) If on the other hand we regard animals as so far beyond the pale morally speaking that they constitute a merely natural hazard to one another (like diseases), a hazard from which our resources are not sufficient to accord them protection, the kinship between man and beast which the vegetarian asserts will also be greatly eroded. And in any case we will want to know why we protect men and women and not (except to a very limited extent) animals against natural hazards. Of course the vegetarian could assert that we should regard nonhuman animals as our kin, and that the restraint of a tiger's carnivorous propensities is a lesser evil than the death of a gazelle (or vice versa). At this phase of the argument one can only ask the vegetarian to be consistent, and to point out the price of consistency.

Again, we need not be concerned with the relative value of human and animal life in the abstract, but only with their relative value in the context of decision making by human beings. Even supposing that Hume is right when he says that "the life of a man is of no greater importance in the universe than that of an oyster,"[7] where the decision maker is not an oyster or God (or the universe personified), but a human being, that kind of creature which shares certain essential traits with the agent is entitled to a kind of respect to which those who do not are not. Still further, human beings—or nearly all of them—are capable of a much richer kind of life than nonhuman animals on this planet enjoy, including the very moral agency presupposed in the asking of a moral question. To be deprived of this kind of life (or to have it impaired) is a much greater harm than to be deprived of a merely animal existence. Of course one might say that human beings are unable adequately to judge the richness of the lives of spiders or dolphins, and thus to determine whether their lives are or are not as valuable as ours. But one is forced in any case to judge matters from one's own point of view (from what other point of view might one judge them?) and there is nothing inappropriate—but rather both appropriate and necessary—in human actions being guided by the perceptions of human beings.

49

The proper status to be accorded nonhumans is another matter. "Utilitarianism for animals, Kantianism for people"[8] comes closest to conventional morality on this point, but, like that morality, its implications are extremely unclear. (I would speculate—it is no more than that—that such premises would permit meat-eating among those habituated to the practice, while forbidding bullfighting.) In any case, some sacrifices of the interests of humans to those of nonhumans—for instance in the punishment of cruelty to animals—are surely permissible or even obligatory. As for plants, I should think that any harm to them would be morally *de minimis*, except when we have a case of wanton or perverse destructiveness, or where the interests of humans, including those of future generations, are at stake.[9]

In what follows, I distinguish three principles of interpretation determining the limits of the moral rule against homicide and other moral rules protecting distinctively human rights. One of these, the *species principle*, will be founded on the kinship or solidarity that obtains among members of the same species. It seems best understood as a more precise version of the "Standard Belief" which Roger Wertheimer attributes to nearly everyone: that what warrants the ascription of human moral status to a creature is simply that creature's being human.[10] (I say a more precise version, since Wertheimer believes that one can deny that a biologically human creature is a member of "the family of man," although why he thinks this is not completely clear.) The second, the *present enjoyment* (or present possession) *principle*, rests on the ability of human beings to assert their personhood by appeals or resistance. And the third, the *potentiality principle*, rests on the uniquely rich kinds of action and experience of which human beings are capable, and the uniquely severe loss suffered when the prospect of such a life is frustrated, whether or not the organism whose existence has been ended or whose capacity for such life has been impaired has had some experience of it. The potentiality and present enjoyment principles seem best viewed as attempts to replace the Standard Belief with something thought more satisfactory. Our choice among these principles will determine our judgment of the moral status of fetuses, infants, and the moribund, and thus make a crucial difference to our judgments concerning abortion, infanticide, and euthanasia.[11]

Nonhumans, Robots, and Infants

7. The Species Principle

A FIRST STATEMENT of the species principle as it applies to killing is as follows: those creatures protected by the moral rule against homicide are the members of the human species, and only the members of the human species. This version of the principle protects all human organisms, whatever their degree of maturity or decay, including fetuses and embryos, but not robots or nonhuman animals, whatever the attainments of such beings might be.

The species principle does not mean, as Joseph Fletcher thinks, that "we would be human if we have opposable thumbs, are capable of face-to-face coitus and have a brain weighing 1400 grams, whether a particular brain functions cerebrally or not."[12] Obviously a creature might be morally and biologically human while lacking one of these traits—say a child born without hands (and thus without thumbs)—and it is easy to imagine a species that met the suggested criteria without being in any sense human. Membership in a biological species is a complex matter, but scientists are now well able to recognize biological humanity in the fine structure of an organism, without reference to such things as opposable thumbs. Jérôme Lejeune puts the point nicely:

> Let us take the example of trisomy 21 [a chromosome disorder], observed by amniocentesis. Looking at the chromosomes and detecting the extra 21, we say very safely "The child who will develop here will be a trisomic 21." But this phrase does not convey all the information. We have not seen only the extra 21; we have also seen all the 46 other chromosomes and concluded that they were human, because if they had been mouse or monkey chromosomes, we would have noticed.[13]

In other words, even a human defective is a defective *human*, and this biological humanity is recognizable in the genetic structure of the organism even when the genetic structure itself is defective.

Some vagueness does afflict the species principle when it comes to deciding precisely when—at conception or shortly thereafter, when the unity and uniqueness of the nascent creature is secured—a human organism comes into existence, as well as how much breakdown is necessary before we say that a human organism has ceased to be. Ape-human hybrids and the like also pose a knotty problem. But none of these zones of vagueness render the principle unusable, nor do they provide any grounds for refusing to use the principle to condemn killing where the victim is unambiguously a human organism.

Finally, the species principle provides an adequate answer to the "acorn" argument, which has a surprising persistence in disputes about abortion.[14] Whatever may be the case with dormant acorns, a germinating acorn is, while not an oak *tree*, still a member of the appropriate species of oak. If oaks had a serious right to life in their own right, so would oak saplings and germinating acorns. And the same reply can be made to those who would argue about abortion from the premise that a caterpillar is not a butterfly.[15]

An unsound objection to the species principle is that it employs a biological category, that of the species, in the derivation of moral conclusions. This objection takes two forms: that such derivation is an illegitimate inference from an "is" to an "ought," and that to rely on such categories is to offend human dignity by subjecting human beings, like beasts, to the tyranny of animal nature. Neither version of the objection is plausible.

At most, what cannot be done in deriving an "ought" from an "is" is to assert an *entailment*. Modes of inference weaker than entailment cannot be barred as instances of the naturalistic fallacy lest all moral reasoning be made impossible. "X is a human organism; therefore X ought not to be killed" may be as good as any other significant moral inference. Of course one could treat this inference as elliptical, its missing premise being the moral rule against homicide as interpreted in accordance with the species principle ("One ought not to kill a human organism"). But to spell out this argument in this way may be no more illuminating than treating inductive inference as deductive inference with the principle of induction as a suppressed premise. In any case, this reading does nothing to strengthen the objection to the species principle.

As for the version of this contention which turns on human dignity, the answer to it is best put in the form of a question. Why is it wounding to human dignity to recognize that human beings are, among other things, animals, and to call for some respect for the animal aspect of man's being? Is the sanctioning of unlimited assaults on the characteristic modes of coming to be and passing away of the human species more

52

in keeping with respect for human dignity than the placing of restraints on such activity? To regard the according of moral significance to the animal aspect of man's existence as wounding to his dignity seems to make man's dignity contingent upon his being regarded as something he is not.

A more troubling charge is that of species chauvinism: the charge, that is, that the giving of a higher moral status to members of one's own species than to those of others is akin to regarding members of other races as subhuman. It would not be chauvinism in the strict sense to argue that between two intelligent species, members of one have no rights which members of the other are bound to respect, while each agent is morally required to respect the rights of members of his own species, in particular not to kill them unless he has a very compelling justification. It is, after all, considered worse (all other things being equal) to kill one's brother than a stranger, not because one's brother in himself is morally more worthy than the stranger, but because the relationship between brothers is itself morally significant. Nonetheless we would certainly want intelligent Martians to respect our rights, and might be prepared to respect theirs in return. And, if Martians were enough like human beings that the notion of human individuality could be extended to them, this respect for their rights would naturally take the form, *inter alia*, of regarding Martians as protected by our moral (and quite possibly our legal) rules against homicide.

But this line of thought can be accommodated by a modification of the species principle which does not alter its essential structure. According to this modification, what the moral rule against homicide protects is all members of intelligent species, including, but not limited to, the human. On this account determining whether a given creature is protected by the moral rule against homicide is a two-step process: first, identifying the species to which the creature belongs, and second, deciding whether this species is in fact intelligent. For members of the human species, the human species continues to play a somewhat paradigmatic role, in setting the standard of intelligence which must be approached or exceeded for a species to be considered intelligent, and the same is true for members of other intelligent species. A human being will ask whether Martians as a species are intelligent enough by human standards to be regarded as persons, and an intelligent Martian

53

will make the corresponding inquiry concerning human beings. In any case, all creatures protected by the original species principle are protected by the modified species principle as well.

Three problems of application arise for the modified species principle, of particular importance in assessing the claims which might be made on behalf of chimpanzees, whales, and dolphins. First, supposing one member of a species reaches the human level, what effect does this achievement have on the status of the other members of the species? Second, what kind of standards are to be employed in determining whether a given species is to be regarded as intelligent? Since we cannot, in answering these questions, rely on the considerations of lineage which settle nearly all questions of species membership, they will require very careful examination.

It seems that we want to regard an individual cat which has, through some chance or other, attained human intelligence as protected by the moral rule against homicide. To do so consistently with the species principle requires the adoption of one of two strategies: (1) the existence of such a cat renders the entire species *Felis domestica* an intelligent species, and all of its members protected by the moral rule against homicide (consider the plea such a cat might make on behalf of its less intelligent brethren)[16] or (2) the intelligence of our super-cat might be considered as producing a different species, consisting of him alone, although he is still capable of breeding fertilely with other, less favored, cats. (He may wish to disassociate himself from other cats, and feel humiliated by his bodily likeness to subhuman creatures.) The first of these strategies would be plausible for the claims of dolphins and the like, all of which at least come somewhat close to human intelligence. The second would be more plausible for the claims of cats and dogs.

The second question is what traits are decisive for regarding a given individual as rendering his species intelligent. Self-consciousness (or consciousness of oneself as a subject of conscious states) might be suggested, as a necessary condition of the desire to live.[17] Moral agency is another contender, since moral agents are presupposed by moral discourse as such. Finally, the use of language is the key to the rich kind of life enjoyed by human beings, so that it may be taken as what distinguishes the human from the subhuman. An attractive blend of these last two possibilities is participation in moral discourse: if we

54

discover that Martians argue about the issues discussed in this book, we should be obliged to regard them for moral purposes as human.

The question of which traits are crucial is less important for the species than for other interpretations of the moral rule against homicide, since no attempt is made to draw lines within the human species. But even here it may be crucial—especially on some interpretations of what it is to speak a language—to the status of some nonhumans such as chimpanzees. What seems to be the case is that the distinction between human and nonhuman rests not on any one trait, but on an interlocking set of traits, which will wax and wane as a whole.

Finally, we need to ask (supposing that the relevant traits admit of degree) how much of them is required to make a species one of the human level. (If they do not, we will still have to adjudicate borderline cases.) It is worth noticing that our standards can be more demanding here than for either of the species principle's two rivals. In order to reach minimally tolerable results, the present enjoyment principle will have to demand very little of a creature before treating it as a person; the potentiality principle can ask for more, since what the creature will attain in due course, not what it attains now, is the standard. But the species principle can demand the production of saints, philosophers, musicians, scientists, or whatever else is thought to be the highest embodiment of human nature, since the bulk of the species can gain their morally privileged status through the achievements of their best members, so long as there is not a sharp break between the capacities of the best of a species and members of that species generally.

One kind of creature to which some will wish to ascribe personhood, but which is not protected by the species principle, even as modified, is the robot. In making this remark I distinguish between robots and androids. Androids, although artificially manufactured, are structurally analogous to ordinary living organisms. Such creatures may be human in everything but origin, and thus may be counted as members of the human species—or, failing that, of a biological species other than the human, at the limit with one android to a species. Robots, as I conceive them, whatever clever tricks they are able to perform, are structurally more similar to washing machines than they are to animals (they can be fouled up but not killed) and hence are not human beings within the meaning of the moral rule against homicide.

This result is a reasonable one, in part for the reasons Paul Ziff advances for holding that robots could not have feelings,[18] and in part for the reasons Hubert Dreyfus advances for believing that a robot, in order to be intelligent, would have to have a humanlike body.[19] I rely, that is, on the intimate connections among human thought, perception, language, feeling, motor skill, and bodily structure. But there are also distinct reasons for not regarding the destruction of a robot as morally comparable to the killing of a person of the human species. Beings whose structure is that of an instrument built to service needs will not have the kind of instinctive desire to live that organisms have. It seems clear, for instance, that a robot built under Isaac Asimov's three laws of robotics[20] will be a natural slave, for whom destruction would not be the kind of evil death is for us, since it is built to prefer the safety or even the will of human beings to its own existence. The situation would be altered if robots acquire sufficient judgment to conclude they themselves were (paradigmatically) human.[21] But, since Asimov is vague about the structure and workings of his robots, one can only suppose that such "robots" are what I would call androids.

Of course I have been vague, too, about the line between robot and android. I take it, however, that we can and do distinguish between procreation and manufacture,[22] between repair, even self-repair, and healing, and between growth and addition of new mechanical elements. So long as no limits are placed on the kind of technology employed in the construction of robots, further discussion is not now useful, but must be postponed until human beings are both clever and imprudent enough to produce beings on the borderline between machine and living organism, whose capacities are such as to raise seriously the question of their personhood.

The same issue can be approached from another angle by asking, with Lazlo Versényi, whether a robot can be moral. In giving an affirmative answer to this question, Versényi relies on a dichotomy between the formal—and in his view formalizable—ethics of Kant and Plato and "unanalyzeable, nonempirical and nonrational intuition of moral values; mysterious moral sense; and totally inexplicable insight."[23] Formal ethics is accessible to a robot; intuitive ethics is not worthy of serious attention on the part of moral philosophers. But surely there is a source of moral understanding which is neither merely formal nor wholly irrational—participation in the kind of life characteristic of human beings, including family and social life. It is certainly reasonable to suppose that an adequate set of answers to human moral problems will bear marks of the kinds of contexts in which moral problems are actually experienced by human beings, and also that any being which is either moral or immoral will face moral problems in at least a somewhat similar context.

From this perspective, it is not necessary to reject the role of vicarious experience in moral reasoning—to hold, say, that only women and obstetricians have any business discussing abortion—in order to reject the common move which casts a "Martian" (i.e. a rational being innocent of the messy emotions, loyalties, and conflicts experienced by human beings) in the role of ideal observer for ethical purposes, and to insist instead that ethical understanding requires not only impartiality and dispassionate reflection but also participation in something akin to the kind of life one is being asked to judge.

If robots are structurally incapable of this kind of life, they may be held not to be moral agents even though their behavior suggests conformance to moral principles. What seem to be moral principles may be merely principles of design. And a being incapable, in accordance with the norm for the kind of thing that it is, of ever being a moral agent, might well be rationally denied the kinds of rights human beings or persons have.

I should add that whereas the destruction of a robot would not be murder, it might still be wrong unless carried out with good reason. The reasons would not have to be the same as those required for killing a human being, however; further it is not possible to go without some real life experience of dealing with robots. In any case, the species principle has some prima facie claim to be a satisfactory criterion for marking off the personal from the nonpersonal.

8. *The Present Enjoyment Principle*

THE APPEAL of the species principle, especially as modified and expanded to encompass intelligent nonhumans, to those who are prepared to be generous in their ascriptions of personhood is very great. To the extent, for instance, that we are prepared to regard even the most hopelessly retarded human being as a person, and the killing of such a one as murder, the species principle appears to provide the only plausible grounds for so doing. And even when its full effect is denied, the species principle still has important residues: many who are prepared to defend both abortion and capital punishment balk at the execution of pregnant women, and some defenders of abortion also disapprove of experiments on live aborted "fetuses," as well as experiments on fetuses *in utero* when abortion is intended. [24] And even if we were prepared to admit that the hopelessly retarded might be painlessly killed rather than cared for, still we would be most reluctant to countenance the use of such creatures for the kinds of experiments that are performed on animals, or their being killed for food. Finally, to the extent that we tend to think that there are organisms of the human species that may rightfully be treated as other than human—that may, for instance, be killed to relieve us of the burden of caring for and feeding them—we think in terms of human vegetables, not human brutes. The latter is quite as logical from the standpoint of a denial of the species principle.

Many, however, are not prepared to be so generous in extending the protection of the moral rule against homicide. Nor is this surprising, for the admission that a given creature is a person is morally very expensive, and becomes more so as the lists of human rights grow longer. And caring for those who are persons on the species principle frequently places burdens on those who are persons on narrower principles, of which an unwanted pregnancy may be taken as emblematic. It is therefore well worth asking whether a narrower version of the rule against homicide is possible, one, that is, which is not merely an ad hoc modification of the rule designed to allow us to kill those whose existence we find particularly burdensome.

An obvious possibility is to drop the reference to the species and to require that a creature be in present possession of distinctively human traits before the killing of such a creature will be deemed homicide. Assuming that what we value human beings for is their capacities for rational and social life, perhaps we should place the kind of value which grounds the moral rule against homicide only on those that (now) have these capacities. Or again, we may be impressed by the various ways human beings (and not animals) insist upon respect for their rights (including the right not to be killed), and feel that those who are incapable of making such appeals (or engaging in such resistance) do not deserve to be treated as persons. Let us call this principle the present enjoyment principle.

One consequence of the present enjoyment principle is that the killing of infants is never (morally speaking) murder, never a violation of someone's (serious) right to live, although in many contexts it will be a violation of the quasi-proprietary rights of the parents. One might expect this attitude to carry over into other contexts, so that defenders of infanticide will be more concerned with questions of "ownership" of war orphans, say, and less concerned with the welfare of the infant orphans themselves than the rest of us. This issue is very complex, however, as will become clear later on.

Once the species principle, and consequently the human rights of infants, is questioned, the problem of terminology needs to be discussed. "Human beings," in this context, ceases to be a very useful expression for those protected by the moral rule against homicide. Whatever might be said of fetuses, "infants are not human beings" sounds just too odd. Indeed, I suspect that "human beings" and "human organism" differ in meaning only as do "baby" and "infant": in other words, that while the evaluations implicit in the two terms are different, all human beings are human organisms and all human organisms are human beings. If I am right about this, it will not be possible—without biological or conceptual confusion—to defend abortion on the grounds that an embryo or fetus is not a human being, but it still might be possible to defend the practice on the grounds that such human organisms are not persons. [25]

On the other hand, Michael Tooley's suggestion that the word "person" be used in a purely moral way, to denote those possessing a serious right to live, [26] will not work either, except of course as a purely technical usage. (Compare the legal use of the word "person," for which personality belongs to those entities which are recognized as having rights and duties in law.) The word "person" is less tied to the human organism than is "human being," so that whether infants or fetuses are persons can be treated more or less as a straightforward moral question. But it still has a core of descriptive meaning resistant to eccentric moral views. Even if one holds that no one has a right to live, one must still call oneself a person if one uses the concept at all. On the other hand,

59

no matter how passionate a defender one might be of the rights of trees, to say that trees are people would justify a smile. I shall thus continue to use the expressions "human being," "person," and "human person"[27] to denote those protected by the moral rule against homicide, postponing further clarification to a later point. It is first necessary to develop the central objection to the present enjoyment principle.

9. Infanticide and Our Intuitions

THE MOST STRIKING CONFLICT between the present enjoyment principle and our intuitions—the implication of the principle that infants have no right to live—arises in the specific context of debates about abortion. Many such debates have been conducted within limits imposed by agreed-upon judgments concerning contraception and infanticide. Contraception, it has been agreed, is a morally legitimate way of avoiding undesired parenthood, and infanticide is not. The participants in the controversy have limited themselves to arguing that abortion (or a practice on the borderline between contraception and abortion) is more closely analogous to contraception than to infanticide, or more closely analogous to infanticide than to contraception. But some defenders of abortion have conceded—or even, like Tooley, insisted on and argued for—what has hitherto been the principal contention of opponents of abortion, that abortion and infanticide are essentially the same, and maintained that there are no good grounds for regarding infanticide as a violation of anyone's right to live.

I shall be considering Tooley's views in some detail, since by his willingness to carry the case against fetal rights to its logical extreme, he manages to present the issues underlying the abortion debate with more than ordinary clarity. An examination of the arguments employed by those who have rested their defense of abortion on the fact that the fetus (and not the woman) is unable to envisage a future for itself, talk, enter into social relations, and so on, will show that their premises are brought to their logical conclusion in Tooley's articles.

I shall not here attempt a direct proof that Tooley is wrong, and that infants have a right to live, but shall limit myself to showing that Tooley's attempt to show that the infant cannot be correctly ascribed a right to live (i.e., accorded the protection of the moral rule against homicide) does not succeed. How serious a limitation this is on a moral case against infanticide depends on one's view of the relationship between moral principles formulated by philosophers and socially established moral intuitions of a relatively concrete sort. In my view, the concrete intuitions embodied in our laws and customs, at least insofar as they are shared by the philosopher in his prereflective moments, are entitled to at least as much weight as the moral principles he finds plausible when they are stated in an abstract manner.

Hence, the feeling that exists against infanticide among persons of widely varying religious, political, and cultural attitudes will be taken as a datum for our inquiry. If it persistently resists attempts to accommodate it within our moral theories, we may be entitled to reject it. But if the arguments of this chapter are sound, we have no good reason to abandon our intuitions in this case.

The acceptability of an appeal to socially current intuitions may well be the chief issue between defenders of infanticide and me. But I think it can be shown that it is reasonable to appeal to such intuitions, and unreasonable to bar such appeals. That our moral intuitions are shaped by others—our parents, teachers, peers, and so on—before we are capable of thinking about morality for ourselves, I do not deny. But to regard this fact as in some way constituting an argument for the conclusion that the beliefs and attitudes so formed are as likely to be false as true is to deprive ourselves of any basis whatever for a moral theory. For there are indefinitely many moral theories, the doctrine that right conduct consists in maximizing pain and minimizing pleasure for instance, which are never seriously entertained by philosophers, because they deviate so wildly from the moral intuitions shared by the philosopher and his community. And there are results, such as that it is our duty to kill as many people painlessly as we can, which suffice to invalidate even the most superficially attractive moral theory if they follow from this theory as a result. Moreover, to argue that a moral intuition is suspect because of its source in family or social life is to render one's moral conclusions irrelevant to that life, and thus to moral problems as human beings in fact experience them.

One can best view the enterprise of moral theory as continuous with the pre-theoretical enterprise of working out the implications of what one has been taught in the area of morals, resolving real or apparent contradictions in these teachings, and defending, modifying, or abandoning various teachings in the face of challenge (a process that can take one rather far from what one has been taught). One can see the various schools of moral theory as resulting from taking as paradigmatic one kind of teaching (and hence of intuition) rather than another. Intuitions regarding fairness produce one moral theory when taken as central, intuitions concerning the moral relevance of certain consequences another, intuitions concerning the wrongfulness of homicide perhaps yet another. Of course intuitions vary considerably, both individually and culturally, accounting in part for the variety of moral theories advocated in the history of philosophy, and it is probably impossible to accommodate them all into a coherent account. But every time a strong moral intuition is overruled, the theory that overrules it must gain strength by organizing and illuminating many others. As for divergence among intuitions, the best that can be done is to look for intuitions shared by the parties to the dispute, and work from these intuitions to agreement on the other points where this is possible.

The underlying point is quite simple: since it is self-defeating to question one's own rationality, how we in fact think is evidence for how we ought to (will, if rational) think. And this point holds good in moral reasoning as well as anywhere else, so that common moral belief— including such beliefs as that it is wrong to kill babies—will be a touchstone of moral philosophy. [28]

The difficulty is that many people find themselves unable to accept the whole of the morality in which their parents tried to raise them, or of the conventional morality of their society. Nothing I have said implies that such people are wrong (nor that they are right). Indeed, it is impossible for anyone who is at all reflective to accept *all* the moral data that reach him from his parents, his peers, the newspapers, and so on, because these data are full of contradictions, even within the same source. The difficulty with a merely conventional morality in the present world is not that it is craven (someone might decide that the task of working out a personal moral position is hopeless and that he will simply play by the rules) but that it is not feasible. But this observation does not mean that ordinary moral judgments are irrelevant to the task of creating a satisfactory moral theory.

There remains the problem of cultural relativity. [29] The arguments of this book are directed principally to those who participate in modern Western culture, in which infanticide is not, yet at any rate, accepted, and whose more conventional selves will therefore condemn the practice. As for cultures in which infanticide is traditional, distinctions will have to be drawn. If a society is ignorant of the facts of human reproduction and can regulate its fertility only by infanticide, we can say either that in this case (not our own) the rights of the infant must yield to the superior rights of society or else that the harsh conditions of this society's life render abstention from infanticide, although still morally required, more than is to be expected from human beings not gifted with heroic virtue. [30] Alternatively, the participants in this culture may be in a moral blind alley where whatever they do will be wrong; one might doubt the intelligibility of this position, but it ought to be mentioned for the sake of completeness. [31] On the other hand, if female infanticide is practiced because females are less socially valued than males, or male infanticide because females are more salable as prostitutes, our resources of tolerance may be exhausted, and we may be forced to regard the culture where these acts take place as morally insensitive in this respect, just as we may in the end be forced to make a similar unfavorable judgment about our own society.

In general, the casuistical principles appropriate for dealing with the differences among cultures and those appropriate for applying general moral norms, given the diversity of experience and situation within the same culture, are in principle the same. The same considerations apply, for instance, as we look back, from the standpoint of contemporary reluctance to impose capital punishment, on those stages in the history of Anglo-Saxon jurisprudence when people were executed for larceny and other minor offenses, and capital punishment frequently took forms modern sentiment finds especially intolerable. All such judgments require us to take a moral result reached within our present culture as normative, but let the skeptic about the legitimacy of this procedure consider that the attempt to weed out taboos and be rational about morality in a systematic way is by no means culturally universal.

In any case, no degree of unwillingness to condemn cultures other than our own could lead us to abandon a condemnation of the killing of infants by those who participate in our culture. The most that relativistic arguments can show is that members of divergent cultures are each entitled to continue with their own customary evaluations. And that argument, of course, is as good in defense of our evaluations as it is for those of the ancient Greeks or the South Sea Islanders.

None of this discussion gives us any arguments against someone who sees nothing wrong with infanticide. The arguments of this section have been strictly defensive, consisting in attempts to ward off any attempt on his part to show that we, in holding the contrary view, are irrational. Some considerations in affirmative support of the rights of infants will be advanced below (section 13), but I have no expectation that these considerations will prove decisive. Perhaps the best that can be done is to urge the defender of infanticide to obey the laws which (still) protect infants from lethal attack, on the grounds that he, being dependent on our legal system for the defense of his person and property, ought to conform to those laws enacted for the protection of others, even when he disagrees with their scope. The rest of us can continue to presume that infanticide is wrong, quite independently of such arguments.

10. *Infanticide and Rights*

TOOLEY'S STRATEGY for showing that an infant should not be ascribed a serious right to live is indicated in the following passage: "My approach will be to set out and defend some basic moral principles specifying conditions an organism must satisfy if it is to have a serious right to life. It will be seen that these conditions are not satisfied by human fetuses and infants, and thus that they do not have a right to live."[32] Tooley's account of these basic moral principles gets quite complex, but for the purposes of the present critique the following simplified version will prove sufficient: "An organism possesses a serious right to live only if it possesses the concept of a self as a continuing subject of experiences and other mental states, and believes that it is itself such a continuing entity."[33] The underlying premise of Tooley's argument is his account of the concept of a right. Again, his analysis is complicated, but the following statement will suffice for our purposes: "My basic argument . . . rests upon the claim that there is a conceptual connection between the rights an individual can have and the circumstances under which they can be violated, . . . and that, in general, violation of an individual's right to something involves frustrating the corresponding desire."[34] The central thesis of Tooley's discussion follows immediately from this basic premise: since infants lack consciousness of themselves as continuing beings, they are incapable of desiring that they continue in existence. Accordingly they do not have a right to continue to live.

Against this reasoning I argue, first, that a man may have a right to something he does not desire, and second, that an organism can have a right to something it cannot desire.

Consider the (moral) right not to be punished as a criminal except in accordance with the law. This is a right that can be violated even when the person so punished is a neurotic seeking punishment or a religious fanatic seeking to emulate Christ. It would certainly be prima facie wrong to punish someone as a criminal for a crime he did not commit, or for an act not made criminal by law, just because he consents to and indeed ardently desires such a result, even if this desire is in no sense a temporary aberration but represents his considered decision as to the sort of life he wants to live. And it would seem (to me at least) that the reason it is wrong is that it is a violation of the neurotic's or the fanatic's rights.

(A possible other explanation is that the legal system does not exist to provide this kind of service. It is easy enough to imagine a situation where the exchange would be mutually beneficial, however. Suppose the police have given up hope of uncovering a brutal killer, and there is a danger of lynchings.)

To be sure, to hold that this is the case requires at least an exception to the principle *volenti non fit injuria* as employed by moralists, but this maxim will require heavy qualification in any case. One would hardly wish to apply it to children. Philosophers should resist the temptation to regard a proposition as self-evident because it is expressed in lapidary Latin.

But, of course, the neurotic or the fanatic possesses the concept of not being punished except in accordance with law. So that Tooley's central contention—that for someone to have a right, he must possess a concept of that to which he has a right—remains. A number of counterexamples to this contention are available.

1. Consider once again the right not to be punished except by due process of law. If the infant children of a man convicted of treason were

65

considered traitors themselves, and punished in some way as a result, their moral as well as their legal rights would clearly have been violated, even though they lacked any concept of due process or that of which they were deprived by their punishment.

2. Tooley himself cites the right of a child to an estate, which he is not now capable of wanting. He responds: "My inclination is to say that the correct description is not that the child now has a right to the estate, but that he will come to have such a right when he is mature, and in the meantime no one else has a right to the estate."[35] But this account will not do, given Tooley's account of what a right is, or indeed any reasonable account. For by no means is it always wrong, even prima facie, to take something to which one does not have any right. If I am gathering (unowned) blackberries, I do not have any right to blackberries I have not gathered, but both I and others who do not have any right to them may with perfect rectitude take them and thus deprive each other of the ones we take. (The idiomatic "have no right" implies [roughly] that I would be breaching someone's rights if I took that to which I had no right.)

True, Tooley might adapt a remark of Joel Feinberg's and argue that the property rights of an infant are "placeholders or reservations for the rights he shall inherit when he becomes a full-fledged interested being."[36] But while there is no strict logical difficulty about this proposal (a position of advantage or power can be kept open for someone not now in being, to hold when he comes into being) the application of it to our case is most implausible. For surely the infant has interests even now, in getting enough food if nothing else, for the sake of which his estate could be expended. That is to say, even an infant can enjoy wealth, although he is not yet capable of understanding that this is what he is doing.

If either of the foregoing examples is accepted, the close connection Tooley attempts to establish between right and desire and hence self-consciousness will be defeated. A being can have rights without a consciousness of that to which it has rights, and even without any consciousness at all. Hence no argument of Tooley's will succeed in showing that an infant does not have the right to continue its existence. Of course one does not *have* to accept them; one might hold that infants have no rights at all. But this position is grossly implausible, and in any case it is not Tooley's position.

66

Tooley wants to hold that infants have rights—for instance, a right not to be mutilated—and lack only a right not to be killed. He thus admits the soundness of objections of the above sort, and attempts to meet them (1) by asserting that someone's rights can be violated because the person will in the future come to desire that the act which constituted their violation had not taken place, and (2) by adding to his account of rights a complicated stipulation concerning potential desires, which Tooley sums up as follows:

> The basic idea . . . is simply that actions to which an individual doesn't object—either because he is incapable of desiring at the time that they not occur, or because he lacks relevant information, or because his desires have been "warped" by psychological or physiological means—may nevertheless violate his rights if there is some time at which he is or will be capable of wishing that the action had not occurred, and at which he *would* so wish if he had all the relevant information and had not been subjected to influences that distort his preferences. [37]

But Tooley's theory of rights, even as modified, cannot deal with a child's right to an education. Such a right cannot be treated as a right contingent upon maturity, since being educated is a way of achieving maturity. And it is not because the child's desires are "warped," but only because they are unformed, that he does not desire the things, the subtler kinds of aesthetic experience for instance, which it is one of the functions of an education to get him to desire. The most hopeful part of Tooley's account is the "lack of information" clause. But since education consists in important part in *giving* the child the information that (it is hoped) will make him desire certain things, to explain his lack of a desire for an education in terms of his lack of information is rather unsatisfactory from Tooley's standpoint. Arguing that a child has the right to the information that will make him glad to have received this information, and desirous of receiving more, is rather close to arguing that a baby has a right to live, since letting him live will make him glad to have been let live, and desirous of living longer.

I shall not pursue this line of reasoning any further, however, since it should be clear that, given sufficient equants and epicycles, all our common moral beliefs except that infants have a right to live can be accommodated. Making the points above is still worthwhile, however, since the extreme complexity of the connection between the concept of a right and that of a desire prepares us for the further complexity, and ultimate greater simplicity, of ascribing rights based directly on interests to those who now have no desires, but would eventually have them if we did not now kill them.

For, if, when considering the morality of mutilation or deprivation of property, "one should take into account not merely *future* desires... but also *potential* desires,"[38] it seems arbitrary to exclude from consideration those potential desires which are kept from becoming actual not by warping the preferences of the person whose desires they are, but by seeing to it that he never develops these preferences by killing him. (Compare my killing of a female infant with my conditioning her so that she will throw herself on her husband's funeral pyre.) And it is on the face of it extremely paradoxical that it should be permissible to kill but not to mutilate, to remove the head because it will not be missed but not remove the testicles which will. For instance it follows from Tooley's account that if one injures an infant one is well advised to finish it off, since the injury is for Tooley a violation of a right, the injury-plus-killing not. And mutilation is no violation of a right, for Tooley if the infant is known to have a disease which will kill it before it comes to miss its lost organs or powers, since there will then be no actual individual whose interests will have been violated. But if we castrate a boy child, who is then run over by a bus on the way to choir school, a wrong will be turned into a non-wrong by accident, although one might still hold that those who castrated the infant did wrong by creating a *danger* that there would be a discontented adult eunuch.

The chief point, however, is that since an infant normally will come to be glad that he wasn't killed at birth, it is at least bizarre to maintain that it is all right to kill him at birth since he will not miss the life that he thereby loses. Tooley's argument seems, in the end, to amount to little more than the saying that dead men—or dead babies—tell no tales. In any case, if one asks *why* one should accept Tooley's theory of rights, in all its complexity, the answer turns out to be that it supports the moral conclusions Tooley wishes to reach, including, of course, the conclusion that it is all right to kill babies. That it supports this conclusion is for many of us sufficient reason to reject his theory.

At this point a restatement of the principal issue in contention is desirable. It seems to be common ground that only those creatures

68

which have interests can have rights, and that one can have a right only to that which is in one's interest. The difference between Tooley and myself seems to be that Tooley thinks that an interest must be grounded in a desire, albeit in some cases the desire may only be a possible or future desire of an existing individual. [39] That is to say, if an act is to be a violation of someone's rights, it must be contrary to desires he could experience *now*, or desires he *will* experience in the future. I am maintaining, to the contrary, that at least sometimes desires are expressions of pre-existing interests, and that it is unnecessarily strained, when someone entertains clearly self-destructive desires, to refer to his potential desires to explain how his desires and interests are in conflict. (I do not suppose that someone could have an interest in having something he could never view except with aversion.) Accordingly, an infant can have an interest in continuing to live, although he can possess no articulate desires of any sort, and if we kill him he will never develop any. His existence as a self-maintaining system of a complex sort is sufficient to ground the claim that he has an interest in continuing to live, and hence also (if our common moral notions are not in error) a right to do so.

I have framed my critique of Tooley in terms of his analysis of the concept of a right. But the criticism might also be made in terms of his concept of a self. [40] Tooley comes close to identifying a person with his consciousness, so that either we cease to exist during periods of unconsciousness (as Hume came close to holding) or else (as Descartes held) despite appearances we are never unconscious. (On Tooley's difficulties with the notion of an unconscious person, see section 13.) A Cartesian standpoint might explain Tooley's rejection of the species and potentiality principles, since it is by virtue of his body that an infant is potentially self-conscious and belongs to the human species. Those whose concept of the self is different can accept these principles (or one of them) and hold that infants have a right to live.

11. Other Views on Infanticide

PERHAPS THE PREMISE of the previous discussion—that if infanticide is wrong it is because it is the violation of the infant's right to live—is incorrect. If this were true, Tooley's analysis could be accepted, at least insofar as it applied to rights, and our common belief that infanticide is wrong preserved. Moreover, the burden to be borne by defenders of abortion in distinguishing abortion from infanticide would be reduced, since we are more tolerant of arbitrary distinctions when rights are not in question. Accordingly, I shall consider some compromise views, which attempt to preserve Tooley's insight (or supposed insight) while making some sort of accommodation for most of our feelings about the killing of babies.

One version of this line of thought has been pursued by Mary Anne Warren. [41] Conceding that the logic of her defense of abortion (which is roughly the same as Tooley's) applies as well to infanticide, Warren goes on to insist that while infanticide is not murder, it is nonetheless prima facie wrong both "because even if [the infant's] parents do not want it and would not suffer from its destruction, there are other people who would like to have it and would, in all probability, be deprived of a great deal of pleasure by its destruction," and because people generally value infants and are prepared to support orphanages to provide for their care. The crucial difference between a fetus and an infant is for Warren that the care of fetus, but not an infant, requires the use of a woman's body and thus a restriction on her freedom.

It is clear that Warren's line of reasoning will not sustain anything like traditional inhibitions on infanticide, especially since many of her remarks about infants (that they give pleasure to those who rear them, that people are made unhappy at the thought of their being destroyed) are true also of kittens, which are routinely killed in our animal shelters. Warren sees that "it follows from [her] argument that when an unwanted or defective infant is born into a society which cannot afford and/or is not willing to care for it, then its destruction is permissible." It seems to me that she is committed to a similar result in many other circumstances, perhaps even when the parents, while not wishing to rear the child themselves, have a fixed aversion to the thought of its being reared by anyone else. For unlike natural resources and great works of art (Warren's examples), babies after all are, when viewed as commodities, replaceable. To emphasize the radical uniqueness of each human being would be to move sharply away from Warren's way of thinking about infants and fetuses.

A line of thought similar to Warren's is developed in another way by S. I. Benn. [42] Benn accepts Tooley's conclusion concerning the rights of infants, and goes on to argue that, if consistent, Tooley must reach the same result concerning very small children, since they no more than infants can envisage a future for themselves. He proposes to defend our common belief—or at least to provide a framework in which it can be intelligently discussed—by adducing rule-utilitarian considerations. "It is," he suggests, "because the person that he *will* be (provided he grows up) will be emotionally stunted or impaired if he is deprived of love and tender care as an infant, it is for the sake of those that *will* grow up into persons that we take care of all babies now. For not to do so for some— those that we regard as expendable or dispensable—might well lead us into a callous unconcern for others too." Obviously, Benn is not arguing that an infant which is killed is going to grow up into an emotionally stunted adult. His point is that if we killed some infants, we might end up treating the others coldly, thus stunting the adults resulting from the ones we do not kill.

If we view the critical moralist as exercising something like a power of judicial review, employing one standard or other for the scrutiny of moral intuitions as the judge employs standards for the scrutiny of statutes, Benn's argument provides, I think, adequate indication of a reasonable basis for our feelings about infants. But, taken as an autonomous standard from which norms concerning infanticide could be derived apart from any prior commitment to preserving socially established intuitions unless they are shown to be irrational, it relies on premises we do not and cannot know to be true. The only way of finding out whether a society having our society as part of its history could combine a lethal chamber for some infants with appropriately tender care for others, is to allow such a situation to develop and see what happens. And then, of course, it would be too late.

If infants did not have a right to live, we would not lightly behave as if they did. If, let us say, extreme mental defectives are not persons, we might still feel obliged to extend to them the rudimentary right not to be killed, to avoid having to set up a standard of quality which a human organism would have to reach in order to be considered a person. A relatively small number of courtesy persons might be established in order to guarantee the rights of real ones. But to apply this line of thought to infants would be irrational, since it would mean that for every actual person there would have been at least one courtesy one.

Again, assuming at least some value is placed upon nascent life, it would be wasteful to perform a eugenic abortion where there is some doubt whether the fetus is defective, if the defect can be diagnosed at birth and the infant then killed without violating anyone's rights. I conclude that if infanticide (by or with the consent of the parents) is wrong, it is because to kill an infant is to violate that infant's rights. Since I have already argued that our common moral intuition concerning infanticide is to be preserved, we must ascribe to infants a right to live.

Ronald Green advocates a position akin to Benn's, that (some) beings not in present enjoyment of distinctively human capacities have rights conferred upon them by those that now have them.[43] The chief difference between this position and Benn's is that the protection of such creatures is not a mere matter of social prudence. Once conferred, "these rights are real moral rights, they are agreed upon by the same persons who formulate any moral rule: the community of rational agents." Nonetheless, conferred rights are distinguished from rights pure and simple by more than the consideration that a moral rule becomes viable only through its acceptance by those who are presently moral agents (a class that does not include infants). The ultimate ground of such moral rules lies not in the interests of the creatures protected by them, but rather in those of rational agents: "the effect of conferring or denying rights on our general capacity for sympathy; the effect on the possible interests of possible agents; and, finally, the character or moral worth of rational agents generally."

The second of these considerations has no application to infants, since moral agents know that they will never be infants in the future. The question is whether the terms of the original position will let them use this knowledge. (Green appeals to their interests as parents, but of course no parent need kill his own children unless he wants to: if that other parents commit infanticide bothers him he can simply develop calluses.) The others all refer to the good of the moral agent conceived of in ideal terms: his being a sympathetic, morally worthy kind of person. In appealing to the agent's good conceived in these terms, Green departs from the usual contractual position, which limits itself to what Rawls calls the "primary goods" of the parties to the social contract—a tradition Green himself appeals to when he dismisses the concern felt by opponents of abortion for the fetus as "informed by a complex moral and religious viewpoint . . . inadmissible . . . in the considerations of impartial rational agents." We are of course under no obligation to renounce our ethical views when entering into the negotiations for the social contract, but if we do not do so, the frame of reference from which Green derives the concept of a conferred right will be undermined. An ideal of consideration for those too weak to bargain for their rights is for many as compelling a basis for the ascription of rights as is the social contract. And it is on this basis that I would affirm the rights of infants.

To argue that the social contract does not provide an adequate basis for assessing the claims of infants does not mean that the vague but important insight which underlies both social contract theories and moral relativism must be denied application in this area: that our moral judgments about killing babies (and other issues) rest in significant part on an understanding among ourselves that certain things are of value, and that some acts violate, offend, or damage these values. Nor does the rejection of the kind of argument advanced by Warren, Benn, and Green with regard to babies commit me to the rejection of such arguments in all contexts (see section 15).

What I have done so far is to expound the species principle, and to state and give grounds for rejecting the present enjoyment principle. In particular, I have argued that there is no good reason to deny, as holders of the present enjoyment principle must, that infants have a right to live in principle no different from that enjoyed by adults. With this background, we are prepared to confront the question of abortion.

III /

SCOPE OF THE PROHIBITION:

Fetuses and `Human Vegetables"

I NOW TURN to an exposition of and defense of the potentiality principle, an attempt to do justice to the competing claims of the potentiality and species principles, and an argument that at least the central cases of abortion are morally unacceptable.

12. Abortion

I SHALL ASSUME here that infants are protected by the moral rule against homicide. From this assumption it seems to follow immediately that fetuses, and other instances of human life from conception onward, are also so protected, so that, unless justified or mitigated, abortion is murder. For there seem to be only two possible grounds for asserting the humanity of the infant: (1) The infant is a member of the human species (species principle). (2) The infant will, in due course, think, talk, love, and have a sense of justice (potentiality principle). And both (1) and (2) are true of fetuses, embryos, and zygotes, as well as of infants. A zygote is alive (it grows) and presumably is an instance of the species *homo sapiens* (of what other species might it be?), and it will, if nothing goes wrong, develop into the kind of creature which is universally conceded to be a person.

But a number of arguments still have to be answered before the humanity or personhood of the fetus can be asserted with confidence. All of them are reflected in, and lend plausibility to, Joel Feinberg's remark: "To assert that a single-cell zygote, or a tiny cluster of cells, as

74

such, is a complete human being already possessed of all the rights of a developed person seems at least as counter-intuitive as the position into which some liberals [defenders of abortion] are forced, that newly born infants have no right to continue living."[1] These arguments are (1) that if a fetus is a person because of its potential and its biological humanity, spermatazoa and ova must also be considered persons, which is absurd; (2) that personhood is something one acquires gradually, so that a fetus is only imperfectly a person; (3) that there is an adequately defensible dividing point between the human and the nonhuman, the personal and the nonpersonal, which enables us to defend abortion (or "early" abortion) without being committed to the defense of infanticide; and finally (4) that the opponent of abortion himself does not take seriously the humanity of the fetus, an argument *ad hominem.* Insofar as one relies on intuition to establish the wrongness of infanticide, one must come to terms with the contention that the assertion that a fetus is a person is itself counter-intuitive.

1. Michael Tooley argues that if it is seriously wrong to kill infants or fetuses because they potentially possess human traits, it must also be seriously wrong to prevent systems of objects from developing into an organism possessing self-consciousness, so that artificial contraception will be just as wrong as infanticide. But only organisms can have a right to life, although something more like an organism than a mere concatenation of sperm and egg might have a right to something like life. And the same point can be reached if we speak not in terms of a right to life but of a moral rule against certain kinds of killing, for only an organism can be killed.

There is another, more complicated, argument against the contention that a spermatazoon and an ovum, not united, might be protected by the moral rule against homicide (or would be if infants and fetuses were). Since the moral rule against homicide is a rule that protects rights, it cannot obtain unless there is some specifiable individual[2] whose rights would be violated were it breached. A sperm conjoined with an ovum in this way is not in any sense an individual; therefore it cannot have any rights. For this reason the prevention of such a combination's being fruitful cannot be a violation of the moral rule against homicide. An ejaculation contains many more spermatazoa than could possibly be united with ova, and it is difficult to see the sperm-plus-ovum combinations which do not prevail as somehow deprived of something on which they have a claim.

But it is hard to reject all rights-claims made on behalf of inchoate subjects. It is commonly held to be prima facie wrong to exterminate entire species of animals, and such a wrong could be committed without destroying any individual animal (e.g., by rendering all members of the species sterile). It seems that many of us want to accord to the species as such a right to continue in existence as a species. (Compare the notion that genocide, the destruction of an entire race or ethnic group, is a crime over and above, and indeed apart from, the destruction of individual members of such a group.) How seriously we take talk of the rights of species depends on how seriously we take the interests of species. It will not do to refuse to admit the existence of such interests on the grounds that "a whole collection, as such, cannot have beliefs, expectations, wants, or desires,"[3] since such conditions are not necessary to the existence of interests. We can easily view the perpetuation of a species through its characteristic mode of reproduction as an act, not only of the individual organisms that engage in reproductive activity, but also of the species itself, acting through its members. It is thus possible to attribute an aim of preserving itself to the species as a whole and to see this aim as frustrated when a species becomes extinct.

If so, it seems also that human beings have at least a general duty to procreate, to the extent that it would be wrong to encompass, or to adopt maxims which entail, the dying-out of the human species. (What I have in mind are those who hold that truly virtuous or enlightened persons will abstain from sexual activity or reproduction, a view which has the result that the human species will be continued by fools or sinners, if by anyone.) Thus, it seems, unrealized human possibilities do have some sort of claim on us. Still, the distinction between an individual organism and an unrealized possibility of such an organism is surely great enough to block any attempt to bring such unrealized possibilities within the scope of the moral rule against homicide.

One can reply similarly to the contention that, since every cell in the body is a potential person (by cloning), and no very great moral weight attaches to the cells in the body, no very great moral weight attaches to potential persons. But even with cloning, an ordinary human cell is not only a merely potential person: it is also a merely

76

potential organism. Belief that creatures which are potentially personal are persons is not the same as believing that anything from which such a creature might arise is also a person. One might, in view of the possibility of cloning, argue that a one-celled zygote is only a potential organism, essentially no different from an ovum or an ordinary cell; but the embryo and the fetus are clearly actual organisms, even if they are supposed to be merely potential persons. Hence, if to be potentially personal is to be a person, they are actual persons as well.

Spermatozoa and ova might be said to be living individuals in a sense. But it is clear that a spermatozoon cannot be considered a member of the human species or a being potentially possessing the traits we regard as distinctively human in the way a fetus or infant can. A developed human being issuing from a sperm alone is a possibility far outside the normal powers of the spermatozoon in the way a developed human being issuing from a fetus or infant is not outside the normal powers of those creatures.

The case of the ovum is more complicated, since parthenogenesis, reproduction from ovum alone, takes place in at least some species. But, apart from considerations involving twinning and recombination (to be discussed below), fertilization still remains a relatively bright line available for distinguishing prehuman organic matter from the developing human organism. Finally, we must remember that sperm and ovum are biologically parts of *other* human individuals (the parents).

2. Perhaps, however, it is a mistake to look for a bright line between prehuman organic matter and a developing human being or person. Perhaps personhood is a quality the developing human creature acquires gradually. This suggestion will always have a considerable appeal to the moderate-minded. For it avoids the harshness, or seeming harshness, of those who would require great suffering on the part of the woman carrying a fetus for the sake of that fetus's rights, while avoiding also the crudity of those who regard abortion as of no greater moral significance than cutting one's toenails, having a tooth pulled, or swatting a fly. Moreover, that abortion is morally less desirable the closer it is to birth—and not simply because a late abortion is more likely to harm the woman—is one of the few intuitions widely shared on all sides of the abortion controversy, and thus not to be despised. That abortion should become harder and harder to justify as pregnancy proceeds,

without being ever as hard to justify as is the killing of a person, is a suggestion which ought therefore to be given the most serious attention.

The gradualist suggestion raises a problem of quite general scope. Not only as regards the distinction between prehuman organic matter and a human person, but also as regards that between human beings and brute animals,[4] and that between a dying person and a corpse,[5] our thought is pulled in two different directions. On the one hand, we find it natural to look for sharp, if not radical, breaks between different kinds of being, for evolutionary quanta so to speak. On the other hand, we are suspicious of sharp breaks and look for continuities at every point in nature. On a merely theoretical level, Kant's suggestion—that we regard the principle of continuity and the principle of speciation as regulative ideals or heuristic principles which, although contradictory if asserted together, are nonetheless useful in prompting the advance of knowledge; in other words, that we should look for both continuities and gaps[6]—is most attractive. But it is of very little use to us here.

For what we are looking for is a way of making abortion decisions that offers some hope of rational agreement. And there seems to be no stable, nonarbitrary way of correlating stages of fetal development with justifying grounds. At the stage of development when the embryo most closely resembles a fish, the moderate on the abortion question will want to ascribe it stronger rights than he does fish, but weaker rights than he does full human beings. And the moderate, as I conceive him, regards an infant as a human person, though the difference between a human infant and an infant ape is not palpable. Turning to "indications," it is far from clear why incestuous conception, for instance, plays the kind of role it does in justifying abortion to many moderates.[7]

There is a form of the moderate position which seems to escape this line of attack. Marvin Kohl defines and defends a "moderate feminist" view of abortion, according to which "a living potential human being has the prima facie right to life but... the actual right may be reasonably denied in cases of abortion on request."[8] In other words, although the killing of a fetus requires justification, any reason which might prompt a woman to request an abortion is sufficient.

Kohl concedes that there is nothing in his view to prevent a woman from having an abortion for no reason at all, or more precisely, nothing in his view to permit Kohl to disapprove such abortions. But he sees no

78

need for such a preventative. To suppose that a significant number of women will have frivolous abortions, thinks Kohl, is to be guilty of "the most deadly anti-women bias of all, namely: that unless women are carefully controlled they will kill their own progeny without reason because they are not fully rational creatures." In this way, Kohl combines a moderate assessment of the fetus with an avoidance of line-drawing. The issue of how much justification is required for killing a fetus is left to the good sense and discretion of the pregnant woman.

There are three answers to Kohl here: one qualitative, one quantitative, and one conceptual. The qualitative point is that while it is of course extremely unlikely that a woman will have an abortion for a lark, there is also evidence that women and couples (I do not know what Kohl considers a significant number) will sometimes request abortions for uncompelling reasons. There have been reports of women having abortions because the child turned out to be of the "wrong" sex, and because a one-in-twenty chance of a cleft lip was diagnosed.[9] Quantitatively, where permissive attitudes toward abortion prevail, the number of abortions has been known to exceed the number of live births. To defend such results one has to abandon all pretense of moderation about abortion and contend that the fetus has no right to live, even a prima facie one, against its mother. For—and this is the conceptual point—there is a connection between the concept of a right and the maxim that no one shall be judge in his own cause. I should remark in conclusion that I do not regard either women or men as fully rational beings. A writer on ethics who denies the irrational (even perverse) side of the human make-up, including his own, is doomed to irrelevance. In any case, questions of sexual bias, however important they may be in other contexts, are of very little relevance here. For the unborn, at least as much as women, may be victims of prejudice.

Moreover, if personhood or humanity admits of degrees before birth, then it would seem that it must admit of degrees after birth as well. And even if we can manage to block such inferences as that kings are more persons than peasants, Greeks than barbarians, men than women (or women than men), or those with Ph.D.'s than those with M.A.'s, according to this theory we should still expect that adults will be considered more fully human than children. But few hold and fewer still teach that a ten-year-old child[10] can be killed on lighter grounds

79

than an adult. Indeed the killing of small children is often considered worse than the killing of adults. (Although a parent who kills his child is likely to receive a less severe sentence than someone who kills an adult, this remnant of the *patria potestas* is the result of excuse or mitigation rather than of justification.)[11]

Some philosophers, it is true, might contend that there are degrees of humanity, but that full-fledged humanity is attained well before the age of ten. The question then is at what point full-fledged humanity is attained. Tooley's suggestion—twenty-four hours after birth—is clearly dictated by considerations of convenience rather than by the nature of the newborn. Some might say that first use of speech is a plausible criterion, but the development of linguistic capacities is a process, if anything is, not completed, if ever, until much later in a human being's development than his tenth birthday. If one wishes to fix a point after birth when someone becomes a full-fledged person, it could seem plausible to some thinkers to choose a point after the age of ten—when the nervous system is fully developed, at puberty, or at the conventional age of majority. In any case, the gradualist does not avoid the central problem—that of determining when we have a person in the full sense on our hands.

It has also been argued that a graduation from personhood into nonpersonhood can be observed at the end of life.[12] But the consequences of such a view are scarcely tolerable. For what the analogy with abortion leads to is the killing of old people (1) without their consent, and (2) for the sake of relieving *others* of the burden they pose. Whatever our conclusion might be concerning voluntary euthanasia, and whatever difficulties there might be in fixing a precise moment of death, we cannot admit that anyone who is humanly conscious, or will or may regain human consciousness, is anything but a full-fledged person. This point can be restated in more technical terms as follows. The concept of a person is normally both open-textured and flexible in its application—a corporation for instance may be treated legally as a person for some purposes and not for others. But when the concept of a person is given one particular use, to mark out those creatures whose existence and interests are to be given special protection in the court of morality, there are special reasons weighing in the direction of clarity and rigidity. Whatever the extent to which the interest of a given person might legitimately be sacrificed for the good of the community, it seems intolerable that a creature should be regarded as not a person—and hence of next to no account in moral deliberation—simply because it is or appears to be in the interest of others to so regard that creature. At any rate, to proceed in such a manner would be to overthrow some of the most fundamental elements of our moral tradition.

The difference between early and late abortion is best accounted for, I believe, not by the more nearly human status of the mature fetus as compared with the younger one, but rather by the closer imaginative and emotional link between the mature fetus and a born child and hence between such a creature and an adult human than is the case for a young fetus or embryo. Hence, while whatever norms are appropriate to our treatment of fetuses might be applied with greater strictness to them when they are mature than when they are young, nonetheless the fundamental moral status of all fetuses might still be the same.

We might also be faced with a gray area, not an area in which the unborn creature is gradually becoming a person, but one in which its status as a person or as prehuman organic matter (like an ovum) is open to reasonable doubt. The question for interventions in such a gray area would be on which side—of excessive risk or excessive caution—we prefer to err, and the decision might well depend on which end of the gray area we were at, just as the justifiability of firing a gun at an unidentified animal depends on how likely it is that it is a human being rather than a dangerous beast, without its being necessary to invoke the possibility that it might be something in between. In such cases the doctrine called probablism—that the agent is entitled to take the benefit of an honest doubt—and its rivals in the history of casuistry[13] become of relevance. It would seem that one's decision must be based not only on the strength of the doubts in question, but also on the relative importance of the interests at stake, so that even a fairly small possibility that what one is doing is taking the life of a person requires interests of considerable importance to override it.

Germain Grisez takes a more stringent view of this issue. He argues that if someone kills an embryo, not knowing whether or not it is a person (but having some reason to suppose that it is), he is in no different a moral posture than someone who kills what he knows is a person. In his own words, "to be willing to kill what for all we know might be a person is to be willing to kill it if it is a person." And he observes of possibly or probably abortifacient methods of birth control: "If one is willing to get a desired result by killing, and does not know whether he is killing or not, he might as well know that he is killing."[14] (This last case is an extremely complex one, since several layers of doubt may be superimposed upon one another: whether the method chosen results in the destruction of zygotes, whether there is a moral distinction between the prevention of implantation and the outright killing of the zygote, and whether the zygote is a human person within the meaning of the moral rule against homicide. This last doubt is itself complex, having factual, conceptual, and moral elements difficult or impossible to disentangle from one another.)

It does seem to me, however, that there is some difference, although not a large one or one it is desirable to emphasize, even between someone who says, "I know I am killing a person" and someone who says, "I may be killing a person, and I'd just as soon not find out whether I am." The latter might, after all, find out what he is doing despite himself, and stop doing it. But someone who says, "I may be killing a person, but I'm not satisfied that I am, and if you satisfy me, I'll stop" is in neither of these positions. (He may still be *wrong*, of course.)

3. We are now prepared to address the question of the homicidal character of abortion head on. If we assume the personhood of the human infant when born, is there a point later than fertilization when the life of a human person may be said to begin?

a. One possible dividing point is that stage at which twinning, and the combination of two developing zygotes to form one organism, is no longer possible. If something which we could not help but regard as a person were to split, or merge with another person, in such a manner, we would be compelled, in order to ascertain what (if anything) was the continuation of our original person, to rely on such criteria as memory and character. Bodily continuity would not give an unambiguous result. But since a developing zygote has neither memory nor character, we are left without means of resolving questions of personal identity. The potentiality of acquiring memory or character may suffice to ground a claim of personhood, but only with an organism whose unity and uniqueness is firmly secured.

One can hardly leave the question in this state, however, since the question of dividing (and fusing) selves cuts very deep into the contested question of personal identity. Faced with the possibility of a dividing self, there are, I think, three different possible responses. One can employ such a possibility to undermine our idea of a person, of one being persisting throughout the human life span.[15] Such a course would seem to overthrow a great deal of our moral universe, not least our ethics of homicide. A second strategy is the heroic course of regarding the self before a division as in fact two selves, so that each subsequent self will have the whole pre-split history as part of its past. The implausibility of this position need hardly be labored. The third possibility treats the question of who a given person is (in split cases) as relative to the temporal perspective from which the question is asked. Asked from before the split, the question leads us to pick out a Y-shaped "lifetime," including the pre-split self, and both subsequent branches. Asked from the perspective of afterwards, the question leads us to pick out one of the post-split selves, including the pre-split self as part of its history. The labored quality of this solution means that it can coexist with our concept of a person only when splits remain extraordinary (or a mere possibility): it is a precondition of the kind of language of selves that we have that selves normally neither split nor fuse.[16] Hence there is a legitimate presumption against positions which require us to admit splitting or fusing selves, and hence also the capacity for fission and fusion enjoyed by the one-celled zygote is a legitimate moral difference between it and an infant or older embryo which warrants our regarding it as not a person. It hardly seems plausible to regard a distinction linked to our very concept of a person as arbitrary.

If this cut-off point is accepted, we are committed to the existence of bits of human biological material which are neither human organisms, nor parts of human organisms, but things which are becoming human organisms. But this of itself provides no warrant for extending the category of "human becoming" to embryos and fetuses generally.[17] For the behavior of the zygote is quite clearly an anomaly, and any way we choose to deal with it is going to produce some degree of conceptual discomfort. At least where the context is an ethical one, the category of "human becoming" seems to be the least uncomfortable way of dealing with the problem. But being an embryo can still be part of the life cycle of members of the human species, as being a caterpillar is part of the life

83

cycle of members of various species of butterfly. For the justification present in the zygotic case for introducing an anomalous concept is not present in the embryonic one.

b. A plausible but troublesome dividing point is suggested by a difficulty of persuasion which the opponent of abortion commonly faces: the invisibility of his client, the fetus. (Consider the frequent occurrence of abortion in lists of crimes without victims.) This difficulty is met, at least in part, by photographs of fetuses *in utero* and of the results of abortion now widely available. But such persuasive devices have a very important limitation: they are of use only when the unborn creature has some semblance of human form.

This line of reasoning suggests that a necessary criterion of personhood is the possibility that the creature regarded as a person be the object of at least a modicum of human sympathy, and that such sympathy cannot in principle be extended to embryonic life lacking any semblance of human form even when the standard of comparison is an infant rather than an adult. (Capacity to evoke sympathy is not of course a sufficient condition for personhood, since we can and do feel sympathy for dogs and horses.) One might buttress this suggestion by noticing its affinities with the historically important distinction between the formed and the unformed fetus[18] and by citing such remarks as that "only of a living human being and what resembles (behaves like) a living human being can one say: it has sensations; it sees; is blind; hears; is deaf; is conscious or unconscious."[19] Further support might be drawn from the psychological observation that fellow-feeling precedes a sense of justice, sympathy a willingness to accord rights.[20] For versions of the case against abortion, like John T. Noonan, Jr.'s latest attempt,[21] which lean heavily on the response to the fetus that is possible by the educated imagination, the appearance of a human-like form would seem to be the crucial dividing point.

On the other hand, it is essential that the limitation on human sympathy in question be in some sense intrinsic and inherent. To allow merely contingent limitations upon our sympathy to delimit those who are entitled to rights would be to sanction every kind of prejudice. One cannot for instance justify—though one can of course *explain*—the difficulty many people have in regarding the fetus as an object of serious moral concern by appealing to the limited nature of the encounters mature humans have with it. [22] At least, when such concern is *possible*, sufficient basis for regarding such concern as appropriate is provided by the consideration that the fetus is a member of the human species which will in due course do the things we normally think of as human. And I know of no way of proving that fellow-feeling for zygotes is impossible, apart from a showing (not available without independent reasons for not regarding the nascent human organism as a person) that such sympathy is so radically inappropriate as to be humanly unintelligible. Certainly some people have believed, if only because the logic of their argument required (or appeared to require) it, that zygotes were human persons.

Supposing fellow-feeling for zygotes to be impossible (in the relevant sense of "impossible"), we are faced with the question of at what point fellow-feeling for the nascent human organism becomes a possibility. And the answer to this question may well depend on the mood in which we approach the data (in particular the photographs). In any case, the latest cut-off point which seems at all defensible on this kind of ground is six weeks. After that point, while one might have difficulty feeling sympathy for a fetus (or indeed an infant or an adult of another race), there seems to be no way of maintaining that such sympathy is impossible or unintelligible.

c. None of the other proposed intra-uterine dividing points is in the end credible. The beginning of heart or brain activity gains its plausibility from the criteria of death, but the cessation of such activity is a criterion of death only because it is irreversible: when, as in the embryonic case, such activity will begin in due course, there is no reason to regard its absence as decisive on the personhood issue. Growth alone, combined with the possibility of future activity, seems sufficient to justify the finding that the distinctively human kind of life is present, unless we are able to find some other reason for denying the immature embryo the status of a person, or are prepared to revert to the present enjoyment principle and treat infants as well as fetuses as subpersonal.

Writing in defense of a brain-activity criterion, Baruch Brody asks:

> Imagine the following science-fiction case: imagine that medical technology has reached the stage at which, when brain death occurs, the brain is removed, "liquefied," and "recast" into a new functioning brain. The new brain bears no relation to the old one (it has none of its memory traces and so on). If the new brain were put back into the old body, would the same

human being exist or a new human being who made use of the body of the old one? I am inclined to suppose the latter. But consider the entity whose body has died. Is he not like the fetus? Both have the potential for developing into an entity with a functioning brain (we shall call this a weak potential) but neither now has the structure of a functioning brain. [23]

The answer is that there is this crucial distinction between the two sorts of "weak potential." The weak potential of the fetus includes genetic information, with which the fetus will, in due course, generate a brain of its own. The weak potential of a brain-dead individual is merely the capacity to sustain a brain which can be imposed upon it from the outside.

Of course the absence of brain activity means that the unborn organism is not conscious, but once again this lack of consciousness, being merely temporary, has no decisive moral weight. Conversely, the responses to stimuli observed in very young embryos do not of themselves establish personhood—that must rest on the capacity for distinctively human development—whether or not these responses indicate consciousness in the usual sense. They do, however, like human form, provide a possible basis for sympathy.

d. Quickening has moral relevance of a secondary sort, since it affects the way a woman perceives the life within her, and hence also the social results of the widespread practice of abortion. But it does not represent any biologically or morally significant stage in the development of the fetus itself.

The decisive objection to viability is not that it is unclear precisely when a given fetus is capable of prolonged life outside the womb—with the result that legal definitions of viability are often too late. It is not necessary to demand that the line between persons and nonpersons be perfectly precise, so long as it is clear enough to enable us to make intelligent decisions regarding abortion and other such issues; it is necessary to demand only that it not be arbitrary. Nor is it decisive that viability is relative to medical technology. (So, on many views, is death.) The decisive objection to viability is that there is no reason to suppose that the fact that a given creature cannot live outside a given environment provides a reason why depriving it of that environment should be morally acceptable. (And the independent viability of even a born human being is of course a highly relative matter.) The moral significance of viability, like that of quickening, is secondary. It results from our ability to relieve a woman of a burdensome pregnancy while preserving the fetus alive—by premature birth rather than abortion in the usual sense. But the relevance of this point is limited, since prematurity has its hazards.

e. Although birth is given considerable significance by our law and conventional morality (otherwise this section would not have to be written), it is still difficult to see how it can be treated as morally decisive. Considered as a shift from one sort of dependency to another, I believe it has little moral importance. The severance of the umbilical cord removes the child, not from the body of his mother, but from the placenta, an organ of his own for which he has no further use. The social and administrative importance of birth is well accounted for in terms of practicality and discretion irrelevant to the abortion issue. One example is the reckoning of United States citizenship from birth rather than conception; another is the practice of not counting fetuses in the census.

And the grounds given by H. Tristram Engelhardt for distinguishing between fetus and infant, "that the mother-fetus relationship is not an instance of a generally established social relation," whereas "the infant, in virtue of being able to assume the role 'child,' is socialized in terms of this particular role, and a personality is *imputed* to it,"[24] are in fact an argument for drawing the line some time, say twenty-four hours, after birth. It would be possible to postpone the imputation of personality (signalized by naming) for such a period in order to look for defects and decide whether to kill the infant or spare it. On the assumption, argued for in Chapter II, that newborn infants are persons, Engelhardt's argument must therefore be rejected.

Finally, treating birth as the dividing point between the human and the nonhuman places a rationally indefensible premium on modes of abortion designed to kill the unborn infant within the womb, since once removed from the womb a fetus is born, and thus human by the suggested criterion, and is therefore entitled to be kept alive if prospects of success exist. Some might try to get around this by stipulating that whether a creature of the human species counts as an infant (with a right to life) or an abortus (which doesn't have one) depends on the intentions with which it is delivered. This kind of proposal seems quite arbitrary, however.

4. A final objection to the claim that abortion is homicide is the argument *ad hominem*. Ralph B. Potter, Jr., phrases this objection:

> Neither the church nor the state nor the family actually carries out the practices logically entailed by the affirmation that the fetus is fully human. The church does not baptize the outpouring spontaneously aborted soon after conception. Extreme unction is not given. Funeral rites are not performed. The state calculates age from date of birth, not of conception, and does not require a death or a burial or a birth certificate nor even a report of the demise of a fetus aborted early in pregnancy. Convicted abortionists are not subjected to penalties for murder. The intensity of grief felt within a family over a miscarriage is typically less than that experienced upon the loss of an infant, an older child, or an adult. [25]

But alongside the indications of a less than personal status for the fetus in our laws and customs listed by defenders of abortion, there have been many indications of fetal personhood. Since Potter mentions baptism, it is worth remarking that the Roman Catholic Church ordains the baptism of embryos of whatever degree of maturity, although problems of feasibility naturally arise in cases close to conception because the nascent organism is so small. And Protestants who do not baptize fetuses need not be expressing a lesser evaluation of unborn life, but only a non-Catholic baptismal theology. (Certainly many Protestants have condemned abortion, as have many non-Christians, who of course do not baptize anyone.)

There have been many indications that the fetus has been considered a person in the law of torts and the law of property. One might also notice the holding of a New York court that a fetus is a patient for the purposes of the doctor-patient testimonial privilege, [26] as well as the traditional reluctance to execute a pregnant woman and the accompanying feeling that the killing of a pregnant woman is a peculiarly reprehensible act. And men and women sometimes feel significant grief over the loss of an unborn child. Even contemporary sensibility has little difficulty personalizing a fetus—calling it a "baby," and using the pronouns "he" and "she"—in the context, say, of instruction in the facts of reproduction or in the techniques of prenatal care. Finally, the

88

existence of inherited norms forbidding abortion itself testifies to a recognition of fetal rights. [27]

Some (although hardly all) of the above features of our laws and customs might be explained in other terms. A fetus might be treated as a person with a condition subsequent, [28] in other words as having rights (now), subject to the rebuttable expectation that it will mature. So artificial a concept—while no doubt acceptable in law—should not be introduced into morality without very compelling justification. A few might tend to think of a fetus as a person when its interests and those of its mother work together (for instance in the getting of food stamps), [29] while doubting its status only when the mother herself desires to be rid of her child. But it is difficult to see how this could be justified.

Moreover, the practices that seem to point away from fetal personhood can be explained in other ways. To the extent that funeral practices are designed to deal with a severed relationship, they are not necessary when no such relationship has been established. The same can be said of the rule of inheritance cited by Joel Feinberg as counting against fetal personhood: "A posthumous child . . . may inherit; but if he dies in the womb, or is stillborn, his inheritance fails to take effect, and no one can claim through him, though it would have been different if he lived for an hour after birth." [30] It can be explained in part as a special rule of intestate succession designed (*inter alia*) to guarantee that spurious or doubtful pregnancy will not confuse inheritance. The disposition of its property is in any case a matter of indifference to a dead fetus. Finally, the reluctance of the courts to treat the fetus as a human person in criminal-law contexts other than abortion requested by a pregnant woman [31] can be explained as reflecting an unwillingness of courts to read criminal statutes more broadly than their language requires.

Nor is it necessary that the opponent of abortion insist that abortion be treated, legally or socially, as murder. The difficult situation pregnancy often poses for a woman, and the difficulty many people feel in regarding the fetus as a human person—in particular the understandable difficulty some women have in regarding the fetus as a person separate from themselves—suffice to mitigate abortion to a moral analogue of (voluntary) manslaughter. Another analogy is the special offense of infanticide which exists in a number of jurisdictions. [32] On the other hand, while these mitigating circumstances are quite powerful when the well-being of another human being—the mother—is at stake, the opponent of abortion need have no hesitation in regarding as murder (and demanding the severest punishment for) the killing of embryos where what is at stake is only scientific curiosity—for instance when embryos conceived *in vitro* are disposed of, or when embryos are conceived *in vitro* with the intent that they should be so disposed of if they survive.

When conventional morality is ambiguous, the rational course is to resolve its ambiguities in the most coherent way possible. And the result of so doing is to ascribe a right to live to the fetus or embryo from the sixth week of gestation at the very latest, since this is the latest point at which the possibility of arousing sympathy might be said to begin. It should be added that, where there is even some probability that the life at stake in a decision is that of a human person, some morally persuasive reason, even if not so grave a one as is required to warrant what is clearly homicide, is required if that life is to be rightly taken.

13. The Fetus and the Comatose

INFANTICIDE IS NOT the only difficult case for those who defend abortion by invoking the present enjoyment principle. Any attempt to win a quick victory over the claims made on behalf of the fetus (by pointing out that the fetus is unconscious—although this is not true for all fetuses—has no concept of itself, and lacks the ability to reason, act, speak a language, enter into social relationships, or itself have obligations) runs at once into the consideration that a reversibly comatose human organism is in these respects as bad or worse off than the fetus, and yet is regarded as a person possessing the right to live. And one intuitively plausible ground for asserting the personhood of the comatose—that they will wake up and do such things—is also a ground for asserting the personhood of the infant or the fetus which will grow up and do such things.

In view of the personhood of the (reversibly) comatose, it is also possible to reject Richard B. Brandt's contention that, since a child does not remember its life in the womb (the same is true of the period shortly after birth), the fetus is not the same person as the child and so not a person at all. [33] While it is true that memory has an important part to play in the definition of personal identity, it is also true that I remain myself (and so a person) during periods I cannot remember, whether on account of unconsciousness or for some other cause.

Tooley rests the rights of the comatose on their desire—entertained by them before they went under—to continue to live.[34] Such an account places the rights of the unconscious on the same footing as the rights of the dead—a procedure that requires the closest scrutiny. (In cases other than the desire to go on living, the unconscious may learn of the satisfaction or frustration of their desires. But this consideration can be neglected when what is under consideration is an unconscious person's right to live.)

The questions are two: (1) Do the dead in fact have any rights? and (2) If they do, are these rights strong enough that the rights of the unconscious may be safely placed on the same basis? And the first of these questions itself divides into two: (a) Are the dead the sorts of beings that logically speaking can have rights? (Do the dead have interests?) and (b) If they can have rights, should we in fact ascribe rights to the dead as a matter of normative ethics?

There are three kinds of right the dead might plausibly be said to have. These are the right to have promises that were made to them when they were alive kept, the right to have their remains disposed of respectfully and in accordance with their wishes, and the right to dispose of their property by will (subject to the overriding claims of the community). None of these is a clear case of the concept of a right.

That one may sometimes be under an obligation to keep one's promises to the dead is clear, but the point of emphasis is on the obligation, not on the right (although living human beings may of course acquire rights through obligations). We may stipulate that any obligation which is in any sense to someone (e.g., created by a promise to him) creates a right, but short of that, it is surely more natural to say, when reluctantly watering a dead friend's flowers, "I promised him I would do it and a promise is a promise," and not "Having these flowers watered is his right." Norms concerning the disposal of human remains have more to do with the sentiments of the living—to be sure, sentiments we feel that they ought to have—than with the rights of the decedent, and the rights of the heirs are more at issue in litigation over wills than the rights of the testator. Perhaps the best course is to follow

Feinberg's suggestion and to take the interests, and therefore the rights, of the dead as "a fiction that most living men have a real interest in preserving."[35]

But assuming *arguendo* that it makes sense to ascribe rights to the dead and that it is rational to make such an ascription, it is clear that any rights which we might wish to ascribe to the dead are relatively weak and easily overridden. The point is obscured in the case of the deathbed promise, since the binding force of a promise is in part a function of its solemnity. But surely the fact that a dead person could never have his expectations defeated by our breach of a promise made to him does serve to weaken the obligation to keep such promises. And courts generally treat—or ought to treat—the interests of the living, including those living people who now wish to make wills, as of far greater weight than the alleged rights of the dead when deciding will cases. We would not, I think, be prepared to discount the rights of the unconscious in a similar manner. And even if one rejects the account of the ethics of wills here suggested as too neglectful of the respect due the dead person, it is most implausible to hold that the dead are to be treated as if they might awaken at any moment.

If, as is common among philosophers at least, death and irreversible coma are identified, the distinction between the unconscious and the dead for the purpose of the ascription of rights seems clearly to rest on the consideration that the unconscious will, unless interfered with, wake up and (say) desire certain things. And the wrongfulness of killing the unconscious (which effectively precludes their feeling any frustration at their loss) would seem to rest on the very basis Tooley wants to reject—possible future desires of an individual who will not exist if we act as we contemplate acting.

Another way of treating those who have gained consciousness of themselves and temporarily lost it as having a right to live, while denying as Tooley does, rights to those, such as infants and fetuses, who do not yet have it, is to rely on both past and possible future desires.[36] Such desires, framing periods of unconsciousness, might prove enough to ground a rights claim of the required strength.

But notice that an appeal to possible future desires is very dangerous for the defender of infanticide and abortion like Tooley. Some rationale is required to preclude a claim based on possible future desires alone, if the denial of a right to live to fetuses and infants is going to be anything but arbitrary.

I cannot exhaust all possible rationales, but the most plausible would seem to be something like the following: unlike the fetus or the infant, the comatose person has established himself as a person by talking, acting, and forming relationships with other persons. So long as a possibility remains that he will resume his place in the human community, his status as a person continues. The fetus or infant, on the other hand, having never established itself as a person, is not one. The model is that of marriage or club membership: a condition begun by doing some things, and ended by doing other things. But here the model is defective: there is nothing corresponding to divorce, resignation, or expulsion from the human community. Although one may forfeit some of the rights of a person, a person remains a person so long as he is. (If we think of Jones's corpse as "Jones," we also think of it, with equal haziness, as a person.)

Another possible account treats personhood, as Ashley Montagu once said, not as an endowment but as an achievement,[37] an achievement (like the earning of a university degree) which confers a certain status on someone as long as he is. But since the relevant achievement seems to be the performance of personal acts, and to recognize something as having performed a personal act is to recognize it (already) as a person, this line of thought will not work. Since only persons can perform personal acts, personhood cannot be an achievement and must be an endowment. The traits with which personhood is somehow linked are *capacities,* and part of the logic of a capacity is that it must be had before it can be exercised.

I conclude (1) that the rights of the unconscious must be based on something more than their past desires, and (2) once their (possible) future desires are admitted as grounding rights claims, the case of the unconscious person is inadequately distinguishable from that of the infant or fetus. Hence Tooley's defense of abortion and infanticide is in a crucial respect defective. Of course he might hold that the distinction *is* adequate, that some other rationale for simultaneous reliance on past and future desires can be found, or that no such rationale is necessary. But given the strongly counter-intuitive character of his conclusion about babies, these moves are not plausible.

Those who attempt to apply the present enjoyment principle to problems of homicide tend to neglect the unconscious, perhaps because periods of reversible unconsciousness (periods of total unconsciousness certainly) tend to be relatively short. One can easily imagine someone in a deep, long-lasting coma (or state of suspended animation) from which he could be revived, but only after nine months or a year. Most of us would regard such a one as a person—and the killing of such a one as homicide. If so, the case for regarding fetuses as human persons is quite strong.

14. The Potentiality Principle

THE CASE JUST MADE for regarding the fetus or embryo as a human person does not depend on identifying a person with a human organism. One could ascribe personhood to members of other intelligent species, and deny it to so-called human vegetables, while ascribing it to the (normal) fetus. The underlying premise of such an ascription is what has been called the potentiality principle.

Like the species principle, but unlike the present enjoyment principle, the potentiality principle accounts quite without difficulty for our ascription of humanity to infants and the unconscious and requires ascribing humanity to fetuses as well. According to this principle, there is a property, self-consciousness or the use of speech for instance, such that (i) it is possessed by adult humans, (ii) it endows any organism possessing it with a serious right to life, and (iii) it is such that any organism potentially possessing it has a serious right to life even now— where an organism possesses a property potentially if it will come to have that property under normal conditions for development. It is often convenient to speak of those who are regarded as persons under the potentiality principle, but not under the present enjoyment principle, as "potential persons." But this usage is misleading. For even a normal, awake adult can be thought of as a person for essentially the same reasons as an embryo: both are capable of using speech and so on, although the embryo's capacity requires the more time and care before it is realized.

Notice that, whereas the potentiality principle in terms extends a right to live to all creatures potentially possessing self-consciousness or the use of speech, it could be narrowed to require that such organisms also possess certain additional properties $P_1 \ldots P_n$ (e.g., exclusion of twinning, the presence of brain activity, or existence outside the uterus) to have a right to live. A defender of a narrowed version of the principle would, of course, have to show that the additional properties $P_1 \ldots P_n$ provided a morally relevant reason to ascribe rights to those having them and to deny rights to those not possessing them. I have had occasion to consider the merits of some suggestions along these lines above.

The basis of the potentiality principle is quite simple: what makes the difference between human beings and other life is the capacity human beings enjoy for a specially rich kind of life. The life already enjoyed by a human being cannot be taken away from him, only the prospect of such life in the future. But this prospect is possessed as much by an infant or fetus as by a full-grown adult. But it is not possessed by the irreversibly comatose, and thus they are morally speaking dead from the standpoint of the potentiality principle.

Tooley motivates his rejection of the potentiality principle by citing what he calls the Frankenstein example:

> Let us suppose that technology has advanced to the point, first, where it is possible to construct humans in the laboratory from inorganic compounds. Second, that it is possible to freeze animals, including humans, and then to thaw them out without damaging them. Third, that it is possible to program beliefs, desires, personality traits, and so on into an organism by bringing about certain brain states. Given these technological advances, suppose that we put together an adult human in the laboratory, carrying out the construction at a temperature at which the organism is frozen. We program in some happy set of beliefs, desires, and personality traits. If we now thaw out this organism we will have a conscious, adult human with beliefs, desires, and a distinct personality. But what if, as a result of all this work, we have developed ravenous appetites, and rather than thawing out the organism, we grind it up for hamburgers. Our action might be economically unwise and subject to culinary objections, but would it be open to moral criticism? In particular, would we be guilty of murdering an innocent person? I think most people would say the answer is no. [38]

One reason those who consider such a case are likely to give for regarding such a creature (which I shall call a frozen android) as not a person is that it is artificially produced, not generated from human parents. But once it is granted that the artificial production of a creature need not make it a nonperson, it seems reasonable to consider the potential of the frozen android as making the proposed action one of murder. The more important point is that the eccentricity of the example, its distance from any problem I or my audience will ever confront, makes it difficult to sort out our moral and our nonmoral responses to it, and hence makes considered moral judgment on such cases nearly impossible. The best course is to decide them by analogy to, or by generalizations derived from, cases where our intuitions are surer. Thus if indeed the frozen android is a fair analogy to an infant, or if there is no plausible principle which distinguishes an infant from a frozen android or a frozen android from an infant, the rational course is to allow our intuitions concerning infants to control our result as to frozen androids even if this leads to a result which seems strange. The same is true of another example of Tooley's: the kitten injected in such a manner as to give it, upon maturity, the capacities of an adult human.[39] My own judgment would be that the analogy holds and that frozen androids and injected kittens should both be accorded the right to live.

Tooley's chief criticism of the potentiality principle starts with what he calls "the moral symmetry principle with respect to action and inaction," which he phrases as follows:

Let C be a causal process that normally leads to event E. Let A be an action that initiates process C, and let B be an action involving a minimal expenditure of energy that stops process C before outcome E occurs. Assume further that A and B do not have any further consequences, and that E is the only part or outcome of C which is morally significant in itself. Then there is no morally significant difference between intentionally performing action B and intentionally refraining from performing action A, assuming identical motivation in both cases.[40]

Tooley argues that, if this principle is accepted, there is no essential moral difference between killing an infant and refraining from fertilizing a human egg, since in the one case the development of a self-conscious creature is prevented by action, and in the other case by inaction. So that if we accept the potentiality principle, we are forced to the conclusion that "any woman, married or unmarried, does something seriously wrong every month she intentionally avoids becoming pregnant,"[41] even when the means chosen for avoiding pregnancy is sexual abstinence.

I shall postpone my formal defense of the distinction between action and inaction until the next chapter. In this context, I shall limit myself to arguing intuitively that the moral symmetry principle is unacceptable, and give grounds for believing that the intuitive sense we all have that there is an important difference between not starting a life and stopping one once started is in fact sound. In order to reach the widest possible audience, I shall forgo arguing that, if the moral symmetry principle requires us to believe that there is no essential difference between infanticide and contraception, that of itself is sufficient to require us to reject the principle. That I forgo such an argument does not mean that I find it unacceptable. Certainly the intellectual costs of rejecting the principle are not great.

Consider the following method of interrogation, designed to get information out of those of great physical courage but sensitive conscience. The person interrogated is informed (correctly) that a child will be tortured until he talks: when he talks, the torture will be stopped. Now imagine this method being employed by an interrogator whose motive is simply patriotism against a captured soldier whose motive for not talking is also simply partriotism. Both say "I regret this child's suffering, but my country demands it." The causes of the war and the probable effects of victory for one side or the other are left unspecified and thus may be taken as irrelevant. One might think that the victory of those who are prepared to use blackmail of this sort would be a bad result, but supposing that the comrades of the person interrogated have used similar tactics does not alter the ethics of the situation. The motives and justifications of the two parties can thus be treated as the same. But to hold that the interrogator and the captured soldier are in any sense morally on a par is monstrous, or at any rate highly counterintuitive.

Some pragmatic[42] considerations reinforcing our sense of difference between stopping life and not starting it follow. Obviously, not all ova can reach maturity if the human race is not going to be swamped. Avoiding the fertilization of most ova, whether by contraception or by some other means, is clearly preferable to destroying the product of conception at some later stage in its development (e.g., in infancy). No one but a very imaginative philosopher is likely to see any connection between the former kind of action and the killing of adults (which nearly all agree is to be avoided), whereas the similarity between killing a baby and killing an adult is underlined by our murder laws among other things. Hence it is reasonable to ascribe to infants and fetuses a right to live while denying that ova have a right to be impregnated. Of course, to argue in this way is to concede that abortion has some good effects, in that it helps prevent overpopulation, but on any view of ethics I can think of, a wrong act—even a gravely wrong one—can have some good consequences.

One might also treat the coming-into-existence of specific human individuals by sexual reproduction as constituting the results of a kind of natural lottery. In the absence of a compulsion to attempt a task one cannot satisfactorily perform, or mindlessly to employ all technical devices available, it seems best, for instance, to leave the proportion of males to females in society to chance rather than controlling it technologically. Likewise the decision whether a given possible person should enter the population is best left, for the most part, to a combination of chance, personal decision motivated at most in part by a desire that a possible person should enter the population, and other elements alien to technocratic manipulation. But once a child has been conceived, the natural lottery has been completed, and it is time for talk about rights.

To these considerations may be added the considerations adduced in section 11; briefly, the importance of maintaining in our society a concern for the welfare of babies. While such considerations do not themselves establish that immature human beings have a right to live in their own right, they do contribute to a cumulative argument having this conclusion. No such considerations are available tending to support the conclusion that ova have a right to be fertilized.

It may seem that pragmatic arguments such as I have offered are inconsistent with an insistence that an infant has a right to live not subject to consequentialist manipulation. But this is not so. I have been trying to show that our moral intuitions regarding infants possess a reasonable basis and thus to quiet skepticism concerning them. I do not wish to reduce these intuitions to their consequentialist ground or to deny that the right to live embodies a norm resistant, at least to a

98

considerable extent, to consequentialist considerations. There are good consequences to be hoped for from protecting some interests from direct consequentialist overriding and bad consequences to be feared from failing to do so. In any case, even at the level of strictly consequentialist argumentation, the death of an infant seems a very different sort of result than some possible human being's not being conceived.

Finally, a word about the logic of the potentiality principle is in order. The potentiality principle relies heavily on the distinction between what happens in the ordinary course of events, as opposed to by miracle, freak accident, or extraordinary human intervention. Philosophers have sometimes expressed considerable difficulty with such distinctions, and if such difficulties were allowed to prevail, the potentiality principle would collapse, since anything that could be given self-consciousness or other distinctively human traits by some extraordinary manipulation would then be a person. But most of us can understand that a kitten's growing up into a rational being—even if it should happen without human intervention once in a million years—would not be part of the normal course of events, whereas the similar maturation of a human fetus or infant is. Although I have cited the case of a very rare occurrence, the distinction I have in mind is only in part statistical. Pregnancy for instance is a normal result of coitus, even though it results from coitus with relative infrequency. Hence also statistics on infant mortality and fetal loss are of little relevance to the question of what the normal development of a human infant or fetus is.

Nonetheless, the distinction between a potential person and something which might become a person under extraordinary conditions is dependent on the prevailing conditions of human experience and would change its complexion if these conditions were to be drastically altered. Joel Feinberg observes:

> If we lived in a world in which every biologically capable human female became pregnant once a year throughout her entire fertile period of life [without external intervention], then we would regard fertilization as something which happens to every ovum in "the natural course of events." Perhaps we would regard every unfertilized ovum, in such a world, as a potential person even possessed of rights corresponding to its future interests. It would perhaps make conceptual if not moral sense in such a world to regard deliberate nonfertilization as a kind of homicide. [43]

99

What the ethics of such a world might be is a matter concerning which it is only possible to speculate. (The case for drawing the line at the beginning of recognizably human form rather than at "conception" would probably be much strengthened.) In any case, it should be possible to acknowledge that changes in human experiences, purposes, and techniques could produce changes in the application of concepts like "right" without regarding every new biomedical development as altering the parameters of moral discourse so fundamentally as to render all older ideas irrelevant. Hence we have good reasons to use the potentiality principle to ascribe personhood to immature human organisms, such as fetuses and infants, and not to spermatozoa and ova.

15. The Potentiality and Species Principles

THE POTENTIALITY and species principles both protect all normal human infants and unborn children, along with the reversibly unconscious and, of course, normal, awake adults. They differ importantly as to scope, however. According to the potentiality principle, a gravely retarded human (unable, let us say, ever to communicate with us at all as a person), and an irreversibly comatose human organism whose heart beats of its own accord are not persons, whereas they are members of the human species and as such are protected by the species principle. (The status of someone whose heart beats on only because it is artificially stimulated is unclear even on the species principle.) While generous impulses and an unwillingness to take the moral risk of acting on the narrower principle may predispose us to adopt the species principle, a surer foundation for choice is greatly to be desired.

In what follows, I shall offer a tentative synthesis of the two principles, which I hope will be at least to a minimum degree intuitively acceptable. I shall use the potentiality principle to specify the extension of the expression "person," while continuing to use "human being" as a morally significant expression. That is to say, I shall distinguish two classes of creatures, delimited by the two versions of the moral rule against homicide: persons, that is, creatures having the capacity or potentiality of doing distinctively human things; and human beings, that is, members of the human species. (What is true of human beings could also be true of members of other intelligent species.) I shall suggest that a prima facie obligation to abstain from killing both kinds of creatures exists, but the obligation to abstain from killing persons is both primary and more stringent.

Respect for persons is morally fundamental. To deprive a person of his capacity to perform personal acts—to reduce a person to a thing, or displace him by one—is an act that can only be justified under the most stringent conditions. And killing is precisely such a reduction of the victim from personhood to thinghood or the annihilation of a person in favor of a thing. It is unclear whether the language of reduction, or the language of annihilation and replacement, is more appropriate here, because of the suggestion that someone whose existence as a person has ceased may yet survive as a human being. For most purposes, reduction of a person to a thing may be taken as a portrayal of death which, while somewhat mythical, since it supposes that a person is somehow identical with his corpse, is a good enough approximation that ethical conclusions can be drawn from it.

But the principle of respect for persons also extends, by what might be called the "overflow principle," to things closely associated with persons. Thus corpses ought not to be treated as ordinary garbage, and one might also argue that a modicum of reverence should be accorded the processes by which persons come to be. This line of thought explains the (otherwise quite bewildering) expression "the sanctity of life" (as opposed to the sanctity of the living individual), as well as the connection many have seen between questions of homicide and such questions as artificial insemination. Nothing more is claimed for the overflow principle here than that it helps explain a number of our intuitions, and helps suggest a way of bringing together the species and potentiality principles in a way that appears to do justice to the claims of each.

Human beings who are not persons (the expression "person" being used in the semitechnical sense explained above) are entitled to a degree of respect because of their close association with persons. First, all human beings are entitled to be presumed to be persons until it is absolutely clear that they have no capacity for personal activity. Second, even those human beings who clearly have no such capacity ought not to be killed except where the reasons for so doing are very strong and the resulting danger to the principle of respect for persons very small. Thus, for instance, even the most severely mentally retarded ought not to be killed, since to do so would endanger those (the majority of the retarded) who can, with effort, be brought to a human level of existence (roughly, can be taught to talk). On the other hand, one might perhaps allow the abortion to be performed upon fetal indications, to avoid great suffering on the part of the parents, in cases of grave and irremediable mental defect (not, it deserves emphasis, on grounds of physical defect: an oddly shaped human being is no less a person for that reason). For fetuses are not very closely imaginatively linked with born persons. On these premises, disorders like Tay-Sachs disease, which by killing in early childhood prevent the development of significant human capacities, provide (given certainty of diagnosis) just enough justification for abortion on fetal indications. Down's syndrome (mongolism), on the other hand, does not. For some mongols at any rate manage to attain the capacity to speak to us as persons. [44]

Again, an irreversibly comatose human being ought not to be hurried into the grave in order to advance the hospital schedule. But if his heart is needed to save the life of another, it might be taken from him for that end. (Notice, however, that all comas are, in the absence of very clear evidence, to be presumed reversible: one might, of course, terminate life-support systems on grounds of futility somewhat before the point of certainty, though the decision is a very grave one.) Where the body is kept going only by massive artificial aid, one might, indeed, conclude that what one has here is not even a human organism but a corpse with a beating heart.

To refuse to admit this concept—say, on the grounds that the death of a human organism just *means* "the system of those reciprocally dependent processes which assimilate oxygen, metabolize food, eliminate waste, and keep the organism in relative homeostasis are arrested in a way which the organism itself cannot reverse"[45]—leads to paradoxical conclusions. These conclusions are that if the organism were to stop functioning in the way just mentioned and then be revived, we would have a case, not of saving life, but of reversing death. The most radical implication of advances in medical technology may be that one cannot define death simply by reference to an organic state, but must bring in the available medical resources as well.

The flat EEG, which has played a considerable role in recent discussions of "brain death," has a double relevance in this connection.[46] As an indication of cessation of brain function, it is a possible criterion of organismic breakdown; it is also evidence of irreversible unconsciousness and thus of personal death. Conceivably, however, decisive evidence of irreversible unconsciousness could be obtained without flat EEG or other indices of the organism's breakdown. In that case the problems discussed in this section would become quite acute.

I appear to have somewhat compromised the rejection of graded personhood that I insisted on in section 12. The tendency we have to require a sharply marked-off class of persons, outside of which creatures can have only very few and very weak rights but within which the greatest scrupulousness is required in respecting the rights of persons, perhaps cannot be maintained without qualification given the complexity of human situations. But a principle whose complex application is the result of the union of two identifiable, simpler principles is still preferable to a way of applying the concept "person" which invites opportunism, that is, ad hoc adjustments of rights in an arbitrary manner throughout the whole range of its application.

Implementation of the perspective just outlined does raise difficult problems, however. These problems do not arise in the case of abortion on fetal indications (extreme mental defect), since our institutions have for a long time distinguished, however shaky the ultimate justification for so doing, between abortion and the killing of the born. They arise in connection with the use as organ donors of those who have lost the capacity for human activity.

On the one hand, organ transplants do save lives, and it seems undesirable, at least if one can in good faith regard the donor as a cadaver, to make exceptions to the moral rule against homicide in order to justify them. On the other, there are serious worries involved in blurring the questions "Is he alive?" and "Should he be let die (or killed)?" and with definitions of death which vary according to the definer's purposes.[47] Some of these worries—for instance the possibility of "the protracting of the in-between state . . . and extracting from it all the profit we can"[48]—might be laid to rest by stressing the principle of respect for human remains. But the central difficulty—the doubtful legitimacy of manipulating the time of death for transplant purposes—is still troublesome.

We might react to this difficulty by reverting to the species principle, with the result that the moral rule against homicide will protect not only all born human organisms, but also all human fetuses however defective they may be. We may feel that even the most gravely retarded human being—and even a human being who is unconscious and certain never to regain consciousness—is a person entitled in his own right not to be killed, though futile measures to prolong life would still not be required. (This is how we would feel, certainly, about someone lying on a railroad track, drugged to remain unconscious until the train ran him over, and quite possibly how we would feel about a premature infant with a beating heart whose biological death was imminent. It is when the cause of permanent unconsciousness is structural damage that our intuitions are unclear.)

We might justify our adoption of the species principle in the following way. No matter how unlikely it may be, it is never a fantastic supposition—never one requiring a miracle, freak accident, or technological intervention of a radical sort—that a human being should attain or regain consciousness at the personal level or become able to perform distinctively personal acts. On this interpretation, the species and potentiality principles merge fully.

Even so, it will still be possible for a human being or person to be succeeded by a mere animal in some sense continuous with him. A werewolf, who as a wolf has only the mental capacities of a wolf,[49] should he become stuck in the wolf phase of his existence, would be a mere brute animal, although we might still treat the resulting wolf differently out of respect for what it had (in some sense) been.

The upshot of this discussion is that it is very difficult to choose decisively between the species and potentiality principles. And the choice between the principles is very important—philosophically, since it marks the crucial divide between those who believe that human beings have worth simply because they are human, and those who believe that they have worth because they are able to produce systems of philosophy, cities, works of art, and sophisticated manuals of sexual technique; and practically, since the choice and the calculation underlying it will crucially affect our attitude toward the severely mentally retarded (and perhaps others). On the other hand, there are important issues for which the results of accepting the two principles are the same.

One of these is that the abortion of a normal fetus (and many defective ones too) can only be justified in ways which would justify the sacrifice of the life of a mature human being. The same result can be reached without formal invocation of the principles, relying instead on a presumption against narrowing the scope of moral concern, and the analogy between a fetus and an infant (section 12), or between a fetus and an unconscious or reversibly comatose adult human (section 13). We must now ask what circumstances (if any) might justify countenancing the death of a fetus, an infant, or anyone. [50]

IV /

THE PRINCIPLE
OF DOUBLE EFFECT

THE PRINCIPLE of double effect is of relevance to life-and-death issues in all contexts. It is employed in commonsense moral judgment and in traditional moral theology. I explicate the distinction between the direct and the indirect production of bad effects (such as someone's death), and defend its moral relevance, along with that of the distinction between producing a bad effect and merely not preventing it, against the strictures of Jonathan Bennett and others.

16. Some Examples

COMMONSENSE MORALITY distinguishes what we do from what happens as a result of our actions, a bad act from an act with foreseen bad consequences. If increasing the educational level of a community means also increasing its suicide rate, we do not regard furthering education as tantamount to driving people to kill themselves. Traditional moral theology has enshrined this distinction in the principle of double effect, which allows good or indifferent actions to be performed in pursuit of a good end, even though evil consequences will follow, provided the evil consequences are not means to the good end, and provided due proportion between the good sought and the evil accepted is observed. [1] In other words, an agent is permitted to produce an otherwise forbidden result—the death of an innocent person, for instance—by way of an act itself innocent. In such a case the evil effect is said not to be intended by the agent, but rather only permitted by him. It should be clear that the distinction between doing something and only bringing the effect about as a consequence is crucial to both the formulation and the application of the principle.

In this section, I attempt to elucidate further the principle by means of examples; in the next section I connect the principle with certain general points concerning the descriptions of actions and the relationship between ends and rules in morality; then I defend the principle and its underlying distinctions against the strictures advanced by Jonathan Bennett in his article "Whatever the Consequences."[2] In considering the examples it should be remembered that they are intended not as examples of correct moral conclusions, but of possibly relevant moral distinctions. Other considerations may justify the direct taking of human life, as well as, of course, rendering indirect killing impermissible.[3]

1. A common view holds that it is permissible to refrain from extraordinary means of preserving a patient's life; moreover, if the patient is in great pain, it is permissible to give drugs which, while relieving pain, also hasten death. But it is not permissible to kill the patient in order to stop his pain. Thus while one may give as much of a drug as is necessary to make the patient's condition tolerable, one is not permitted to give him a larger dosage in order to "get it over with," to employ a gun instead of drugs when drugs are not available; or to rely on mercy killing as a solution to the problems of nonfatal, but painful, physical disease, insanity, or old age.

The way this line is drawn clearly rests on a description of the doctor's act in terms of act and consequence, intended and merely permitted effect, enabling the moralist to say that to give a patient a large dose of pain-relieving drug is not to kill him, or at any rate to kill him directly, but only to do something which leads to his death as a foreseen but unintended consequence.

2. Another case from medical ethics concerns abortion. Since I shall be discussing abortion under the assumption that it is a form of homicide, I shall, in this and the next two chapters, refer to the fetus as the unborn child. I shall also refer to the unborn child by the pronoun "he" (in the sense of "he or she").

Official Roman Catholic moral theology forbids both the direct killing of an unborn child within the womb and his direct removal from the womb before the child can live outside on his own, even though one of these procedures should be the only way to save the mother from imminent death, and even if the unborn child has no chance of survival if an abortion is not performed. But an organ of the mother—the uterus or one of the Fallopian tubes—may be removed on the grounds that it is diseased. Still, the unborn child may not be removed and the organ left in place, though such a procedure would be no more certainly fatal to the unborn child than the approved one, and the mother's fertility could thereby be preserved.[4]

The way in which these "indirect" abortions are justified is as follows: what the doctor is (directly) doing is removing a diseased organ and thus preserving the mother's life. The removal and death of the unborn child is only a permitted side effect. If one insisted that the description of the doctor's act should contain all its foreseen consequences, then it would be one of killing the unborn child pure and simple and the justification would fall to the ground. But equally if the doctor declined to intervene, his action might be described as killing the mother (by omission), so that the whole question would have to be decided on different grounds.

It may be thought that such patterns of thought are peculiar to Roman Catholic severity about abortion. But they appear elsewhere. In an article entitled "A Defense of Abortion," Judith Jarvis Thomson argues that, even assuming that the unborn child is to be accorded the status of a human person, it does not follow that abortion is (always) wrong.[5] For what is at issue is not only the right of the unborn child to live, but the right of a woman not to lend her body to his support if this support is burdensome beyond a certain undefined point. If the Society of Music Lovers plugs a famous violinist into someone else's circulatory system, the victim of this procedure may unplug the violinist—at least if the burden of the violinist's presence is sufficiently great—even though the violinist will certainly die. Analogously, she argues, abortion—the severance of the means of support which the unborn child has in his mother's body—is justified in cases of rape, clear threat to the mother's life, and, she strongly suggests, many other cases as well (although not in *all* cases where it may be requested).

To this argument she adds the following qualifications:

> While I am arguing for the permissibility of abortion in some cases, I am not arguing for the right to secure the death of the unborn child. It is easy to confuse these two things in that up to a certain point in the life of the fetus it is not able to survive outside the mother's body; hence removing it from her body guarantees its death. . . . I have argued that you are not morally required to spend nine months in bed, sustaining the life of the violinist; but

this does not mean that if, when you unplug yourself, there is a miracle and he survives, you have a right to turn round and slit his throat. You may detach yourself even if this costs him his life; you have no right to be guaranteed his death.

And she concludes: "The desire for the child's death is not one which anybody may gratify, should it turn out to be possible to detach the child alive."

In practical terms, while it might in Thomson's view be legitimate to remove a viable child from his mother's body, it would not be legitimate to kill the newborn child (or abstain from saving his life except in circumstances when one would do so even if the child had not been delivered by abortion). Nor would it be legitimate to prefer saline injection to hysterotomy as a technique of late abortion, on the grounds that the former technique is very unlikely to produce a living child. Moreover, Thomson's example makes it clear that one need not, if he is committed to the defense of abortion, accept also the use of the fetus for purposes of medical experimentation. The right to detach oneself from the violinist does not entail any right to use him for such purposes.

An abortion can take place in two ways: the child can be removed from the womb and then die, or he can be killed within the womb—cut up or poisoned for instance—in order to facilitate his removal or bring about his expulsion. Thomson's defense of abortion has much greater plausibility for the first kind of abortion than for the second: we are inclined to say that though in the first case we may be only "guaranteeing," in the second case we must surely be "securing," the death of the unborn child. If I may not kill the violinist after he is detached, it seems that I may not kill him before he is detached either. Even less may I kill him as a means to getting him detached. The only way I am permitted to kill him is *by detaching* him.

But another interpretation of Thomson's argument is possible. She can be read as maintaining simply that the only killing permitted is that indispensable to the removal of the intruder. If the violinist is conscious and resists, it may be necessary to kill him before unplugging him, and if the unborn child is so situated that dismemberment is necessary to removal, he too may be killed before he is removed. Indeed, if the death of the unborn child is inevitable, however he is removed, the killing may precede removal simply as a matter of convenience.

This interpretation ill accords with Thomson's argument, however. When she argues that the right to live does not necessarily include the right to have that which is minimally necessary to life (because what is minimally necessary to one's life may be something one has no right to have) and goes on to say that even the right not to be killed may involve the right to have something one has no right to (the use of another's kidneys, for instance)—so that deprivation of such supports, though it kills, does not violate one's right to live[6]—her argument needs to be limited to a justification of the deprivation of the means of support as such and not of any preliminary dismemberment. Nor is it plausible to read Thomson as arguing for the proposition that the death of the unborn child may be sought as a means, but not as an end, for in that case the death of the unborn child could be sought as a means to the mother's future peace of mind, a course Thomson clearly disallows.[7] No, the only killing her argument supports is the strictly defined exercise of the mother's right to expel an intruder from her body. It follows at once that Thomson's line of defense is useless in at least one kind of case, where the abortion is performed to prevent the birth of a defective or otherwise unwanted child and thus would be pointless should the unborn child unexpectedly survive.[8]

Moreover, if Thomson's line of argument is to be used to justify particular abortions, three kinds of obstacles will have to be overcome. The least serious point is that, even when the unborn child is not cut up or otherwise destroyed in the process of the abortion, the abortion might still be construed as the infliction of a fatal wound if the placenta is damaged. For the placenta, unlike the apparatus which connects the violinist to the philosopher, is biologically a part of the unborn child. (While intentional wounding probably does not of itself completely preclude the application of the principle of double effect, it does make that application more difficult: consider the claim, for instance, that a physician who cuts the heart out of a living man does not intend the man's death, only the availability of his heart for transplant.) On the other hand, the placenta is arguably not an essential organ of the unborn child, since it is discarded at birth.

One can formulate the issue as follows: to intentionally inflict grievous bodily damage, expecting to produce death, is to intend to kill. But whether damage to the placenta is grievous damage to the body of an unborn child (aside from the probability or certainty that it will produce death) is very unclear. Second, in all cases except conception arising from rape, the woman has voluntarily assumed the risk of pregnancy (where contraceptives are employed, the risk of contraceptive failure). She may, of course, be fully justified in taking such risks, and in doing what she can to avoid pregnancy, but her so doing nonetheless places her in a very different situation from someone who wakes up with a violinist plugged into him. Finally, unlike having a violinist plugged into one, pregnancy is a normal episode in the life of the female of the human species, one for which a woman is physiologically (and in many cases psychologically) adapted, and which contributes to a personal relationship of the very greatest human importance—that between mother and child.

The upshot seems to be that the analogy between Thomson's example and a pregnancy arising from rape, and only such a pregnancy, is close enough that she can be regarded as presenting a respectable argument in defense of some kinds of abortion in such situations. One wonders how much practical importance the argument has, however, since prevention of implantation probably does not involve the sacrifice of the life of a human person (section 12 [3a]), and hysterotomy is customarily employed only late in pregnancy, when it would normally make better sense (so long as the death of the child is not directly encompassed) to let the pregnancy reach its natural close and put the infant up for adoption afterward. Moreover, rape victims could be given financial and emotional support during pregnancy and thus compensated, however inadequately, for the use of their bodies, whereas unborn children cannot be compensated for the loss of their lives.[9] Still, despite the difficulties I have found in Thomson's argument, it does seem that, should anti-abortion laws be reestablished, they might appropriately include exceptions for pregnancies arising from rape, including statutory rape if the victim was actually incapable of consenting to intercourse.

I should mention two attempts to refute this conclusion. Harry H. Wellington challenges the applicability of the concept of assumption of risk, remarking that "sexual intercourse is not voluntary in the same way that going to a baseball game or agreeing to be plugged into a violinist is voluntary."[10] But it is hard to see how this remark is relevant to the justification of abortion. The question is not of blaming a woman for risking conception, or denying the woman aid in her difficulties, but only of allowing or refusing her the right to solve her own problems at the cost of another life. (I deal only with burdens upon the woman herself, since these are the ones suggested by Thomson's argument.) In such a case the relevant principle is that we should accept some responsibility for our acts, whether impulsively, habitually, or deliberately done.

On the other side, John T. Noonan, Jr., presents two criticisms of Thomson's analogy.[11] One consists in citing a case[12] in which a farm family was held liable in tort for putting a sick supper guest out into the cold. The plaintiff in this case was a guest, at least for supper, and hence not analogous to someone who owes his presence to a violent assault. And, in any case, there is a difference between putting someone up in one's house and putting him up in one's body.

Noonan's second argument is a slide, and goes as follows:

> Pregnancies due to bad planning or bad luck are analogized to pregnancies due to rape; they are all involuntary. Indeed many pregnancies can without difficulty be assimilated to the hard case, for how often do persons undertake an act of sexual intercourse consciously intending that a child be the fruit of that act? Many pregnancies are unspecified by a particular intent, are unplanned, are in this sense involuntary. Many pregnancies become open to termination if only the baby consciously sought has immunity.

The slide is as much Thomson's as Noonan's, since she argues from rape cases to an unspecified larger class. But if there is anything at all in the notion of assumption of risk, this slide can be stopped at the outset.

Thomson does not explicitly rely on the description of abortion as something other than (direct) killing, or argue that the death of the fetus is an unintended but foreseen consequence of the mother's legitimate exercise of her right to control what goes on in her body. But she does at one point distinguish between "guaranteeing" and "securing" the death of the unborn child—a distinction which cannot be made on consequentialist grounds alone. And the whole thrust of her article is to establish a priority of the mother's right to control her own body over the unborn child's right to live, by describing the abortion as primarily an act of deprivation of support rather than of killing.[13]

112

3. Another set of problems involves the principle of noncombatant immunity in time of war. [14] Though combatants may be rightly killed in a just war, it is commonly held, the killing of noncombatants, however justified strategically, remains simply murder and is thus wrong. But it is practically impossible to conduct hostilities without killing some noncombatants, in the sense that their death results from one's actions. And failure to conduct hostilities may also lead to the death of noncombatants (i.e., those on one's own side). Hence it is necessary, in order to uphold the principle, to say something like the following: given sufficient strategic justification, and a sufficiently just war, one is permitted to kill civilians *indirectly*; it is only *direct* taking of the life of noncombatants that is forbidden.

A particularly useful case in this connection has been posed by Paul Ramsey. [15] Consider the proposal—made during World War II—that the extermination facilities maintained by Nazi Germany be bombed. Some might object that the tactic would not work: the Nazis would find other ways of killing Jews, Gypsies, and others they called "subhumans," so that the best strategy was to concentrate all efforts toward removing the Nazis from power. But, if this objection is answered, another objection arises: would not the proposed action be a war crime, since the bombs would kill the inmates of the extermination camps, who are in every sense noncombatants, and some of whom might survive the war if not killed? The principle of double effect provides a way of solving the difficulty in an intuitively satisfying manner: the deaths of the concentration camp inmates are the unintended effects of a good action, the destruction of instruments of death.

4. Suppose I am in possession of a secret I think vital to the welfare of millions of people, and an enemy, in order to wrest it from me, decides to start killing children (say), promising to stop as soon as I talk. Thus, if I do not divulge the secret (let us assume that I cannot get out of the situation by lying), my refusal will cause the deaths of others. But to regard me as inflicting the children's deaths, even as justifiably and unwillingly inflicting them, is morally intolerable, and a system of ethical concepts that requires such a description is a quite unnecessary boon to the imaginative sadist. The same is true of a principle that would treat me as responsible for the children's deaths in the way the interrogator is.

113

Notice that my argument here does not require that I should in fact be right in refusing to talk (the secret may not be important at all) or even (although it is difficult to see how one could make the defense) that the interrogator be wrong in killing the children. The point is not that I am justified in what I am doing and the interrogator is not, but that he and I have different things to justify, and he has a great deal more to justify than I.

The foregoing case turns on the following feature of our moral discourse. It matters to us not only what moral result we reach, but also on what grounds we reach it. Moreover, its plausibility rests in part on the intervention of a free and deliberate (although quite predictable) human act—the decision of the interrogator to continue the killing if the secret is not revealed, and to stop it if it is. The case would be still plausible, but less compelling, if the interrogator has so arranged matters that my telling of the secret would stop the killing mechanically.

17. The Principle Developed

SOME GENERAL REMARKS on the principle of double effect are now in order.

1. The principle relies on certain ways of describing human actions. These divide into two parts: reliance on the distinction between *act* and *consequence*, and reliance on the distinction between the *foreseen* and the *intended* consequences of an act.

With regard to the first, some have argued that the distinction between an act and its consequences, between doing a thing and causing a thing, is a merely verbal one, a matter of convenience of speech. One consideration supporting this claim is that there is considerable fluctuation with regard to what we say an agent did, as opposed to the consequences of his act.

But a more accurate account of the relationship between action and consequence is the following:

a. There are actions (of a person, as opposed to, say, of an organ) which are never consequences of another action, what Arthur Danto calls "basic actions."[16] An example is raising one's arm in the usual way, as opposed to raising it with one's other hand. At least as the world is presently constituted, such actions in themselves (apart from their

114

intentions or effects) are morally neutral. For anything one does to someone (oneself or another) will consist in the movement of one's body or some part of it, and the effects on oneself or another which follow from that movement as a consequence.

b. There is never (in interesting cases at least) just one correct description of a given act. The basic action of raising one's arm may also be voting, voting against a piece of legislation, expressing one's lack of confidence in the party leadership, and guaranteeing that one will not return to Congress after the next election.

c. The term that denotes an act may often be elided into the terms that denote (the production of) a consequence of the act: "Doing X with consequence Y" can often be rephrased as "doing Y," "stabbing someone lethally" as "killing him."

d. Certain kinds of acts—the taking of human life, for instance—are of such moral significance that terms denoting them may not be honestly elided into terms denoting their consequences, which fail to reveal the morally significant character of the original act. Once it is granted that "killing a man" is a proper description of a given action, it may not be redescribed as "saving a city," or even "saving a city at the cost of a life," even if the result of the man's being killed is the saving of a city.[17]

e. The elision of acts into their consequences is limited by a variety of other considerations. If doing X is the exercise of a certain office, only those who act as holders of that office can be described as doing it. Only legislators can pass a bill. The intervention of another human act under some circumstances makes it inappropriate to elide acts into consequences, but under other circumstances does not. Even a man who drives his wife to suicide is not said, without more, to have killed her, though he may be said to have as much as killed her. But it is possible to act through an agent, and not just give orders to one's agent which have the consequences one wishes to take place. Thus in Shakespeare's play Richard III kills the princes, though he personally never lays hands on them.

f. In some cases frankly moral considerations keep us from saying that a man does what his actions cause: if a paralyzed man manages a smile and his faithful wife is overcome with joy and dies of a heart attack, we should not say that he has killed her, or even that he has caused her death (though we might say that his smile caused her death), for we feel that such an ascription would be morally monstrous.[18] Another consideration is continuity with (or carry-over from) previous action. A trolley driver who, the brakes of his trolley having failed, fails to turn it onto a spur, with the result that it runs into a number of people, kills them (accidentally); if the trolley-driver dies of the shock, a passenger who understands the situation and can intervene, but fails to, only lets them die.[19]

These six points can be summed up in the following two:

a. When we say "X did Y" we base our statement on a mixture of narrative, explanatory, and what may be called ascriptive considerations.[20] We are in part concerned to describe what happened, in part to explain it, and in part to assign responsibility for it.

b. In some cases whether we say "X did Y" is a negotiable matter, determined by ascriptive considerations; in some it is not. If I drive a man out of my shelter into a snowstorm, and he dies, whether you say that I killed him depends on whether you wish to hold me responsible for his death. But if I shoot him lethally in the head, I kill him, and no justification or excuse I may offer will alter that fact. Where the ascription of an act is negotiable, we can say that it was performed *indirectly*; where it is not, that it was performed *directly*. Thus the distinction, employed in connection with the principle, between direct and indirect homicide can be elucidated.

The second distinction having to do with the description of actions is between the intended and the foreseen consequences of an act. One argument against making such a distinction lies in the common law doctrine that a man intends the certainly foreseen consequences of his acts.[21] In the words of one court, "intent and desire are different things, and once it is proved that an accused man knows that a result is certain, the fact that he does not desire that result is irrelevant."[22] But law or no law, this doctrine is unacceptable as an explanation of what we ordinarily mean by "intend." Even a lawyer would not say *probably* foreseen consequences of an action are intended by an agent, that a doctor who performed an operation which he knew might save the patient but would probably kill him, where the patient's death was otherwise inevitable, intended the patient's death. And even where the consequence is foreseen with certainty, the point still holds. It is clearly wrong to say

116

that a man who gets drunk, certainly foreseeing the next morning's hangover, intends to give himself a hangover.[23]

Glanville Williams defends the common law doctrine in the following extraordinary passage:

> To say that intention includes foresight of the certainty of consequence is not always true for ordinary speech and ordinary life. If a conscientious objector to the military service denies the callup, he may realize that prison is the inevitable outcome, but he would not in ordinary speech be said to intend to go to prison. However, ordinary language is not decisive for legal use. When the procuring of a consequence is prohibited by law, a person who so conducts himself that he brings about the consequence, realizing that his conduct will inevitably have the result, must be taken to intend it, i.e., he must be regarded as caught by a prohibition against intentionally causing the result. This may be a departure by legal language from ordinary usage, but is dictated by common sense.[24]

The law may use language in its own way. But to appeal to common sense in order to justify neglect of a distinction made in ordinary language is a remarkable procedure. Perhaps what Williams means is that such a person is as culpable as one who in ordinary language would be said to intend the effect, or that the law should treat him as such to block possibilities of evasion. This is often so—not, I think, always—but this result can be reached without pretending that the effect of his action was intended.

We thus have grounded three formulations of the principle: *It is sometimes permissible to perform an act having as a consequence (e.g.), that someone dies, where it would be forbidden to kill. It is sometimes permitted to do indirectly what one may not do directly. It is sometimes permitted to act, foreseeing a consequence one is not permitted to intend.* These formulations may be taken as roughly equivalent.

I should say also that while the distinction between the intended and the merely foreseen is the most natural way of specifying what underlies the principle, any other formulation which allows the requisite distinctions to be made is also allowable. Thus we can, with Bentham, speak of what is directly intended as opposed to what is only obliquely intended,[25] or with the jurisprudent John Austin of intention with or without desire (including desire as a means),[26] or with Meiland of

117

"purposive" as opposed to nonpurposive intention. [27] All that is required is that the right distinctions be drawn.

It is important, however, that the *right* distinctions be drawn. The problem lies in the drawing of lines. A man who refuses to divulge a secret, with the result that another person continues to be tortured, can claim to be causing the pain only indirectly, if that, even if he foresees with certainty that unless he talks the pain will continue. But a doctor who removes his patient's head in order to stop his migraine cannot claim that the patient's death is only an indirect result of his operation. (Notice that the proper question is whether the agent intends the victim's death, in other words whether he intends that the victim should die. A lifeguard faced with a choice of which of two swimmers to rescue may intend *not to save* the more distant one, but it would not be strictly correct to say that he intends to *let him die*, since to intend to let someone die is to intend that he die.)

Yet whether one can claim that one is not intending a (nonviable) fetus's death, only its removal from the womb and the consequent relief of its mother's unbearable burden, or whether one who orders the bombardment of a fortified hospital can claim that he only intended the death of the soldiers in it, not that of the patients, or whether a group of explorers can claim that they did not intend to kill the fat man who bars their exit, only blow him out of the mouth of the cave, is not so clear.

John Finnis suggests that the following questions be asked to determine whether the taking of a life (or an act which leads to or permits loss of life) can be justified by appeal to the principle of double effect:

(1) Would the chosen action have been chosen if the victim had not been present?

(2) Is the person making the choice the one whose life is threatened by the presence of the victim?

(3) Does the chosen action involve not merely a denial of aid and succor to someone but an actual intervention that amounts to an assault on the body of that person?

(4) Is the action against someone who had a duty not to be doing what he is doing, or not to be present where he is present? [28]

Question 1 seems to state a sufficient condition for the application of the principle, provided that due proportion is observed. The case where a cancerous uterus is removed despite the unborn child within it and the case where the secret is kept despite the children's deaths which will result are clearly cases where death can be said to be inflicted at most indirectly. The case of the fortified hospital raises due proportion problems only, although these problems of course may be severe, since the hospital would still be bombed if the patients were evacuated. On the other hand, it is not clear that if I fire a bullet through A in order to kill B, I can claim that I am killing A only indirectly. (If I fired at B, foreseeing that the bullet would pass through his body and kill A, my situation would be much better.) Still, it does seem that under some circumstances it will be right to kill an innocent shield (say B is about to kill forty people, and shooting him is the only way to stop him). And regarding the killing here as indirect is as satisfying a way of articulating the justification for the act as any.

But many of the classic double-effect cases involve problems that arise precisely because the victim is present or in a certain condition, and so cannot be settled with the help of Finnis's question 1. When pain relievers are given to a man in great pain, although they hasten his death, the giving of pain relievers would hardly be possible were he not present. And the detaching of Thomson's violinist is only possible because he is there.

Question 2 seems motivated by a desire to conflate double effect with self-defense. Such a conflation which seems to me to rest on a confusion, despite St. Thomas's original formulation of the principle in a self-defense context. If I shoot someone in the head because he is trying to kill me, it does not seem plausible that I am not killing him directly, or that I do not intend his death, however justified I may be. (There is no doubt an acceptable sense in which I am not intent upon his death.) Nor does there seem to be any significant difference between my right to defend myself and my bodyguard's right to defend me.

Question 3 is really two questions: Is the act a denial of aid? and is the act an assault? These questions can receive independent answers. An act which is a denial of aid and not an assault—refusal to use extraordinary means to save life, for instance—can be justified with the help of the principle of double effect, provided due proportion is observed. (Refusal to use ordinary means is a violation of due proportion, or, alternatively, a violation of duty to save life distinguishable from a duty not to kill.) An act that is not a denial of aid but an assault—

shooting someone in the head, for instance—must be justified on other principles if at all. But there are acts which are both denials of aid and assault—shoving a possible homicidal maniac back into the snowstorm, when he has entered part of the way into one's shelter, for instance— and acts which are neither denials of aid nor assaults—the administration of pain relievers, for instance.

With respect to this criterion, Thomson observes: "It is, simply, a *mistake* to think that not saving is indirect killing. An indirect killing is perforce a killing, whereas it is quite possible that a man has never killed, and yet there are many lives that he did not save."[29] The truth in this remark is that when the case for saying that someone killed someone else only indirectly, if that, becomes very clear, we cease to say that he killed him at all, even indirectly. Indirect killing shades off into not killing at all. But there are cases where not-saving is killing: I have decided to expose my unwanted child; I look for him and find that he has in play wandered into the child-exposure pit, from which the customs of my tribe forbid any but the parent to rescue a child; I do not rescue him and he dies. It may even be direct killing: My son, whom I hate, is caught out in a snowstorm; he tries to enter my shelter, but I push him out of the doorway. Indirect killing is action which may or may not be described as killing, depending on the degree of sympathy felt toward the actor and his action. And not-saving is sometimes, although of course not always, indirect killing.

Question 4 seems to bear on due proportion only. No doubt I have greater liberty to expel (even at the cost of their lives) those who have no right to be where they are, than I do for those who have a right to be there. But only considerations of due proportion forbid my saying that the lethal expulsion of someone who has a right to be where he is is only direct killing.

Finnis remarks in conclusion:

> Too generalized or rule-governed an application of the notion of "double effect" would offend against the Aristotelian, common law, Wittgensteinian wisdom that here "we do not know how to draw the boundaries of the concept"—of intention, of respect for the good of life, and of action as distinct from consequences—"except for a special purpose." But I think that those whom Aristotle bluntly calls the wise can come to clear judgments on most of the abortion problems.[30]

Aristotle, the common law, and Wittgenstein—together they make for formidable authority. But I am still not altogether happy with Finnis's appeal to "the wise." After all, one of the questions at issue in vexed ethical discussions is who to count as "wise." Of course no philosophical discussion can hope to settle all casuistical questions, but more specificity on the application of double effect seems still to be desired.

I ought also to note the version of the principle of double effect developed by Germain Grisez. Grisez uses the principle as the *sole* justification of deadly deeds, while giving it a somewhat larger scope than is customary. "My position," he says, "is that human life can never rightly be directly attacked, but that the concept of indirect killing covers more cases than has generally been supposed."[31] He follows Thomas Aquinas in viewing killing in self-defense as a species of indirect killing, but departs from St. Thomas in holding that no one may directly or intentionally kill a human being, even by public authority and for the common good. For this reason he condemns capital punishment in principle, not merely because it fails to deter more effectively than does life imprisonment.[32]

Grisez argues that "a good effect which in the order of nature is preceded in the performance by an evil effect need not be regarded as a good end achieved by an evil means, provided the act is a unity and only the good is within the scope of the intention."[33] Thus the fact that I ward off the person attacking me only by killing him does not mean that I need intend his death, or that I achieve the good end of my safety only by the bad means of procuring his death. If this is the only way I can save myself, my saving myself is one indivisible act. On the other hand, if I killed a third party to save my life, my killing the third party would be a distinct act from my saving myself and so direct killing.[34]

One can agree that the temporal order of the good and bad effects is not decisive. In fact, where the purpose of one's act is the saving of someone's life, it is hardly to the point to speak of the time of the good effect at all, since the good effect continues so long as the saved person continues to live. On the other hand, the unity-of-the-act criterion is unclear, since what is precisely at issue is the legitimacy of redescribing one's act to include the production of the good effect but not the bad one. It seems just as plausible to say "I'm not directly killing Smith when I shoot him in the head, only saving myself from Jones's attack" as

121

to say "I'm not directly killing Jones when I shoot him in the head, only saving myself from Jones's attack." In both cases my act could be described, in a narrow context, as killing a man, and in a broader one as saving my life by killing a man. We tend to distinguish the two cases—believing that attackers may rightly be put at their peril whereas innocent third parties should be immune from lethal attack—but our distinction does not seem to have much to do with direct vs. indirect killing. I conclude that self-defense is a principle separate from double effect, and that nothing is gained by conflating the two modes of justification.

In the case of abortion, Grisez presents the following working criterion to distinguish the direct from the indirect killing of the unborn: "what would be done . . . if there existed an artificial uterus into which the . . . baby might be transferred."[35] Genuinely therapeutic abortions, even when they involve "the crushing of a baby stuck in the birth canal,"[36] are indirect, since such a uterus would be used if it could be (some therapeutic abortions still might be excluded by the principle of due proportion, however). But where abortion is used to get rid of a privately or publicly unwanted child, or to dispose of a defective one, the death of the child is clearly required by the abortionist's purposes, and therefore the feticide committed is direct.

One can agree that the fact that an artificial uterus would not be used if it could be indicates that the unborn child is being directly and intentionally killed. It seems a bit strange, however, to call the crushing of an unborn child's head indirect or unintentional killing. What would be done with an artificial uterus hardly seems relevant to this issue. A population controller might be perfectly happy to save the lives of the unborn—if there were another planet on which they could live. (Reflecting on the possibility of distant planets shows, I think, that it is logically possible to wish that someone cease to interact at all with one's world while still not wishing his death.) So that even abortion as a means of population control could be presented as indirectly lethal if wild enough suppositions were allowed. Accordingly, it seems best to limit the concept of indirect feticide to the removal of the unborn child from the womb, without further damage to him.

In order for a killing to count as indirect it is, I think, necessary that there be some scenario according to which it does not produce its lethal effect, and that this scenario, though it need not be actually possible in the situation, must still not deviate too far from possibility and toward fantasy. Thus someone who throws himself on a grenade to save his comrades does not kill himself directly, since, should the grenade fail to go off, the end of his action would not be frustrated. And the possibility of the grenade's not going off, even if the agent is certain that it will not be realized, is not fantastic. (But cannot his intentions be phrased as follows: I intend that, *if* the grenade goes off, it should spend its force in my flesh. And is it not fantastic that a grenade should spend itself in someone's flesh and he survive? Not necessarily. If someone had extraordinarily tough skin, he could stop a grenade without injury, whereas if he failed to stop it, his comrades, lacking such skin, would die.) But someone who donates his heart to save another does kill himself directly, although for altruistic motives, since it is fantastic to suppose that a man should get along without a heart. [37] (It is not fantastic to suppose that a cadaver donor might arrive to provide the living donor with a replacement heart, but such a donor would make the living donor's contribution unnecessary.)

Someone who finds the fantastic-scenario criterion too vague might attempt a more liberal one, according to which one might call killing "indirect" if it is logically possible that the act in question could be performed without producing the death of the victim. [38] One consequence of this criterion is that the death of the unborn child in craniotomy cases can be indirectly produced, since the child might (logically speaking) survive the operation. Also the death of a heart donor might not be directly produced, since it is logically possible that someone might live without a heart. Again: one might cut off someone's head in order to be able to show it to a blackmailer, and still kill him only indirectly. For it is logically possible that the head could be sewn back on the body and the victim survive. (One might have independent moral objections to making someone appear dead, of course, but it is hard to see how these would be sufficiently strong to be of relevance in the difficult cases—except insofar as making someone appear dead means killing him.) Since all morally interesting acts can be described in more than one way, and since killing is not a basic action, there will always be a description of an act which does not entail that it produces someone's death. (Whether abortion logically entails the death of the unborn child, or whether it is merely a kind of act which is nearly always lethal, depends on one's definition.) It seems that the only kind of killing which cannot be described as indirect in this way is killing for the sake of killing, or for the sake of an ideal—of manhood, say—of which experience in killing is a necessary part.

We can thus conclude that S indirectly kills V if and only if

I. S's act or abstention A produces V's death.
II. Either
   A. A would have taken place even if V had not been present, or
   B.
     1. S is not motivated in doing A by a desire for V's death, or a desire for something of which V's death is a necessary part.
     2. There is no available means of producing the end sought by S without also producing V's death.
     3. There is a non-fantastic scenario by which the end sought by S could be obtained without V's death.
     4. A does not take place in a way which would preclude the scenario's taking place if it could take place.

This analysis leaves a number of questions unanswered. How far a scenario may depart from what actually could happen without being fantastic is not specified. One thing is clear: it is never fantastic to suppose someone will change his mind even when we know that he will not. What counts as fantastic will be relative to medical technology, among other things. Until recently an artificial uterus could be dismissed as fantastic. Microsurgery to save the life of a child whose head has been crushed in delivery still can.[39]

Nor are we told when an effect may be said to be produced by or result from an abstention. About these questions Finnis is right: the adjudication of difficult questions must be left to "the wise." Moreover, the whole analysis neglects the fact that the concept of indirect action usually is applied only when it would be at least prima facie wrong to produce a result directly. The norm of due proportion has also been left out of account.

2. The principle of double effect is usually associated with what Jonathan Bennett calls moral "conservatism" and Thomas Nagel "absolutism"—the doctrine that there are simply and specifically specifiable kinds of actions it is never permissible to perform. (The qualifica-

tion "simply and specifically specifiable" is required, since otherwise one could always make one's description in all morally relevant respects complete, with the result that any wrong act would be assigned to a class of acts all of whose members were wrong, and since an act-utilitarian—surely the very opposite of an absolutist or conservative—would hold that it is never permissible to act in such a way that utility is not maximized.) A conservative or absolutist system of course has need of the principle to escape moral blind alleys; since if whatever one does an innocent person will die, one has to distinguish somehow an act which takes such a person's life and one which only permits (leads indirectly to) loss of the life. G. E. M. Anscombe puts it:

> If I am answerable for the foreseen consequences of an action or refusal as much as for the action itself, then these [absolute] prohibitions [such as that forbidding the taking of innocent human life] will break down. If someone innocent will die unless I do a wicked thing, then on this view I am his murderer in refusing: so that all that is left to me is to weigh up evils. [40]

But the principle need not be limited to such an ethic. A system may allow its prohibitions to be overruled on merely consequentialist grounds, where the bad consequences of acting in accordance with its dictates are sufficiently ghastly, while in more ordinary situations retaining its deontological shape. For such a system indirect killing will remain much easier to justify than direct, so that the principle of double effect will still have a use.

3. Even when the principle of double effect is employed, the norm of due proportion between means and ends is to be observed. Not every indirect killing with a laudable purpose can or should be justified. If due proportion is violated badly enough, then that the result is accomplished indirectly makes no moral difference. That, in brief, is the answer to Rogers Albritton's suggestion that the destruction of a village containing many civilians and only a few guerillas might be defended on the grounds that what one was doing was not killing everyone in the village to get the guerillas, but obliterating the area where the guerillas were hiding. [41] But one might press further: in situations where due proportion is neglected, that one did not intend the death of the innocent but only foresaw it as a result of one's actions is *not pleadable*. [42] (Of course, there will be a borderline area where indirectness of intention is accepted as mitigation but not justification.)

It is now possible to say something further about the legal practice of ascribing intention to those who foresee but do not intend the consequences of their acts. Since in many of these cases due proportion is utterly neglected, it is not unjust to treat such cases as ones of intention. But it does strike me as unjust to double constructions of intention: for instance, while there is no injustice in treating those who intend serious bodily harm as intending death, and no injustice (special cases of justification apart) in treating those who foresee death as intending it, it does strike me as unjust to treat someone who foresaw serious bodily harm as if he intended death. So much, then, for the uses of the principle and its connection with the description of actions.

18. The Principle Defended

THE TIME HAS COME for a consideration of Jonathan Bennett's strictures. Bennett addresses our problem in terms of an absolute prohibition of abortion, a context which is unfortunate in three respects. First, many people deny that the unborn child is at all a human person, and thus will see no real moral dilemma here. Second, a solution is available which permits abortion in threat-to-life cases without renouncing the ban on the taking of innocent life. If "innocent" is given the sense it bears in the theory of the just war (i.e., *not harming*), we may deny that an unborn child which endangers his mother's life is innocent at all in the requisite sense. Third, Bennett's placing his discussion in the context of a critique of moral absolutism obscures the fact that his argument is much broader in import, denying as it does the intellectual basis of even a moderate deontology. (This is especially evident from his contention that the principle that it is always wrong to take the life of an innocent human being, no matter what the consequences of not doing so, "is in the last resort on a par with 'It would always be wrong to shout, whatever the consequences of not doing so.' ")[43] His contention is that the fact that in one course of action a man would be killing an innocent human, and in another the death of an innocent human would follow from his action only as a consequence, gives no grounds for holding it to be wrong to act in the first way and right to act in the second. There is no overlap, he argues, between the senses in which the distinction between action and consequence has moral import, and the senses which apply to the cases where the principle of double effect is typically used.

In my reply to Bennett, I shall employ the kind of rule-utilitarian or rule-consequentialist argument used, for instance, by D. H. Hodgson.[44] In other words, I shall argue from the premise that when the utilitarian or consequentialist chooses rules, institutions, and attitudes, these rules and so on will not have a purely consequentialist shape. I shall not call upon the kind of general utilitarianism[45] or consequentialism which relies on the fact that a number of human actions or abstentions—votes or individual failures to support a station playing classical music, for instance—taken cumulatively may have consequences no individual one of them has. Since no agent will be able to control the actions of his fellows in the relevant cases, this kind of consequence would seem to bear on the morality of individual acts only through the utility of certain rules (and so forth). Nor will I, like J. J. C. Smart (following Sidgwick), separate the morality of action and the morality of praise and blame.[46] That kind of consequentialist reasoning about moral rules is open to the charge that it involves the creation of a moral elite which deludes the masses concerning the structure and content of morality.[47] Rule-consequentialism is for me a procedure for choosing moral rules, which, once chosen, are to be adhered to in practice by the agent himself as well as publicly defended by him. One consideration to be taken into account in rule-consequentialist reasoning is the tendency toward self-deception inherent in, and the power of, climates of opinion over, all human beings, including (perhaps especially) intellectuals.

I should add that the employment of rule-consequentialist reasoning against Bennett need not be founded on a deep commitment to consequentialist ways of arguing. All that is required is a desire to meet the consequentialist on his own ground. Those whose approach to moral questions is non-consequentialist do not require this particular kind of argument. Also, even someone who feels that he must retain an act-consequentialist perspective should consider my arguments in determining what sorts of conventional moral rules he should support and wish to see enacted into law.

The easier distinction to defend against Bennett is that between acting and refraining. Bennett contends:

When the killing/letting-die distinction is stripped of its implications regarding immediacy, intention *etc.* —which lack moral significance or don't apply to the example—all that remains is a distinction having to do with where a set of movements lies on the scale which has 'the only set of movements which would have produced that upshot' on one end, and 'movements other than the only set which would have produced that upshot' on the other. [48]

First, our pre-reflective moral consciousness does make a distinction between acting and refraining. Bennett is aware that he is arguing a radical thesis, that most of his audience will find the slogan "better two natural deaths than one murder" fanatical, perhaps, but not radically incoherent in the way Bennett argues that it is. Moreover, we do not merely invoke the distinction between acting and refraining in order to defend challenged courses of conduct: we also make such distinctions as between neglecting to inform one's enemy that his next step will carry him over a cliff and actually pushing him over. (Compare this with the couplet "Thou shalt not kill but needst not strive/Officiously to keep alive," which originally had a cynical sense but is now widely accepted as a principle of medical ethics.) That we feel this way is an ordinary fact, and moralists of whatever stripe are obliged to take account of facts, even when they disapprove of their origins.

Second, the distinctions we draw spontaneously when we consider our actions are to be taken into account when we frame moral rules, construct institutions, and shape attitudes (including the way we see ourselves as moral agents). Because we have fewer clear opportunities to save life than to kill, and because, even though the legitimizing of not-saving in one context is likely to encourage a feeling that not-saving in other contexts is legitimate, it is not so likely to license killing, a license not to save will be far less socially dangerous than a license to kill.

Third, consequences of moral relevance flow not only from our individual acts but from the moral rules we adopt, the attitudes we have, and the institutions in whose setting our acts take place. Not only obedience to a set of rules has effects; the adoption of such a set of rules has them as well. Indeed, an action may have (on the whole) good effects only so long as it is not carried out in the belief that it is right, or publicly defended. And a set of rules, attitudes, and institutions which distinguishes killing from letting-die will take into account facts about human beings of relevance that one which fails to does not, and hence, is likely to have better effects. If this is so, a utilitarian is bound to adopt such a (non-utilitarian) system of ethics.

Another virtue of the distinction between action and inaction is shown by an example advanced, in a contrary sense, by Michael Tooley. [49] He asks us to consider a machine containing two children, John and Mary. If one pushes a button, John will emerge unharmed, but Mary will be killed; if one does not push a button, Mary will emerge unharmed, but John will be killed. Tooley suggests that the right thing to do would be to flip a coin to determine whether to push the button or not. On the contrary, I believe the right thing to do would be to do nothing, and let John die rather than kill Mary. Absent any specification of how John and Mary got into their respective places in the machine, there is no need to flip a coin. The coin has already been flipped. The chances which brought about their positions count as a kind of natural lottery, and to flip a coin would be like flipping a second coin because the first coin told us to let John emerge, and yet we have some irrational prejudice against him.

Letting nature take its course is frequently a way of dealing with questions concerning which we are radically limited in our competence, such as which of two human beings is the more valuable. The doctrine of a significant moral difference between action and inaction enables us to appeal to a large number of natural lotteries without even having to make the decision to set up a lottery.

The trouble with an artificially constructed, as opposed to a natural, lottery, is that it is an attempt to attain rationality through deliberate capriciousness. As such, it shares some of the disadvantages of letting things happen as they will (that the outcome is not placed under rational control) and the disadvantages of controlling what will happen (that we are forced to regard the result as our decision). Hence, an artificial lottery is to be preferred to a natural lottery and conscious decision-making on articulated grounds only when it is feared that such decision-making will be tainted by some obnoxious motive, such as racial prejudice, when (as in jury selection, for example) a random selection from a group is precisely what is desired, or when a natural lottery is impossible.

Some may condemn such an attempt to lessen the burden of human decision-making as encouraging irresponsibility, but there is no reason to suppose that the world would be a better place if human beings made a practice of making more kinds of judgment which they could at best justify only shakily, and concerning which they would become either callous or anxious, or if they relied more heavily on the artificial lottery, a very unsatisfying means of making difficult decisions.

Finally, as P. J. Fitzgerald has pointed out, there are excellent reasons for being more reluctant to impose social (including legal) sanctions upon omissions than upon acts.[50] Imposing sanctions upon acts leaves the subject free to perform many alternative acts, whereas to sanction inaction is to narrow the range of his choice to one act (although the line is not sharp, since the one act might be performed in many different ways). It is less of a burden on someone to ask him to refrain from injuring others than to require him to make sacrifices in order to help them.

This argument is not at once relevant to the question of the morality or immorality of acts and abstentions in themselves, but it is easily made so. One need only assume that there is a conceptual connection between the concept of a wrong action and the concept of blame. A wrong action—it seems plausible to say—is at least prima facie an action which may and should be blamed, although further conditions must be met before we blame the actor. To blame is to impose a social sanction, and hence we have good reasons to be far more hesitant in regarding abstentions as wrong. Thus we have good reasons for regarding saving life, for instance by feeding the starving, as a duty of less strict obligation than refraining from taking life,[51] although still of course morally important.

The defense of the moral relevance of the direct/indirect distinction is more complicated, but follows the same general pattern as the defense of the distinction between killing and letting-die. One may agree with Bennett that a morally relevant distinction between act and consequence cannot be based wholly on the agent's confidence in the outcome, its objective inevitability, the causal complexity of the means employed, or the ultimate end in view when the action is performed. The doctor attending a dying patient may well know that giving the patient enough of a pain-killing drug will hasten his death, and the mercy killer may employ a contraption which does its work in a causally complex way with the help of many physical objects. And if I shoot someone in the head, his death results directly from my action whatever my purpose.

The paradigmatic case of an indirect result involves the intervention of another human will. This is the interrogation case cited in section 16 (4): I can say that I am not killing the children or (directly) causing their deaths even though I am quite certain that if I do not talk, they will die. For I can (truly) say: "It is the interrogator who is killing them."

The analysis extends from literal to metaphorical agency. An abnormal condition not of my making will also serve to make an effect indirect and hence a consequence of my act and not part of the act itself. Suppose I turn someone away from my door in a raging snowstorm, because I have some (although far from decisive) reason to believe that he is a homicidal maniac. Then, though I am sure that he will die in the storm, I can say that it was the storm that killed him, not I. (Recall that it is necessary to the case that I regret his death, or at least do not desire it is an end in itself; moreover, if I act without any justification at all, or with very flimsy justification, that the man's death was not a direct result of my action will not be pleadable in the court of morality.) One can see from this sort of case how letting-die may be considered a special case of indirect killing.

It is now time to formally defend the moral relevance of directness. As I did in the case of killing versus letting-die, I will offer a rule-utilitarian argument for its moral relevance, starting from the fact that we, in our precritical moments, do distinguish the direct from the indirect production of bad effects.

I start with the psychological fact that directness or indirectness of result affects how we and others spontaneously think of our actions. We uncritically and intuitively distinguish between shooting someone in the head and doing something which will in a less direct way, result in his death. To be sure, considerations of certainty and the agent's desire for the effect typically enter into our judgment of an act, but directness or indirectness does enter in as well. One way this is so is that one who kills indirectly is less likely to think of himself as a killer than one who kills directly. Likewise one who holds himself at liberty to kill indirectly is less likely to think of himself as lord of life and death than one who feels that he may kill directly.[52] There is even a superstitious feeling that killing someone through an agent is less guilt-producing than killing him with one's own hands, which illustrates the hold the contrast between direct and indirect has on our moral imagination.

That certain distinctions are drawn in prereflective moral judgment is particularly to be taken account of in the framing of rules, the design of institutions, and the shaping of attitudes. For to legitimize acts of direct killing in one context will tend to encourage a feeling that direct killing in another context is legitimate, in a way that the legitimation of indirect killing will not. True, to license indirect killing in one context, to permit a doctor, for instance, to administer pain-killing drugs which also shorten his patient's life, tends to legitimate indirect killing in others. But although in some contexts an act of nonimmediate killing is as certain of its effects as one of immediate killing, this is typically not the case. Someone driven into a snowstorm will in many cases have some chance of finding other shelter. Moreover, the opportunities for nonimmediate killing are fewer than those for immediate, since the possibility of nonimmediate killing requires some special circumstances not of the killer's making. Hence a license to kill indirectly is less dangerous to the public weal than one to kill directly. Hence by the standard rule-utilitarian maneuver, our moral rules ought to reflect our precritical distinction between direct and indirect killing; and these rules ought to be obeyed.

I have spoken about our "prereflective" attitudinal distinction between direct and indirect killing. Someone might argue that this distinction is irrational, and that the task of the moralist is to wean his fellow men from it, so that while we must perhaps shape our rules and institutions in accord with it for the time being, we may look forward to a happy day when man will be freed from such institutions and conduct his life in accord with the dictates of straightforward consequentialism. Not so: for the distinctions cited are rough guides to distinctions which the consequentialist must admit have real moral weight. Intentional action that has the direct effect of producing someone's death is more likely to have been prompted by a desire for that death, to have been carried out with the certainty that it would produce the death or result inevitably in death, than a mere refraining from saving his life, or action having this effect through conditions or actions not of the agent's making. Hence so long as moral decisions need to be made quickly, and on less than full information, these distinctions will be required.

Moreover, that the distinction between acting and refraining and between direct and indirect action is susceptible of consequentialist justification does not mean that it is dependent for its moral relevance on consequentialist considerations. Our distinction between acting and refraining is as morally fundamental as our sense that certain consequences are bad and that actions which produce them share their badness. And the foregoing demonstration that these intuitions are congruent does as much to reinforce the relevance of consequentialist considerations as the distinction between acting and refraining. Indeed, considering the speculative character of remarks about the probable effects of changes in our moral rules (and so forth), as well as the open-ended character of the lists of goods and evils admissible once it is seen that pleasure is not the only good, the resulting fusion of rule and ideal utilitarianism is best thought of, not as a theory from which moral results can be derived, but as a sometimes useful way of sorting out any set of moral views whatever.

In any case, the classifying of some kinds of killing as indirect, and the defense of the moral relevance of this classification where due proportion between means chosen and ends sought exists, does not settle all issues involved in life-and-death decisions. Many kinds of homicide are thought warranted which can only be regarded as direct, and to these kinds of homicide I now turn.

V /

JUSTIFICATIONS OF
HOMICIDE:

Other Persons

TWO JUSTIFICATIONS of homicide are grounded in the interests of persons other than the one killed, namely self-defense (including the defense of others) and extreme necessity. Justifications of homicide on general utilitarian grounds are rejected.

19. Pacifism

I SHALL ASSUME that indirect killing (i.e., activity or inactivity which does not in itself constitute killing but has as one of its foreseen results the death of a human being or person) is sometimes but not always legitimate. It is illegitimate when it constitutes a breach of another moral rule besides that forbidding killing, and also when the good it achieves is disproportionate to the evil it inflicts, including of course the death of the victim, but not only the death of the victim. Most of us hold that direct killing (action which can only be construed as lethally intended) is sometimes legitimate. Those who deny this claim are commonly called "pacifists."

The least stringent form of pacifism holds that all those wars in which the agent or his contemporaries are going to be able to participate are wrong. A moderate form holds that warfare is always wrong, but is silent about other forms of homicide—abortion, assassination, euthanasia, individual self-defense, paramour killing, or whatever. Such a pacifist would no doubt rely either on the massive loss of human life which takes place in war, or else on the other bad effects which follow from warfare, such as the destruction of ecosystems.

I will be concerned here with what I shall call "strict" pacifism—the doctrine that homicide of any sort is never right. Some expressions for what the pacifist renounces, "force" or "violence" for instance, extend his objection to nonlethal activity. But the pacifist as I understand him is willing under appropriate circumstances to inflict pain or injury, which after all leaves the person in question alive and able to make the best of his situation. (There are of course kinds of infliction of injury and pain which it would be absurd to defend if one were not also prepared to defend killing. It is neither humane nor admirable, for instance, to oppose capital punishment while advocating the "rehabilitation" of the criminal through brain surgery, however little of the original personality will remain when the process is done.)

It is not possible to refute strict pacifism by pointing to situations where, whatever one does, someone will die. For such examples can always be managed with the help of the principle of double effect. Even the example derided by G. E. M. Anscombe, where whichever foot one moves (different) people will die[1] (let us say also that standing still also will mean deaths), can be treated as one in which various life-saving acts or abstentions indirectly produce death. And the same is true, a fortiori, of the dilemmas the pacifist is more likely to face in real life.[2]

Nor will it help to abuse the pacifist with terms like "legalism." Rules are a necessary feature of the moral life, and an overscrupulous adherence to some of them may well have fewer bad consequences, on the whole, than a willingness to break them because it seems best on the whole. Pacifism entails a willingness to accept bad, even very bad, consequences, in particular cases. But if the general acceptance of pacifism would make the world a better place on the whole (as seems at first at least likely), such considerations are themselves not decisive. It is true, as Anscombe points out, that the teaching of pacifism may in fact have *bad* consequences, in eroding the moral restraints which might otherwise govern the use of violence,[3] but this kind of bad consequence may follow, not from pacifism itself, but from certain pacifist rhetorical tactics, such as treating all kinds of killing as equally bad morally. At most it shows that pacifism must be taught with a healthy degree of prudence and discretion. Nor is the pacifist committed—more than anyone else—to the view that obedience to rules is the whole, or the most important part, of morality. He can be as interested as anyone in the ethics of virtue, although virtue for him will of course be different in content than it will be for the nonpacifist.

Pacifism remains, though, in conflict with some of our deeply held moral intuitions.[4] It requires us either to yield to someone who is prepared to kill in order to get his way or else to die, whether what is at stake is either our own life or well-being or that of another. And where another's well-being is at stake, our dying may do no good. One cannot of course rely on the police, for on a pacifist view their activity is wrong as well. That this is so might not be completely clear in a country where the police do not carry guns, but even there the power of the police is backed by the readiness of the state to employ deadly force if less stringent measures fail.

There is, of course, nonviolent resistance, but nonviolent resistance raises some grave difficulties. The problem is not so much its want of efficacy—violent resistance is sometimes futile, too—but the extraordinary degree of moral discipline required for its being carried out, especially if one cannot rely covertly on the possibility of violent intervention by the less inhibited of one's fellows or by the National Guard. In the public sphere a community with grave structural injustices and many less-than-admirable people may have to be protected against far worse, and against a menace that includes blandishments as well as threats. The same is true of any private situation where the pacifist who is attacked is not alone. Prudence and discretion—the teaching of pacifism only to the worthy—is less helpful in this context, since the pacifist presumably wants to hold not that all virtuous people should refrain from killing, but that all people should.

Again, even the most civilized and decorous modes of protest— letters to congressmen and the like—sometimes raise the issue of the use of possibly lethal force. For many such protests call for the enactment of criminal statutes, and even when they do not (e.g., when they call simply for the appropriation of money), the government whose actions one is trying to influence maintains itself (and its ability to meet one's demands) by coercion (e.g., by coercive tax laws). And behind such laws lies the willingness to fight its enemies unto the death should that be necessary to maintain its authority, for instance if those opposed to the welfare state are prepared to offer violent resistance to the seizure of their chattels after defaulting on their income tax. The same is true even more clearly in the sphere of foreign policy, except where what is called for is passivity pure and simple.

To be sure, the pacifist may address the state in the hypothetical mode: "If you must use force, use it in the following way. . . ." But even here he can hardly call for the acquiring of new commitments—the enacting of new criminal statutes for instance—since to do so is in effect to ask the state to move *away* from his position. None of these considerations bears against a pacifist who is willing to renounce all influence on what happens in the world of politics, but it is of course notorious that many pacifists have been unwilling to do so.

None of this prevents one from holding that pacifists are often (or always) right in particular cases and that the vast majority of wars (or all of them) have been unjust on both sides.[5] Nor does it imply that nonviolent resistance is not capable of accomplishing a great deal of good. Nor does it mean that a political movement may not be nonviolent as a matter of principle, and not just of strategy or tactics. For violence remains an evil, even if sometimes a necessary one, and the burden of justification may be fairly placed on those who would employ it rather than on those who would exclude its use.

But as a matter of doctrine, strict pacifism—the doctrine that it is never right to use lethal force—does not seem acceptable, *provided an adequate account of the condition under which the use of such force is legitimate is possible.* For if there were no stable middle point between pacifism and complete unrestraint in the taking of human life, pacifism with all its drawbacks would have to be adopted by any moral and prudent (or rational and benevolent) person.

It is appropriate, before going on to discuss the various ways in which the justification of homicide has been attempted, to consider the reasons which lead many who are not pacifists of any sort to treat strict pacifism with a degree of respect they do not normally accord what they believe to be moral error. The reasons, I think, are in important part these: Since what is central to morality is the human person, the destruction of even one such person is a uniquely grave act. Such an act, and such an act alone, cannot be compensated for, nor can the wound in the tissue of human relations it inflicts ever be healed. While most thinkers hold that this price may on occasion have to be paid, the pacifist reminds us, in an emphatic way, that it is a price, a point easily lost sight of in time of war.

20. Utility

THE SUGGESTION that what justifies an act of homicide is simply that it offers the best result on the whole pinpoints a plausible necessary condition for the rightness of an act of killing—say warfare, judicial homicide, or self-defense—and moreover such a condition seems, at first, implicit in the requirement that indirect killing or letting-die satisfy the requirement of due proportion. The question now is whether it is sufficient.

At this point it is necessary to distinguish what may be called pragmatic utilitarianism or consequentialism from its more rigorous philosophical brethren. The distinction may be illustrated by an exchange on euthanasia between Yale Kamisar and Glanville Williams. Kamisar considered a number of cases in which the law did or, in his view, should recognize the legitimacy of homicide, although it was possible that a mistake might be made. He went on to remark that the need for killing in these other contexts (to save lives) was more compelling than that advocated by the defender of euthanasia, which was only to ease pain.[6] Williams responded that Kamisar's statement was "on Benthamite principles, an inadmissible remark."[7] And of course it is, if by "Benthamite principles" is meant (as is natural) an approach to problems of conduct which takes as fundamental a calculus of pleasures and pains. But so construed, utilitarianism has no claim to represent itself as in some way identical with rationality about questions of morals, or as the only alternative to superstitious, taboo-ridden morality. To put the same point another way, there is no good reason to suppose that one is faced with a choice between leaving morality "in the dominion of vague feeling or inexplicable inner conviction" and making it "a matter of reason *and calculation.*"[8]

The distinction between calculative and pragmatic utilitarianism corresponds closely, and is indeed probably equivalent, to that between ideal and hedonistic utilitarianism. But it is still worth making the distinction twice, for the two ways of making it respond to two different

138

kinds of question. One may ask: What is valuable, only pleasure, or also knowledge, friendship, and so forth? Or one may ask: Is there a lowest common denominator in terms of which the various good things of life can be measured? The hedonistic-ideal distinction speaks to the first of these questions, and is closely connected to disputes about psychological hedonism. The calculative-pragmatic distinction speaks to the second, the calculative utilitarian answering "Yes" (pleasure), and the pragmatic utilitarian answering "No" (or at any rate nothing more specific than goodness).

Calculative utilitarianism is, as I argued in section 5 (1), quite incapable of yielding a sane result about the ethics of homicide. Pragmatic utilitarianism—a rough and ready balancing of goods and evils—does not labor under this kind of handicap, for one thing because it is not a moral theory, but simply the kind of reasoning concerning the public good used by ordinary people, at least when the issue is not one of very great sensitivity. From the point of view of pragmatic utilitarianism, Kamisar's remark is quite admissible (especially when combined with the reflection that there are usually nonlethal ways of easing pain, and even when there aren't, there are usually ways of easing pain which are not *directly* lethal). Likewise the tendency (admitted by Richard Henson),[9] of treating a death as a large bundle of pain when trying to work out conclusions in utilitarian ethics is, while a lapse from the point of a hedonic calculus, from the point of view of pragmatic utilitarianism merely a legitimate way of making vivid the kind of choice to be made.

Perhaps a better way of putting the matter is this: Calculations of the effects of homicide are more likely to reach a securely favorable result where what is balanced against the life of the victim is other lives, rather than something else such as freedom from pain. Such emphasis on the possible incommensurability of death with other evils will, however, lead us beyond pragmatic utilitarianism to something else.

Even from the point of view of pragmatic utilitarianism, however, Alan Donagan's argument retains its bite:

> It might well be the case that more good and less evil would result from your painlessly and undetectedly murdering your malicious, old and unhappy grandfather than from your forebearing to do so: he would be freed from his wretched existence; his children would be rejoiced by their inheritances and

would no longer suffer from his mischief; and you might anticipate the regard promised to those who do good in secret. [10]

For the assessment of goods and evils made by Donagan seems quite as persuasive when made in a pragmatic, as when made (or attempted to be made) in a calculative, fashion.

Notice that Donagan's argument does not in any way rely on a hedonistic theory of value. One's grandfather may be sitting on money which otherwise would be used to further cultural and aesthetic goals of high quality, and his mischief may be an impediment to very valuable friendships. (Or consider a once great philosopher who has ceased to be creative, and is refusing to release his unpublished manuscripts, and who will arrange to have his work destroyed after his death if he is not killed soon.) So that while the admission of nonhedonic values may provide us with reasons for not killing the old man, it will also provide us with reasons for killing him as well.

A possible act-consequentialist response goes as follows: It may be right (productive of the best consequences on the whole) to kill your aged grandfather, but it will also be right (productive of the best consequences) for the authorities to punish you. Not only that: they need not say "We don't blame you, you understand, but we have to do this in order to support our institutions." It may be right (productive of the best consequences) for them to treat you as a depraved criminal. What is more: it may be right (productive of the best consequences) for you to have been so socialized as to be conscience-stricken, and to say (and believe) that your act was one which in no way could be defended. [11] It is hard to see, however, what distinguishes this kind of right act from one which, although productive of the best consequences, is wrong.

We are now prepared for a three-step rule-utilitarian argument, the utilitarianism being as before pragmatic utilitarianism. (1) It is not desirable that our law and conventional morality permit this kind of thing; hence the prudent and moral man will advocate and adhere to moral rules forbidding it. (2) But to adhere to a moral rule is genuinely to adhere to it, and not to hold oneself at liberty to violate the rule when one can do so without detection. (3) Therefore, the prudent and moral man will not kill his malicious, old, and unhappy grandfather.

Step 1 of this argument requires some expansion, since it may seem that if doing X will have good effects on balance, a rule permitting X will have good effects on balance as well. One point to the contrary is the anxiety which the publication of such a rule might engender in grandfathers (and others), but, so long as the rule was narrowly phrased, this might not prove crucial, except insofar as it was linked with the next point: that is, that licensing this kind of killing would be likely to lead to other kinds, and thus to a general rise in the murder-level of the society in question. This may not seem plausible if what one thinks of is knifings in bars, but what one has to worry about here is in-stitutionalized killings, on steadily wider grounds, of those deemed unfit to live. The evils that can be done with some semblance of utilitarian justification are bad enough. While the secret killing of the obstreperous old might not of itself tend to lead to such measures, its possible ap-proval by law and conventional morality would, especially in a society, like our own, where geronticide might not be regarded as a necessary sin, but would perforce enter, as abortion for instance has, under the banners of constitutional right.

At this point a protest is inevitable. The killing of the obstreperous aged does not belong at the beginning of a wedge argument; if any-where, it belongs at the end. Perhaps there are some measures which would be acceptable were it not for their ultimate tendency, but the killing of the obstreperous aged is surely not one of them. Such mea-sures are wrong on their own account, not because of the consequences likely to flow from approving them. I think this protest is right, and that by reflecting upon *why* it is right we can see that, contrary to appear-ances, "more good and less evil" does not flow from killing even an obnoxious and unhappy person just because he is obnoxious and un-happy. But what this means is that we place a kind of value on the continued existence of a human being which, even if not literally infi-nite, suffices to override the considerations mentioned by Donagan. But this is a kind of value we are only likely to discover by reflecting on a moral rule, and thus is not of particular use in giving that rule support. (Notice, incidentally, the very complex way in which our concepts of good results and right action interact here.)

I should now consider the radical attack on consequentialist ethics launched by Germain Grisez.[12] Grisez rejects consequentialist reason-ing in ethics, whatever the theory of value that accompanies it. His rejection is not limited to theories that allow unlimited scope for consequentialist considerations: he also rejects all limited versions of consequentialism, for instance theories that do not employ consequentialist reasoning in the settling of concrete moral questions, but only in determining what moral rules to adopt. Hence also he rejects a consequentialist interpretation of the principle of due proportion as employed in the principle of double effect: for him due proportion means not that indirect killing must do more good than harm, but that it should be consistent with other moral principles, such as those specifying the duties in the doctor-patient relationship.

Grisez's rejection of consequentialism of all sorts arises out of a conviction that the notion of the greatest net good (as consequentialist moralists employ it) is meaningless except as a device of rationalization. One might in limited contexts calculate, for example, the number of lives that will be lost if one course or another is adopted, and one is entitled to prefer goods bound up with persons to goods not so bound up (e.g., the life of a human being to that of an animal). Moreover, some goods—life and health or physical wholeness, for instance—are arranged along a scale such that one is never entitled to prefer the lesser to the greater. But the basic human goods are incommensurable with one another, so that there are no rational grounds on which one may be sacrificed to another. Thus Grisez's critique of consequentialism is closely linked to a moral theory requiring that we pursue those basic goods which seem most appropriate, while abstaining from a direct attack on any of them. For this reason, Grisez holds that it is always wrong directly to take human life, however strong the consequentialist case for doing so may appear to be.

I have the following objections to Grisez's argument. First, it seems to me that the situation as to values is more complex than he supposes. While it is true that one could never be healthier dead, there are cases where he might be faced with a choice between health and life, and it is by no means clear that it is irrational to prefer health. Someone with a heart condition might have to choose, for instance, between a longer life as an invalid and a shorter life of relatively normal activity. And this kind of consideration is relevant to a decision whether to refuse painful and degrading treatments which offer only a short prolongation of one's life, or whether to employ pain relievers which have the side effect of shortening it.

Second, even when one is dealing with goods that cannot be reduced to any common denominator, there may be cases where it would be clearly rational to sacrifice one to others. Granted that skill in games and sports is a human good with an integrity of its own not reducible to anything else, [13] it still seems fanatical to hold, as Grisez does, that it is never right to throw a golf game no matter how high the moral stakes may be, for instance even if one is playing with a tyrant who is in the habit of killing millions of people when upset. Of course it is possible even here to take the hard line: to argue, for instance, that one ought to refuse to play golf with the tyrant (frankly explaining why) and risk the deaths of large numbers of people in hopes that the tyrant will repent and reform. One might feel a certain admiration for a golfer who took this course, if the victims did not include any of one's friends and family. And no doubt one's interest or lack of interest in golf will affect one's perceptions, too. The upshot seems to be that, while there is no way of demonstrating to a persistent skeptic that one is warranted in preferring the lives of many people (even if there is a slim possibility that they will survive one's refusal) to one's integrity as a golf-player, one is surely entitled here to recall Aristotle's warning that the rigor of geometry is not to be expected in morality, and to hold that a decision to throw a golf game under such circumstances is at minimum a permissible resolution of the dilemma. In any case, the element of extortion present in a game with a tyrant need not always be present in these cases: one might for instance give an old and sick person a sense of worth by letting him win a game of golf (or chess) upon occasion and thus avert a possible suicide.

At any rate, even supposing that these are cases where consequentialist reasoning reaches a false conclusion, they are clearly cases where such reasoning reaches a conclusion. No one would defend refusal to throw the game on consequentialist grounds. Hence the weighing of conflicting values does not in all cases reach an indeterminate result. If so, the consequentialism is not meaningless (it tells us what to do in some cases), although it does not follow from this premise that it will tell us what to do in all cases.

Third, opponents of consequentialism, Grisez included, frequently argue that the prevalence of consequentialist modes of thought has had bad consequences. There is nothing wrong with this kind of argument, since, even if one wishes to renounce consequentialist reasoning entirely at the level of choosing and evaluating actions, it is still possible to employ such arguments without inconsistency at the level of choice of rules, design of institutions, and formation of attitudes. But one surely must concede that consequentialist reasoning has had some good moral results—for instance, abandoning the view that it is wrong for a woman to have anaesthesia in childbirth. It thus seems that Grisez needs to argue that more evil and less good has resulted from consequentialism than would have resulted from the adoption of his system. But this kind of reasoning his premises require him to forgo.

On the other hand, that consequentialism leads to bad results may mean that it leads to morally bad results, and that these results are not causal, but logical. (Any moral theory will lead to some morally bad results by being misapplied.) If any consequentialist theory whatever requires us to adopt morally bad results, then of course we have a sufficient reason to reject all forms of consequentialism, although defending the claim that these results are morally bad will often involve defending a (nonconsequentialist) moral theory which condemns them. But since Grisez holds that as a matter of logic nothing follows from consequentialism when values are in conflict, he cannot hold that morally bad results follow in this way from consequentialist ways of thinking.

On the other hand, Grisez is clearly right in asserting that human beings are frequently unable to weigh and measure premoral goods and evils in the way the consequentialist wants them to do. Even at the level of physical pleasure, I see no way of subtracting headaches from orgasms. Nor do I see a way of subtracting the desire of a minority for an unrestricted existence from the desire of the majority to maintain a cultural climate which requires that constraints be imposed on minorities. When it is agreed that knowledge, friendship, and the very existence of human beings are goods independent of want-satisfaction and pleasure, the whole consequentialist calculus becomes in many cases just unmanageable.

In this kind of situation, everything depends on the biases with which one approaches the problems, and there seem to be strong reasons to approach them with a presumption against attacks on fundamental human goods. This means a presumption against killing—both an unwillingness to kill in practical situations unless the case for so doing is overwhelming, and a very cautious attitude to the kinds of arguments in defense of homicide which one is prepared to entertain, particularly when they have not gained unequivocal acceptance in one's community. This means admitting a bit of relativity into the argument, but I am not at all clear that this degree of relativity is objectionable.

The rejection of general utility as a defense of homicide entails the rejection of some commonly heard arguments, such as that abortion may be justified (without inquiring into the status of the fetus) as a means of population control, [14] or euthanasia may be justified to spare the sick person's family, as distinct from the sick person himself, suffering. [15] I now turn to a consideration of the more precise and narrowly defined ways in which homicide may be justified, or a justification of homicide attempted. My evaluation of these modes of justification in part rests on a kind of prudential judgment, with which philosophers are no more gifted than anyone else. It will therefore be possible for someone to be more rigorous or lax than my tentative conclusions, not only as to cases but also as to the kinds of justifications he is prepared to consider, without departing from the intellectual framework here presented. Also, I shall be relying upon intuitions which, although not I think eccentric, are also pretty clearly not universally shared.

21. Extreme Necessity

A NARROW VARIANT of general utility is what I shall call extreme necessity. To argue for an exception to a moral rule on grounds of extreme necessity is to argue that the moral rule in this case protects no significant value whatever while its breach would promote important ones. In the case of homicide, necessity means that if the decedent loses nothing by being killed (being certainly doomed to die very shortly in any case), and others who would die otherwise will be saved by his being killed, then killing is justified. For instance, if for medical reasons there is no way of saving the life of the unborn child, and if he is not killed the mother will die, then abortion is justified. Likewise if the Nazis will kill every pregnant woman in a certain group, and their unborn children in the womb with them, then the principle of extreme necessity would justify abortion. [16] One might put the argument in defense of homicide here in Rawls-like terms: the one who is killed in such cases (the worst off) is at any rate no worse off than he would be if he had not been killed.

One difficulty I shall not be able to resolve lies in the ambiguity of the expression "doomed to die very shortly in any case." By geological and some historical standards, we are all doomed to die very shortly. On the other hand, those who adhere to views of life which hold that there are important goods to be achieved "between the stirrup and the ground" will want to question the claim that there is any shortening of life which can be treated for any purpose as *de minimis.* If this problem is met by requiring that the victim be unconscious (or at least incapable of reason) during the period in question, then extreme necessity will tend to merge into a judgment (cf. section 15) that the decedent is already dead and so not within the scope of the rule against homicide at all. Someone who adopts this position may, of course, still wish to take the safer course and treat those who are dead by his criterion as alive when no other life is at stake.

The more difficult kind of case is where no one is doomed to die unconditionally, but all will die unless someone is killed. Examples are the killing of one person to provide food for his starving comrades (assuming for the sake of argument that cannibalism is not a distinct consideration),[17] and the throwing of passengers overboard to lighten a lifeboat that would otherwise sink.[18] Someone lightening a lifeboat might appeal to the principle of double effect, since after all it is not completely fantastic that those thrown overboard might swim to safety. No such help is available to those who would save their lives by killing another for food. (It might be suggested[19] that one might satisfy the requirements of double effect by eating someone—who is alive and unconscious—bit by bit. But since what is at stake here is fatal wounding, this suggestion is not plausible.)

Baruch Brody argues that in this kind of case one must employ a fair random method to determine who is to live and who is to die,[20] but I should think that in at least some cases—where it is consistent with one's public responsibilities, where conflict and scandal are unlikely to be generated—one is entitled to choose to save those to whom one is more closely tied. Thus for instance a physician may perform an abortion to save a woman, rather than flip a coin in order to determine whether to kill her or her unborn child. For the mother is more his patient than the child is, since he was hired by her or on her behalf. This seems to be the best ground that can be given for preferring the life of the mother in all cases: her death will usually be the more painful and the more socially disruptive one, but not always (cf. section 22 [1]).

There is, however, an important class of cases where extreme necessity does not seem to be applicable. There are largely cases where one is inclined to say "if murder is done, let it not be done by me" rather than "better two natural deaths than one murder," probably because the act of another person severs ascription of responsibility more satisfyingly than does a merely natural event. Even if the suspected rapist will die in any case, whether at the hands of the lynch mob or at those of the sheriff, and though others may die in the riots accompanying the lynching, still the sheriff ought not to kill his prisoner to satisfy their demands, nor even, since he is a sheriff, hand his prisoner over to them. A group of villagers assailed by bandits ought not to kill one of their number to satisfy the bandits, though the bandits threaten (credibly) to kill all if their demands are not met. On the other hand, it does seem that the villagers, who do not have the kind of institutional responsibilities the sheriff has, may hand the scapegoat over, although not go so far as to choose a scapegoat themselves. [21]

Both these cases seem to have something to do with a desire to protect not only lives, but also institutions and patterns of mutual trust. In such cases, the utility of an unbending attitude (which may prevent extortionate demands from being made in the first place) needs to be taken into account.

In a related case, where what threatens is not murder but natural death—whether it would be permissible to take the heart out of a living but moribund person in order to give another person years of useful life—what seems to preclude going through with the operation is the relationship of trust needed between physician and patient. A possible exception to this restriction is a transplant with the donor's consent, but even here one has to take into account the peculiar helplessness of a dying person, and hesitate to impose upon him a procedure irrelevant to his condition. [22]

If it is wrong to kill a dying patient for his organs, it is wrong (a fortiori) to take vital organs from a healthy person, however fairly the victim-donor may be selected. [23] The only defense of such killing that seems possible is that the death of the donor is not intended, but this defense will not work, since (as I have argued in Chapter IV) to intend to take the heart or other vital organ from someone is to intend that he should die.

The case that fails to fit is that of the abortions performed on pregnant women to save them from the Nazis. Perhaps the reason, "If murder be done, let it not be done by me," is relatively unconvincing here is that the Nazis are thought of as almost a natural force—proceeding with their extermination program without interest in the details of what goes on among the subject population. If they were—for reasons of moral sadism, say—particularly interested in getting the physician to perform abortions, he might be forced in conscience to refuse, since the need to protect the ethics of the medical profession against such pressure would then be of considerable relevance.

There are a number of similar examples, not all of them in Nazi environments. May a doctor perform an (otherwise unjustified) abortion at gunpoint if he is sure that, if he refuses and is killed, the child will die in any case? Or if a woman threatens (credibly) to shoot herself in the womb, use a coat hanger, or go to a butcher whose ministrations are likely to be lethal to her as well as to her child? The solution to these questions must rest on a determination whether to allow the killing of unborn children in such contexts will endanger unborn children in others. One thing is clear: the coat-hanger argument (if it is good at all) is only good in particular cases. That women in general (and not that particular woman) were likely to use coat hangers could not justify abortions, since to allow such arguments would be to undermine inhibitions against feticide altogether.

On the other hand, if there are cases where even the institutions we seek to protect would be destroyed if we failed to kill, then this exception to the doctrine of extreme necessity just carved out will not obtain. The case Anscombe ducked—where judicial murder is required to stop an H-Bomb war[24]—is a possible instance, since a nation's institutions will not survive its destruction. The villagers who die rather than choose a scapegoat are presumably members of a larger group who may well learn of their decision, but what we are now supposing is that the group as a whole will be destroyed, even if some of its members survive to form

148

new societies on its ruins. (Consider here the *Fail-Safe* situation—the destruction of New York by American bombs to avert a nuclear war, under circumstances where it would not be fair to speak of extortion.) But since a judicial process which attempts to be fair is a necessity for any civilized community, it may well be morally necessary to offer to kill the scapegoat outright without a trial, or to persuade him to kill himself, but to refuse, whatever the consequences, at least short of the literal extermination of all human life on the planet, actually to hold a scapegoat trial.

On yet the other hand, Caiaphas in the gospels was not justified in procuring the death of an innocent man (with or without a trial) "that the whole people perish not." In the first place, Caiaphas did not know that his action would avert the destruction of the Jewish state, and it in fact failed to do so. Secondly, Caiaphas had reason at least to hope that the destruction of the Jewish state would not mean the destruction of the Jewish community, since the Jewish community had survived such destruction in the past.

A few words need to be said about two weaker senses of necessity. "I had to kill him" may mean, not that the stringent conditions of the principle of extreme necessity were met, but rather (1) that I lacked the personal resources not to kill him, but to suffer some evil instead, or (2) that the consequences of not killing him would be very bad indeed, although since he would survive, the conditions of extreme necessity would not be met. Some blend of these two possibilities is represented by a phrase such as W. H. Auden's "conscious acceptance of guilt in the necessary murder" ("Spain," original version), unless all "necessary" means here is necessary to a given end.

Version 1 is clearly an excuse rather than a justification, and thus of no direct interest at this point in the discussion. [25] Version 2 represents a strengthened version of general utility—something like, but something more than, a prudential judgment that more good and less evil will flow from killing Jones than from not killing him. If killing Jones will save the world enormous evil—say Jones is Hitler's father and we know (never mind how) what kind of son he will beget—are we justified in cutting short his life? A more realistic example is provided by Michael Walzer's suggestion that World War II (in Europe), where the Nazi enemy posed an ultimate and immeasurable threat to civilized values—was a case where "a wager against the rules," in particular the rules protecting noncombatants, was morally required. [26]

One point about the Hitler's-father example is that it appeals to kinds of knowledge human beings just do not have. If we did have that kind of knowledge, our moral life would be very different from what it now is. We might know additional facts which would make the killing of Hitler's father less appealing (there is another, worse, Hitler about to be born somewhere else, and there is nothing which we can do to stop him), or we might adopt a different set of moral rules from those we now have. (The moral rules governing the conduct of an omniscient being are not necessarily those which should govern the conduct of a human being.) The difficulty is that we are to imagine receiving this bit of knowledge out of context, and for such unlikely and bizarre situations one ought to follow the analogy of more realistic cases, strange though the result may seem. More realistic examples, such as that of terror bombing during World War II, are haunted by the specter of the moral blind alley—an unresolvable conflict between two different ways of reaching concrete moral results—which seems to haunt all honest and thorough ethical discussion.

It seems intuitively plausible that very bad consequences might justify homicide even if the stringent conditions of the principle of extreme necessity, and other principles justifying homicide, are not met. But there seems no stable way of walling off this kind of justification and blocking its extension to cases where it is clearly unacceptable. And we must remember that in choosing moral rules we have (or should have) taken into account the human capacity for self-deception, with precisely this kind of situation in mind. Certainly, in view of what has passed since, someone would be extremely adventurous if he claimed that Allied terror bombing during World War II was justified even by act-utilitarian criteria. Indeed, some historians and strategists hold that it was not justified even in terms of defeating Germany, leaving out of account its effect on the international ethos after the war.

Perhaps the best one can say is that such cases are, on the one hand, either very difficult ones, where all but the most heroic will falter, but in which homicide is, despite appearances, wrong; or, on the other hand,

150

cases where justification of a sort as yet undeveloped by us, limited enough to protect the moral rule against homicide from being eaten up by exceptions and qualifications, is available—where we can kill in good conscience without knowing what our justification is. In real cases, we ought of course to look very hard for a way out which will prevent the bad consequences without requiring us to take a life. Indeed, one advantage of absolutistic moral approaches—too little taken into account—is that they compel us to attempt to look for such ways out and thus make it possible to develop methods of achieving our ends without damage to important values.

22. Self-Defense

I HAVE SO FAR CONSIDERED two sorts of conflict situations: (1) where killing X is the only way of saving Y, and where X is doomed to die shortly in any case; and (2) where one can save Y by killing X, or X by killing Y, but if one does nothing both will die. Another kind of conflict situation (3) is where either X or Y will die: X if nothing is done, Y if he is killed to save X. In order to justify killing in this kind of case, one has to have some adequate reason for overriding the results of the natural lottery and preferring X's life to Y's.

The classic kind of justification of homicide in this kind of situation is that of self-defense, or (as it is perhaps better called) incapacitating the pursuer. The expression "incapacitate" I take from Paul Ramsey.[27] It embodies the idea that while killing in self-defense may be, by the criteria set forth in Chapter IV, *direct*, there remains a sense in which the death of the person killed is not directly and centrally willed. One consequence of such a treatment of self-defense (not drawn by Ramsey) is that it is not morally acceptable to define military success in terms of body count, even apart from the increased probability that the bodies counted will be those of noncombatants. The expression "the pursuer" (taken from Jewish tradition) is designed to reflect the view that one may kill in defense of others as well as oneself, although literal pursuit need not be involved (consider strangulation). (For some writers defense of others is the only legitimate kind of self-defense, but it is most natural to regard such writers as proposing that the right of self-defense be placed

151

in suspension since the needs of others might require that it be reactivated.) In any case, I shall continue to use the more comfortable "self-defense" for the principle under discussion.

In the paradigmatic case of self-defense, where Y wrongfully threatens X's life, it seems altogether just that Y should be deprived of his life in order to save X's. Yet we also think that self-defense may be used to justify homicide even where Y is not culpable—where he is, for instance, insane. The wrongfulness of killing the innocent is primarily the wrongfulness of killing the causally innocent, those who are doing no harm, not the wrongfulness of killing the juridically innocent, those who have committed no crime, or the morally innocent, those who are not in a relevant respect morally flawed.

What is required is that Y—rather than (as is often the case with extreme necessity cases) the surrounding human and natural situation—be clearly identifiable as the cause of the threat to X. Thus Robert Nozick's "innocent threats," together with guilty aggressors, are legitimate objects of self-defense, while any action taken against his "innocent shields" will have to be justified (if at all) by double effect or extreme necessity.[28] These principles are, I think, enough to provide a stable and nonarbitrary way of justifying a choice to preserve X's life at the cost of Y's.

How remote the threat can be depends on the situation.[29] It seems that a legitimate government, or an individual in the state of nature, is justified in warding off more remote threats than is an individual in civil society.[30] Also, while innocent threats may be repressed, the threat they pose must be closer than is required when the threat is a guilty aggressor, although not quite so high a degree of certainty is required as for invoking extreme necessity. In any case, sharp limits must be placed on the degree of remoteness and uncertainty of the threat which is consistent with the employment of self-defense, else we should be required to approve the Ottoman habit of killing the brothers of the successful contender for the sultanate.[31]

Further clarification of the principle of self-defense is best provided by a consideration of examples. These I shall choose from the following problem areas: abortion, capital punishment, and war.

1. Where a woman will die if an abortion is not performed, but the unborn child can be saved, abortion is commonly thought to be jus-

tified, and was so thought before abortion-on-demand came to be widely advocated. Though the case is a somewhat problematical one (difficult as it may be in the present cultural context to see it as such), abortion in this kind of situation might be justified where the threat to the woman arises from the unborn child and not from the surrounding environment. Thus medical, though not social or socio-medical, "indications" may in some cases justify abortion.

But another problem presents itself. Not only can the child be seen as a threat to the woman, the woman can also be seen as a threat to the child. If we were to choose to defend the person whom we find socially more valuable, or whose death would be socially more disruptive, we should usually defend the woman—but not always. (Consider an insane woman, pregnant with a healthy child for whom there is waiting a good adoptive home.) Likewise, while the woman's terror is a relevant consideration, such terror will not always be present. (She may be unconscious at the time the situation arises.) Still, nearly everyone will want to save the woman in these cases, even if it means killing the child, and hardly anyone wants to justify saving the child by killing the woman. [32] The justification of abortion in these cases might rest on the closer ties obtaining between the physician and the woman than between the physician and the unborn child—which suggests that the proposed justification for abortion ought to be read quite narrowly.

An attempt at a very broad reading is common, however—culminating in an attempt to justify abortion (irrespective of the status of the unborn child) in a wide range of cases simply as an instance of one's right to protect oneself against harm. A country may defend itself against those who would merely forcibly change its institutions for the worse, a woman may kill a prospective rapist, and in general we may protect ourselves from those who would merely injure us. In the same way, so goes the argument, we may protect ourselves and the kind of life we want to live against the assaults of an unborn child even when our life is not in danger. [33]

Our right to defend ourselves against injury rather than death does not follow from the self-defense rationale set forth at the beginning of this section. If this kind of killing is to be defended, it would seem that the defense would have to follow the lines proposed by Hobbes and Locke. Hobbes, having established to his satisfaction that "a man cannot lay down the right of resisting them, that assault him by force, to take away his life," goes on to argue that "the same may be said of wounds, and chains, and imprisonment," since "a man cannot tell when he seeth men proceed against him by violence, whether they intend his death or not."[34] Locke says:

> He who attempts to get another man into his absolute power does thereby put himself into a state of war with him; it being understood as a declaration of a design upon his life. For I have reason to conclude that he who would get me into his power without my consent would use me as he pleased when he had got me there, and destroy me too when he had a fancy to it.[35]

It is easy enough to see how a plausible case for the use of deadly force to rescue other people from kidnappers or pirates, or oneself to escape from their control, might be built on such premises.

But one thought that emerges from the quotations above is that self-defense is in many instances an excuse rather than a justification, since one who proposes to injure me (especially to steal from me) may in fact have no further malevolent intentions, and I might be able to find this out. In any case the upshot of the discussion is that the right to defend oneself against injury by deadly force rests on the consideration that there is no surety for one's life once someone who is prepared to do severe injury has power over one. No such consideration, of course, can apply in the case of an unborn child, certainly not in a society where adoption is a possibility.

There are, I admit, some very hard cases here. If we could know that a woman would be rendered incurably insane by giving birth, but not by having an abortion, there would be persuasive reasons for regarding such insanity as tantamount to death and permitting the abortion. As things stand, I doubt that we can know these things, and abortion on psychiatric grounds is tantamount to abortion on demand as to the strength of the grounds required, although (due to unequal access to psychiatry) not as regards number. Even in a very appealing psychiatric case, therefore, it seems that abortion cannot be justified, especially since an abortion may turn out to be as traumatic as giving birth. It also seems undesirable to encourage people to get what they want by claiming, even sincerely, mental or emotional disturbance.

Again, one point that seems to be common ground in discussions of mercy killing is that such killing is a case of killing the innocent, despite the ambiguities of "innocence." Marvin Kohl puts the matter this way:

> Unlike the abortion controversy, both parties to this dispute agree that there is no problem concerning the question of innocence. Almost all the intended patients or recipients are viewed as being innocent and, it is doubtless important to add, innocent in all the morally significant senses of that term.[36]

But it is obvious that a sick person may be the cause of considerable unhappiness to his friends and relatives, of damage to their mental health, if you will, and that this unhappiness may be cut short when he dies. If the innocence (in every sense) of such a sick person is not in question, there is no reason to question, as Kohl does,[37] the innocence (in any sense) of most of the unborn children whose life or death is at stake in abortion decisions.

The ambiguities of "innocence"—and the limits that need to be placed on the casuistical exploitation of these ambiguities—may be further elucidated by a consideration of the case of Isaac,[38] a six-month-old child who was crying when a group of soldiers on a search-and-destroy mission approached the bunker where he and about ninety other refugees were hiding. The question is whether the resistance leader did right in killing Isaac to prevent the hiding place from being discovered, and thus to save the lives of the other refugees.

It seems that direct killing at least could be avoided (and Isaac given perhaps a chance to live) by placing one's hand over his mouth to stop his cries. The difficult case is the one where for some reason or other this course is not possible. The question is complicated by a customary principle protecting young children, but not the unborn or the mature.

If, as is probable, the German soldiers will kill Isaac too, we have here a case of extreme necessity, at least if it is certain that killing him, and only killing him, will save the refugees. The nasty case is the less probable one, where it is the policy of the Germans to raise Jewish children of less than a year's age as Aryans or where the results of killing him or not killing him are not so clear. In such a case, while it is clear that Isaac is juridically innocent, he may or may not be "not harming." On the one hand, a causal chain reaches from his cries to threatened harm; on the other hand, the connection between his cries and the threatened harm lies through the acts of other human beings, the German soldiers. (We should not say that Isaac killed the other refugees if his cries led to their deaths.) Perhaps this case can best be treated as a borderline situation, beyond which it is not possible to press self-defense against the juridically innocent.

2. In contrast with the problem of abortion, the problems that follow raise the issue of the nature and status of the state. In order to assess the morality of war and capital punishment, one needs to know, for instance, to what extent, if any, the state is specially privileged to take life, and to what extent, if any, its right to use deadly force arises simply from its de facto power together with principles stating the rights of individuals in a state of nature (assuming of course that the state may wield power legitimately at all). Since one's view of the issues here might well depend on his view of the many powers the state has besides practicing, preventing, and punishing homicide, the discussion could go very far afield indeed. Moreover, the author has nothing like a complete theory of the state handy, and the most subtle and sophisticated account known to him—Nozick's defense of the minimal state (and nothing more than the minimal state)—is too ideologically uncongenial for use here. Perhaps it will be helpful to indicate the objections to Nozick's theory which most closely touch upon the themes of this book.

First, Nozick holds that the state exists to protect the rights of its members, but may not take property from its more fortunate members even to save the lives of the less fortunate. "The right to life," he argues, "is not a right to whatever one needs to live; other people may have rights over these things."[39] But—I would reply—if it is wrong to kill someone, it is extremely implausible that it is permissible simply to let him die, however small the burden of saving him might be. Neither the examples nor the arguments I have advanced in defense of the killing/letting-die distinction will bear so heavy a weight. Moreover, it would be odd if the right not to be killed were enforceable, and the right not to be let die were not, so that if I may kill another to defend myself against him, it seems that I may legitimately steal from another if this is the only way to avoid starvation. But it is more conducive to social peace for the state, acting as the starving person's representative, to tax the affluent but selfish man in order to save the poor person's life. And while this line of thought hardly leads directly to a welfare or socialist state (nothing has been said about equality, or about distributive justice or about monoprly, or about the exploitation of labor), it is quite possible that this any acorn, properly tended, might be made to yield an enormous oak. Need, at any rate, must be at least part of our criteria for a just distribution.

Second, it seems to me that the activities of the contemporary state which are most deplorable, such as waging unjust wars, could be performed by the minimal state, while some of its more admirable ones, such as supporting philosophy, require a "high" doctrine of state authority for their justification. To be sure, the welfare state does objectionable things as well (pressuring the poor into getting sterilized in order to cut down the relief rolls), but that that this is so does not make the welfare state peculiarly subject to corruption. To put the matter in somewhat more emotional terms, if it is granted that even the minimal state might have engaged in the Christmas bombing of Hanoi (or whatever else is your favorite wartime atrocity), it seems disproportionate to argue functional illegitimacy (it is not a question of agreement) when the state undertakes to ban one's favorite psychoactive drug or to impose taxes for purposes one finds uncongenial.

In what follows I shall not defend or attack the legitimacy of this state, but rather explore the consequences of the acceptance of state power. The foil for my discussion will be the anarchist. The anarchist, as I understand him, denies the legitimacy of all institutionalized coercion, including those resting on the possibility or actual use of deadly force. In other words, he identifies the exercise of power by one person or group over another with oppression. He need not—although he may—oppose all forms of authority (e.g., that based on technical competence), nor need he advocate terroristic violence, private revenge on malefactors, or socially disruptive activity. [40]

Except from strict pacifist or anarchist premises, there is no way of denying the state the right to use deadly force against those who are willing to fight it unto death. It will normally prove sufficient to kill only those who are engaged in direct warfare against the state, sparing those who can be kept from crime by imprisonment, assuming that imprisonment for long periods is a morally acceptable penalty. If it is not, say because prisons as such are capable only of brutalizing and corrupting their inmates, we are committed to capital punishment in those cases where the felon cannot be safely left at large. An option of suicide, or alternatively leaving the choice between death and life imprisonment to the felon himself, would not escape the objections to prisons expressed above, since they are objections to the institution of imprisonment. In any case, such an option would not avoid the necessity of sometimes imprisoning or killing an unwilling person, since people do change their minds. (For more on consensual homicide and suicide, see sections 24, 26.)

Even assuming that imprisonment remains a standard penalty, however, the possibility of capital punishment in some cases must be left open. In the cases of murders committed by those in prison for life (including the murder of a fellow prisoner), by persons who have escaped from prison, or by members of terrorist groups, whose members are likely to commit more crimes in order to secure their release, and in the case of some politically motivated crimes where the criminal may be a rallying point for those continuing to wage war against the legitimate authorities, execution might be justified by a straightforward application of the principle of self-defense. Even here mercy is to be preferred where possible, and prudence should take into account the possible bad consequences of creating martyrs, but I know no way of showing that such considerations must prevail in all cases.

(A nasty case has to with one of the less emphasized ends of punishment—the prevention of private vengeance. If someone has committed a crime so hateful to his fellows that his continued existence is a danger to social peace, does this provide a sufficient justification for regarding him as a continuing threat, and so killing him? The ambiguities of the word "innocent" continue to cause trouble: it is plausible to say that he is presently not-harming, but his guilt of the crime in question makes it less plausible to say that he is an innocent. I leave the solution of this case to the reader.)

Caprice and mistake are of course inevitable in the administration of capital punishment, as of all human institutions (from which it does not follow that all decisions to inflict such punishment are even arguably capricious or mistaken). But such considerations cannot be considered decisive in all cases by someone who is prepared to defend war or abortion under any circumstances. Caprice and mistake occur in these areas as well, and the underlying justification for killing is in each case the same. Thus it is not possible for a nonpacifist to endorse without reservation the remark that Charles L. Black, Jr., places in the mouths of the rabbis: "Though the justice of God may indeed ordain that some should die, the justice of man is altogether and always insufficient for saying who these may be."[41] On the other hand, it is no part of my present thesis that there ever has been or will be a just execution, any more than it is strictly part of my thesis that there ever has been or will be a just war or a just abortion. I do think, however, that there is no general argument which shows that capital punishment, war, or abortion is in all cases wrong.

In the foregoing discussion, I have implicitly appealed to a mixed theory of punishment, according to which a just punishment must both (1) be deserved (to avoid the punishment of the innocent), and (2) serve some utilitarian purpose (in the cases above, the protection of the state and its citizens from further assault). Is not another defense of capital punishment—not as a preventative of further crimes by or with the complicity of the condemned man but as a deterrent of crimes by others—at least possible, supposing that we could establish that capital punishment was a better deterrent than life imprisonment?[42] The account given here of possible justifications for homicide is somewhat open-ended, the appeal in each case of justifying a kind of exception being to the prudent and moral man who is unwilling to see the force of the rule against homicide eroded, but interested also in saving lives which would be lost if the rule were held to with excessive rigidity. Thus, it is impossible utterly to exclude the possibility of a distinct mode of justification founded on deterrence. But since, because of the limitations on the kind of knowledge human beings are likely to have, the hope of saving lives by killing in this way would have to be very speculative, it seems best to reject the killing of an ordinary murderer, however brutal, so long as he has been rendered harmless.

Hard cases abound here. The punishment of Adolf Eichmann (assuming problems arising from the principle of legality can be overcome) was amply justified in terms of the symbolic, teaching function of punishment. But since Eichmann was quite harmless when he was apprehended, the death penalty was not justified. But it is hard to see how in practice the Israelis would have been able to keep Eichmann alive and safe in prison; moreover, a sentence less than death might have been interpreted as implying that his offense was not so grave after all. The only way, it seems, the dilemma could have been avoided was leaving Eichmann alone in Argentina, although one must allow the Israelis every excuse for having done otherwise. If Eichmann had been a living center of neo-Nazi sentiment, of course, the situation would have been very different indeed.

3. The position of the state outlined so far makes it clear that the state, if legitimate, has the power and right to repel those who would invade its territory, in other words, the power and right to wage at least defensive war. It also seems probable that a state is justified in acting outside its borders to restrain visible criminality against the common good of mankind—the slave trade or genocide, for instance.[43] Protection of other states against attack, if genuine, would fall into this class.

Notice that the legitimacy of the killing which takes place in war is limited by its underlying justification. Those who may be killed in this way are those—and only those—who are waging war against the state. (There are tragic cases here, for instance a soldier who enters battle privately intending not to fire; his case is like that of someone who brandishes an empty pistol.) Hence it is somewhat misleading (although of course not incorrect) to speak of noncombatant immunity, since what is at stake is not a special rule limiting otherwise justifiable homicide, but an instance of the underlying prohibition against homicide, for which no adequately grounded exception has been provided. It follows that the principle of noncombatant immunity is convention-independent, or at least as much so as the underlying moral rule against homicide, although convention may have a role to play in drawing the line between combatant and noncombatant in doubtful cases. That this is so is of some importance, first, because it is unclear whether a convention protecting noncombatants (e.g., against death from the air) is presently in effect; and, second, because too convention-bound an approach to the ethics of warfare may bar measures, such as the bombing of extermination camps, which we may well wish to advocate.[44]

I turn now to some particular problems in the ethics of war.

a. Not all private political violence (i.e., unlawful force used to gain some political end) is revolutionary. Some may be used not to depose the governing authorities or to deprive them of some portion of the territories they control, but to change their policies (or, in a nonrevolutionary way, their personnel). It is hard to see how such violence could be justified in the absence of a serious revolutionary possibility, however, since the result would be to weaken the government and thus disable it to carry out its revised policies. (If one's ends are merely negative, this line of thought would not apply.) One also must consider violence (e.g., in connection with a labor dispute) which involves the government only indirectly. Such violence is uncomfortably close to that of the private feud, however, so that, again in the absence of a serious revolutionary intention, it is very hard to defend except where it is strictly defensive. For these reasons, I shall assume, although the assumption is quite possibly oversimple, that the question of justifying private political violence is essentially that of justifying revolution.

The argument so far makes it clear that the state is sometimes justified in suppressing rebellion—to hold otherwise would be (except on anarchist or pacifist assumptions) absurdly romantic. But would it not be absurdly reactionary to hold that the rebels are never in the right? The wrong way to justify revolutionary war is to treat violence as including every sort of social evil, so that every sort of social evil can be fought with violence. [45] It is both possible and necessary to distinguish the killing or maiming of human beings from more subtle kinds of harm to them and even from allowing them to starve to death. The right way to justify revolutionary war is to see that the state, when it loses its right to rule, becomes, through its readiness to quell opposition by force, an agency threatening wrongful homicide.

To attempt to determine with precision when a state loses its right to rule would carry us too far from the question of the ethics of homicide. Suffice it to say that, because of the diversity of human situations, the legitimacy of a state cannot be identified either with its prescriptive right, with its acceptance by most members of the society it governs, or with its conformity to democratic or other norms of structural goodness, although these of course may contribute to it. (Indeed, it is very hard to see how revolutionary violence against a state which provides methods of peaceable change—one of the defining characteristics of democracy—could be justified.) We might on occasion at least be prepared to ascribe legitimacy to a government on the stark grounds adopted by a Muslim jurist: "The sovereign has a right to govern until another and stronger one shall oust him from power and rule in his

State. The latter will rule by the same title and will have to be acknowledged on the same grounds, for a government, however objectionable, is better than none at all; and between two evils we must choose the lesser."[46] Or we might accord allegiance to a very unsatisfactory government because the alternative is a government which is more unsatisfactory still.

It seems that a necessary condition for the illegitimacy of a government is the existence of a movement capable of better performing the functions of the state or of making state power unnecessary. It follows that the rhetoric of revolution is illegitimate when it is the recourse of political weakness, and that civil disturbances without serious political intentions—what are called "rebellions" by those who would be indignant if the government took the name seriously and tried those who participate in them (and those who give them aid and comfort) as traitors—are illegitimate as well. A group might claim to be revolutionary (and not merely in the sense that it urges radical change) although its present strength is nowhere near sufficient to confront the state, on the grounds that eventually there will be a revolutionary confrontation between the movement it hopes to form and the state apparatus. But I would question anyone's claim to have read the tea leaves of history in so specific a manner. Meanwhile talk of revolutionary violence has many disadvantages. For one thing, the state authorities are likely to take it seriously.

The argument so far may be sharpened by casting it in the form of what I shall call the Anarchist's Dilemma. Either the anarchist must be prepared to use sufficient force against the representatives of the state to dislodge it from power, or he must resign himself to live as an internal alien in a world shaped by state power. In the one case he is committed to establishing, at least temporarily, a rival state alongside the old state or its remnants. And it is hardly necessary to expand on how deceitful that word "temporarily" is. In the other case, he has removed himself from participation in the task which remains once the existence of the state is taken as inevitable, that of seeing to it that it is a force for good in the world rather than for evil, at least insofar as this task has an institutional aspect.

Suppose that the anarchist in a state of nature discovers that the bulk of his fellows, let us say perversely, are constructing a state—one which will assert its authority over him. He cannot resist their attempt by force (at least not effective force), and his refusal to participate in the building and running of the state will mean that he will lose the chance of making that state a better, or a less bad, state than it would otherwise be.

There remains the hope of persuading the majority not to take part in the building of the state, or to "walk away" from the state once it has been founded. This might have the result of producing a minority of statists who harass the anarchist majority, a majority which is forbidden by its principles to resist effectively. So let us say that *nearly everybody* is persuaded to be an anarchist, and that the remaining statists are so few in number that they are incapable of trying to form a state. But such moral unanimity or near-unanimity does not appear to be an object of reasonable hope. Certainly our disagreements about the ethics of killing, including so fundamental a matter as the extent of the class whose members have a primary right not to be killed, weigh heavily against such an expectation.

I now consider some cases which, while they do not go to the theoretical basis of state power, do raise possibilities that could make the wielding of state power by a conscientious person impossible.

b. Closely related to the problem of revolutionary violence is the problem of guerilla warfare. Guerilla warfare is a problem not for the justification of war but for its conduct. The blurring of the customary distinction between soldier and civilian which occurs in such warfare threatens to undermine the central principle of the morality of armed conflict—the distinction between combatant and noncombatant. In these circumstances it is easy to conclude (as Paul Ramsey seems to) that guerilla warfare is per se illegitimate, [47] and easy, also, to conclude (as Michael Walzer comes close to doing) that counter-guerilla warfare is doomed to be unjust. [48] Of course both claims could be true—we would then be very nearly committed to a form of (weak) pacifism, the doctrine that modern warfare is illegitimate as such. But to adopt one of these alternatives without the other is to be either absurdly romantic or absurdly reactionary.

c. Assassination—the killing of political figures, particularly government leaders, for political reasons—is in essence a form of warfare. Such warfare may be conducted in connection with revolutionary or other large-scale hostilities, or it may be conducted covertly under offi-

163

cial auspices, such as those of the CIA. (Some assassins of course do what they do in order to achieve fame, or at least notoriety, but such cases need not concern us here.) If there were someone whose actions threaten harm to others on a very large scale, and by killing him one could avert these harms (Hitler) or if killing the chief ruler would facilitate a just revolution (Trujillo?), then assassination would seem to be justified if war is justified. Moreover, assassination is in two respects morally better than ordinary warfare: the number of victims is fewer, and the victim is less likely to be, in any relevant sense, innocent (although this last point will be much weakened if the lives of any innocents at all are lost, even as a regretted side effect). Neither of these remarks applies, of course, to terrorism—for instance the placing of bombs in pubs and post offices.

But the situations in which killing one man will make a real historical difference are likely to be very few. One official can easily be replaced by another, quite possibly worse, one. And the use of assassination as a tactic in conjunction with ordinary warfare is constrained by the principle that a just war is (at least ordinarily) limited in its aims, and must therefore be waged in a manner which does not make peace impossible. There are also moral questions concerning covert warfare and assistance to rebellious forces within another state. Finally, it is very hard to see how one can justify the assassination of an official who can be removed by peaceable or legal means.

d. A final problem is that of nuclear deterrence. I do not see how the use of nuclear—or at any rate thermonuclear—weapons can ever in conscience be justified. Even if the other conditions of the principle of double effect are met, due proportion would be utterly lacking in the deaths of civilians that would ensue. Hence there seems no point to counseling a counterforce strategy if the likelihood of nuclear warfare would be even slightly increased thereby.

The interesting question is whether a strategy of deterrence is permissible, whether a state may threaten, in order to ward off serious evil, to perform what it could not in conscience do. (Would it have been wrong even to threaten the use of nuclear weapons to shorten World War II?) The problem would seem to be as much one of the ethics of deceit as of the ethics of homicide. I can only say that if the prospective enemy is minimally sane, an actual belief that his threatened actions

164

will lead to nuclear retaliation is not necessary to deterrence. A possibility that this result will ensue is sufficient. Also, the point of conveying an intention to kill is of course to prevent the conditions on which this intention is predicated from ever obtaining.

To say these things, of course, is not to express any enthusiasm for nuclear deterrence. Living with the prospect of nuclear warfare always present—both the prospect of being killed in this way and the prospect of others' being killed in one's name—can have profoundly damaging effects even if nothing worse happens. It is possible, however, that the alternatives are worse, at least if other states have nuclear weapons and are prepared to employ nuclear blackmail. Whether any present state's nuclear deterrent can be justifiably supported is a question I do not examine.

It is now possible to make a rough preliminary generalization of the conditions under which homicide is justified. First, homicide must be justified in consequentialist terms: that is to say, roughly, that at least as many lives will be saved as lost by a justified killing. Second, a justified killing must be fair or just: it must be possible to provide a satisfactory answer to the question, which we must imagine the victim putting even if he is unable to put it himself, "Why me?" Finally, justifiable killing must be consistent with the functioning of just institutions, or, more precisely, with actual institutions insofar as they are just (or as just as one can reasonably hope for, given the world as it is).

The first of these requirements has some important implications. There are cases where self-defense is an excuse, not a justification. One case is where it is futile, where even if I kill to defend myself, I will die. The application of this result to Warsaw Ghetto situations seems very harsh—although the Warsaw Ghetto uprising itself can be justified by linking it with the Allied war effort—but it also seems inescapable. (These remarks would not apply to situations where one continues a losing struggle in order to gain better terms.) There seems to be no place in a rational morality for "the laundry of honour" which "is only bleached with blood."[49]

Nor does it help to reformulate this line of thought in terms of "a basic human need to live and die with dignity."[50] A desire to uphold the dignity of men and women, and not merely a concern for their comfort, ought certainly to inform our ethical reflections, including those about homicide. But "dignity" provides just too vague a standard to be useful in the justification of homicide. It is easy enough to imagine any number of ingenious arguments on such a premise—for instance, that it is permissible to kill those who disturb one's sleep, where sleeplessness is reducing one to a condition unworthy of a human being. In the same class there belongs a claim for which it is not possible to help feeling considerable initial sympathy—that it is justifiable, morally speaking, to kill a blackmailer.

On the other hand, it is legitimate to kill fifty Nazis to save five Jews.[51] While so doing will lead, in the short run, to more deaths than letting the Nazis live and kill, one needs to take into account the fact that these Nazis are not only a threat to these Jews but to Jews and other "subhumans" everywhere. Even if the official list of subhumans will be exhausted by the killing of these Jews, it is a feature of the Nazis' frame of mind that where "subhumans" do not exist they must be invented.

This discussion completes what I have to say about homicide justified—or said to be justified—in terms of the good of those other than the decedent. I now turn to justifications (or supposed justifications) which rest on either the interests or the consent of the decedent himself.

VI /

JUSTIFICATIONS OF
HOMICIDE:

The Decedent Himself

"JUSTIFICATIONS" OF HOMICIDE that are grounded in the decedent's interest or consent are not persuasive, either separately or together, although my conclusion as to their joint force rests in part on institutional considerations which may not always be decisive. Suicide is an issue that probably cannot be adequately resolved on the kind of premises with which I am working in this book.

23. *Euthanasia (Chiefly Involuntary)*

THE WORDS "MERCY KILLING" and "euthanasia" have been defined in more than one way. Sometimes "euthanasia" has been defined as painless inducement of death—more bluntly painless killing. [1] But although this may be the only way of including some kinds of killings of animals within the scope of the definition, such a definition is not adequate when the subject of euthanasia is a human person. I am not performing an act of euthanasia if I kill my enemy painlessly because that is the best way to escape detection. Conversely, if someone is dying in great pain and the only way available to kill him hurts a little, it would be arbitrary to refuse the name of euthanasia to the proposed killing. Likewise, it will not do to define euthanasia as the inducement of as quick and painless a death as possible; [2] since if the death penalty is ever inflicted, it ought to be inflicted as painlessly as possible, but execution in accordance with this standard is surely not euthanasia. Again, mercy killing has been defined as killing with a certain kind of motive, as killing motivated by pity or compassion. If what we are interested in is mitigation or excuse, then this kind of definition is the most appropriate one. But since in the nature of the case a good motive cannot make an otherwise wrong act right, this definition is not useful in the present context. Also if euthanasia becomes institutionalized (and thus routinized), we might expect to see many acts of euthanasia performed with no motive but to do one's job and earn one's salary. The most appropriate definition for my purposes treats mercy killing as killing for which a certain kind of justification is offered, that is, homicide said to be in the best interests of the person killed. Thus the Nazis practiced euthanasia in just those cases in which they defended their killing people on the grounds that those people were better off dead.

One element sometimes found in definitions of euthanasia is a requirement that the subject be about to die shortly in any case. I do not include this element, for two reasons. First, as a matter of the logic of the case for euthanasia, if a person is better off dead, the longer he has to live, the longer he will be in a state in which it is in his interest not to be, and hence the stronger the case for killing him is. Second, as a matter of practice, euthanasia is sometimes advocated for infants who—if, let us say, their problem is that they have been deformed by Thalidomide—have a long life to live if they are not killed. Accordingly, I shall mean by "euthanasia" the killing of another person (said to be) justified as a kindness or benefit to him. I shall thus view the moral problem of euthanasia as that of the relationship between the duty to be kind—in particular to relieve the distress of others—and the duty not to take human life.

One must distinguish, of course, between voluntary and involuntary euthanasia, between killing with, and without, the consent of the sufferer. And among instances of involuntary euthanasia one must distinguish between merely nonvoluntary euthanasia, in which the expressed will of the decedent is lacking, and compulsory euthanasia, in which the objections of the decedent are overridden.

At this phase of the discussion, however, the ethics of euthanasia will be discussed without reference to the patient's consent, except insofar as this may be *evidence* of the act's beneficent character. Many advocates of euthanasia have been prepared to maintain, with Marvin Kohl, that "unwanted kindness is still kindness."[3] And there are possible subjects of euthanasia—infants and unborn children, for example—to whom euthanasia will have to be administered without consent if it is to be administered at all. And I shall not assume that death is in fact a benefit to the decedent, since one of the questions at issue will be whether it is indeed ever such a benefit. [4] To stipulate that it is, by using an expression such as "beneficent euthanasia," is only to bury the issue under a mass of Greek and Latin roots. [5]

My formulation of the euthanasia issue—as involving a possible conflict between the duty of kindness and the duty not to take life—is not universally accepted. Richard Brandt for instance urges:

> Killing a person is not something that is just prima facie wrong *in itself;* it is wrong roughly only if and because it is an *injury* of someone, or if and because it is the contrary to the *known preferences* of someone. It would seem that a principle about the prima facie wrongness of killing is *derivative* from principles about when we are prima facie obligated not to injure and when we are prima facie obligated to respect a person's own wishes, at least about what happens to his own body. [6]

(Voluntary) euthanasia is not for Brandt, while prima facie wrong, justified by the wretched state of the patient and his consent. It was never even prima facie wrong to begin with, since it is not an injury to the patient and is in accord with his desires.

I have the following objections to treating the obligation not to kill as merely derivative from the obligation not to injure. First, killing is not merely a special case of injury: it is a paradigm. We learn what it is to injure someone through such examples as killing, maiming, infliction of pain, and so on. Secondly, to justify mercy killing on the grounds that it is not even an injury is to distort the situation in a very important way. To be sure, it is not injuring someone to relieve his pain. But mercy killing is not just relief of pain, it is relief of pain (if that indeed is the proper expression) achieved through the *destruction of the sufferer.* As such, it has an ambiguity with ethical implications that will require careful discussion. Finally, better reasons have to be given for not including so prevalent a feature of moral codes as "Do not kill" among our prima facie duties than its omission from a list compiled by Sir David Ross and a desire to make easy the justification of euthanasia.

In this section I am going to defend the widely shared belief that involuntary euthanasia (at least if institutionalized) is little better than ordinary murder, and to argue that the best explanation (or part of the best explanation) for this belief is that death cannot be rationally chosen, at least not on behalf of another. I shall argue, among other things, that when the case for voluntary euthanasia is properly parsed, and limited in the ways necessary to prevent slippage into the other kind, we are left with an asserted right to dispose of oneself that has little bearing on the medical problems to which proposals for euthanasia are attempting to respond.

Before proceeding further, I should like to distinguish direct euthanasia from two related practices, both of which rely for their justification on the principle of double effect. One is the cessation of extraordinary[7] means,[8] justified by a desire to spare the sick person and his family profitless expense and agony, and by a desire that he should live out whatever remains of his life free from medical intrusions. What counts as an extraordinary means is a matter of prudential judgment, which needs to take into account not only the equities of the particular case but also the effect on respect for human life generally of deeming a particular remedy to be extraordinary. If an infant is suffering from an incurable condition, for example, it is a matter for such judgment what kinds of life-prolonging treatment are extraordinary, so long as some aspect of his condition is not taken as a means of securing the infant's death by inaction. I should add that, where a physician decides to cease life-saving efforts, he should not simply leave his patient to die, but should do everything possible to render his condition tolerable while he is dying.[9]

A second practice to be distinguished from mercy killing is the giving of drugs to relieve pain, drugs which may have as a side effect the shortening of the sick person's life. If the distinction between this practice and direct euthanasia is problematic, the reason does not lie in the life-shortening side effects of (say) morphine. No one would regard someone as a suicide who, to control a disease which made him incapable of a normal life, took a drug which enabled him to live normally although for a shorter period. A problem might lie in the fact that such pain relievers also may render the patient unconscious, where this unconsciousness is expected to last until death. Although there is no moral problem in rendering someone unconscious for a time in order to spare him pain (e.g., during an operation), to deliberately render someone unconscious where such unconsciousness is expected to be permanent looks very much like direct killing. It is not direct killing on the criteria set forth in Chapter IV, however, since it is not fantastic to suppose that a patient will sleep through his current bout of pain. And one can easily distinguish the frame of mind—and probable difference in behavior when confronted with a patient not in extreme agony—of a physician who in extremity gives drugs to induce unconsciousness which shorten life as a side effect, from that of someone like Glanville Williams, who expresses frank unease about the possible development of pain relievers (or ways of administering them) which do not have such lethal effects. [10] I shall therefore assume that such giving of drugs is not direct euthanasia.

It is useful to refer to the first of these practices (abstention from treatment) as *passive* euthanasia, and the second as *indirect* euthanasia. Someone sensitized to the word "euthanasia" might object to this terminology, but it is both convenient and in accord with the underlying idea of a good death, which all agree is to be provided the dying by all legitimate means. I should emphasize that my terminology is not meant to imply that there are not important moral differences between passive or indirect euthanasia and direct euthanasia—quite the contrary. And where "euthanasia" appears below without an adjective, the direct kind is meant.

I should add that the distinction of deep moral importance is that between direct killing on the one hand and indirect killing and letting die on the other, rather than that between killing and letting die as such. For letting die is at root no different from killing where it is motivated by a desire that the subject should die, or by desire for a goal to which his death is a necessary means, say, our no longer having to care for him. Still, the withholding of treatment—say, of antibiotics for the treatment of pneumonia where the patient also has cancer—might still be other than directly lethal in its intent, even though it is often supported by the adage that pneumonia is the "old man's friend." Medical treatment always involves possibly offensive touching, particularly if the patient has expressed a wish not to undergo it. The patient might as well be spared such touching if death looms in any case. Also, the distinction between acting and refraining is visible and palpable in a way the distinction between acting with direct intention and without such intention is not. This feature of the distinction permits us to read the relevant intentions more favorably to the agent than when he acts in a way that results in someone's death.

The importance of these distinctions for the case against direct euthanasia is that it helps block the claim that the only alternative to such killing is that patients should suffer prolonged and unalleviated pain. But it is only helpful if the difference between direct euthanasia on the one hand and indirect or passive euthanasia on the other is morally speaking a real one. And the reality of the distinction is something philosophers of consequentialist bent take great pains to deny, frequently suggesting that those who employ such distinctions are less than fully candid about what they are advocating or doing.

But from a merely consequentialist point of view there is of course no transcendent value in ethical candor, but rather an almost unlimited possibility for separation between the ethics of action and the ethics of praise and blame, between esoteric and exoteric doctrine if you prefer. Thus someone who is impressed by the institutional considerations I consider in this chapter (especially section 25 [1]), while not prepared to abandon a directly consequentialist way of choosing individual actions, might well employ these (nonconsequentialist) distinctions in his ethics of praise and blame. Such a person might console himself with the thought that the uses of hypocrisy, like those of adversity, are sometimes sweet. Some movement to such a position may be found in a remark of Glanville Williams, in which he endorses the action/omission distinction as "a useful way of freeing us from some of the consequences of overly rigid moral attitudes."[11]

Postponing fully voluntary euthanasia for the time being, I turn to the consideration of those cases where the subject's supposed interest in dying is invoked to justify killing. Let us consider first the case where he affirmatively objects. If death is indeed in someone's best interests, as defenders of euthanasia maintain, and if he is so perverse as to wish to continue a wretched life, why should we not intervene and do for him what we know is for his good?

By way of reply, an analogy might be drawn from the ethics of human experimentation. Such experimentation, it is commonly held, requires the informed consent of the experimental subject. This view

172

implies that no such experiments can be performed on subjects—the senile, infants, the unborn—incapable of consenting. An important gloss on this principle was placed by the *Jewish Chronic Disease Hospital Case* (1963–1965).[12] There harmless (let us suppose) live cancer cells were injected into patients who gave their consent without being informed of the nature of the cells injected. The authorities concluded that the patients' rights were violated by the failure to inform them, even of something which they would irrationally regard as a source of danger. Attorney-General Lefkowitz put it: "These patients . . . had a right to know what was being planned—not just the bald statement that an injection was to be given, but also the contents of the syringe: and if this knowledge was to cause fear and anxiety or make them frightened, they had a right to be fearful and frightened and thus say NO to the experiment."[13] Hence also—even assuming Epicurus was right and the fear of death is irrational—a person has a right to be afraid of death and to refuse to undertake an experiment as to its nature.

But there is an important distinction between human experimentation and euthanasia. Human experimentation is designed to gain medical knowledge, for the satisfaction of the experimenters' curiosity and the welfare of other patients. Euthanasia claims to be for the benefit of the patient himself. Can we not legitimately force upon, or covertly administer to, a child a treatment we know is for his benefit and of which he is irrationally afraid? And guardians are appointed to give consent to medical treatment on behalf of the incompetent, and whom we consider incompetent is in part a function of what we consider the rationality or the irrationality of their choices. The appointment of such guardians raises knotty problems in its own right, but if there is any case in which it is legitimate to do so, the problem of involuntary euthanasia will remain urgent.

The difficulty lies in the kind of judgment we are being asked to make here—that a given human being would be better off dead. Although there might be no difficulty in deciding that it would be better for *us* if the patient were dead, we have no better grasp of what death would mean for him than he does. To be sure, we may have a better grasp of the prognosis of his disease, but since a rational decision between two alternatives requires a grasp of both of them, we should not attempt to second-guess a sick person in this way.

These remarks suffice to dispose of the case where the sick person affirmatively objects to being killed, but more needs to be said about the case where he expresses (or can express) no opinion on the matter. Marvin Kohl allows for euthanasia under these circumstances in his defense of "noninvoluntary euthanasia." He explains his use of the term: "An act is to be considered noninvoluntary if it is either the result of the fully informed consent of the intended recipient or, when the recipient is not mentally or physically free to choose (as in the case of a permanent coma), the proper legal guardian (or when this is inappropriate society or its representative) acting on the individual's behalf gives consent."[14] On such premises, euthanasia might be administered to an unconscious person, to spare him the pain involved in learning that he has an incurable disease,[15] to an insane or senile person, or to an infant or unborn child. Sometimes, if one waits, the patient will gain, or regain, the use of reason; sometimes not. I shall here discuss chiefly the case where the patient will or may have the use of reason sometime in the future if not killed (having little to add to what I say in section 15 of the status of those who will in no case do so).

One issue raised by Kohl's definition is the validity of "proxy consent," say on behalf of an infant by its parents. Such consent might be acceptable (I am by no means sure of it) where what is at stake is experimentation entailing negligible risk, indignity, or suffering. But I think such proxy consent does nothing to distinguish the killing of infants from ordinary involuntary euthanasia. For the authority of parents over infants and children is essentially provisional, and rests in part on the hope that the children will come to realize that what was done to and for them was indeed in their best interests. Hence parental authority does not include the right to consent, on behalf of the infant, to his being killed and kept from having any opinions at all about his treatment.

The fundamental point, in any case, is this. If the sick person will in time gain or regain the use of reason, there is no excuse not to wait and learn his wishes. Such waiting will entail avoidable suffering on his part, but most of us believe that such considerations are overridden by his right to go on living at least long enough to make up his own mind. The equivalent of a wish to do so may be drawn from the fact that, as an organism, he continues to maintain himself in being. (If he fails to do

174

so, his failure need not be made up for by extraordinary means.) It seems that, even apart from the difficulty of unbiased representation of the sick person's own interests, we can have no sufficiently persuasive grounds to supplant this implicit judgment with one of our own to the effect that the patient would be better off dead.

At this point I should like to consider an argument advanced by T. Goodrich: "An individual does not exist through the process of dying in the same way as he exists through other processes. Dying is just ceasing to exist, and one cannot exist through the process of ceasing to exist. So how can we say that it is for the good of the individual to die?"[16] Notice that Goodrich is not arguing that killing someone cannot decrease the total (or average per capita) amount of pain in the universe. The forms of utilitarianism for which these are the crucial questions have already been sufficiently considered (sections 5 [1], 20). He is questioning whether killing someone can possibly be construed as a benefit to *that person*. Notice also that the problem is not fundamentally one of reference. There is no difficulty in talking about the dead, or in ascribing properties to them. ("Napoleon is a very famous man.") The difficulty lies in regarding the kind of properties a dead person can have, including the property of being dead, as constituting part of his *well-being*.

Kohl's reply to Goodrich is clearly not adequate: "First, the word 'extermination' or its cognates may be synonymous with 'ceasing to exist', but dying is not. Second, there is a difference between stages in a process and the terminal stage of that process (that is, it is one thing to be dying and another to be dead). Finally, just as there is nothing logically odd about saying that we can help a dying patient by making him more comfortable, there is nothing odd about saying that we can help a person by hastening the process of dying."[17] Kohl's first reply (or step) is false—except on premises which Kohl manifests no desire to invoke. (Perhaps Kohl is thinking of Jones's corpse as "Jones.") To die *is* to cease to exist, although one usually leaves behind what are significantly called "remains." Second, there is indeed a difference between a process (of dying or cessation of existence) and its result (being dead, having ceased to exist). But it is hard to see how this consideration supports Kohl or refutes Goodrich. Perhaps what Kohl means is that, since the dying person exists at the time euthanasia is administered, he can be benefited *then*. But to talk about benefiting someone is normally to speak of his condition both before and after the benefit is conferred, so that Goodrich's argument still holds good. Finally, in his third reply (or step) Kohl seems to be resolutely refusing to see the problem, since that there is any parity between killing someone ("hastening his dying process") and making him comfortable is precisely what Goodrich intends to deny. Perhaps what Kohl means is that, just as one can help someone by reducing the amount of pain he feels at any one time, one can also help him by reducing the time during which he has to suffer it. But this would be to beg the question as well, since, if Goodrich is right, there is no parity between shortening the stretch of a person's life during which he experiences pain in favor of a painless period of existence and shortening such a stretch by replacing it with an endless "stretch" of nonexistence (at least if we avoid identifying a person with his consciousness).

Still, human beings do sometimes wish that they were dead, desire death (even pray for it), and so on, in a way which suggests strongly that they consider death to be a condition superior to their present one. And they also use—and seem to understand—such expressions as "better off dead" and "a fate worse than death." And they go further: one sometimes hears such remarks as that it would have been better for a certain person if he had never been born or conceived, and the conception of offspring under some conditions is sometimes thought of as an injury to *them*. Conversely, people are sometimes "glad to be alive" in a way which suggests a comparison with the alternative. Such expressions may represent a straining at the limits of language, or a covert appeal to the notions of pre-existence and survival. But they do manage to cast at least some doubt on the obvious-seeming proposition that to talk about someone's welfare is always to talk about actual or possible state of *him*. The upshot seems to be not that killing can never be intelligibly said to be a form of kindness, nor that it might under appropriate conditions be as unambiguous an act of kindness as helping someone across the street, but that the status of a benevolently intended act of killing is of necessity conceptually ambiguous. This particular ambiguity could be relieved by talking, in a hard-line consequentialist way, not of benefit to the patient, but of the balance of good over evil in the universe.

This line of reasoning brings us to three questions: whether human life has value as such, which may be set against its sufferings; the

176

relevance of the customary treatment of animals; and the relevance of the difficult but important concept of human dignity.

On the first point, Kohl argues that those of us who defend neither extreme vitalism, according to which every life must be preserved as long as possible by whatever means, nor direct and active euthanasia, are guilty of an inconsistency. Such people, he thinks, agree with him that "almost all men hold life to be a good (perhaps an almost intrinsic good), but few would perceive or hold it either a good in itself or the highest good"[18] when passive euthanasia is discussed, but insist that life has intrinsic or absolute value when active euthanasia is in question.

Some confusions need to be cleared up before we proceed further. To hold that something is an intrinsic good (good in itself) is to commit oneself neither to the proposition that it ought never be done without nor to the proposition that it is always good whatever the circumstances. To hold that pleasure is an intrinsic good is to hold neither that we must enjoy all the pleasure of which we are capable nor that all such pleasures—for instance, those of sadists—have value. So Kohl could admit that life in general has intrinsic value, while denying that some particular life does, or affirming that the value of some particular life is overridden by the suffering its persistence entails. (I do not pretend to know what Kohl means by an almost intrinsic good.)

This said, I do wish to defend the view, which seems to be implicit in most of our views about homicide, that a human life is an important intrinsic good. One can explain *why* human life is such a good by appealing to its rich potentialities, but its relation to those potentialities is not that of means to end. Even in Kohl's case ("the life of child like David Patrick Houle—a child who was born with, among other things, improperly formed vertebrae, a malformed left side and hand, no left eye or ear, and, who, if he had survived, would have been partly deaf, palsied, blind, and mentally retarded"),[19] it still can be affirmed that such a child's life is an intrinsic good. People as bad off as he (or almost so) do sometimes want to go on living, and this desire of theirs is a natural desire, one bound up with their very structure as human animals, and one it is arbitrary to declare irrational.

The question of *how important* an intrinsic good it is will be complicated by the child's mental retardation, which, if severe enough, might tempt us to regard the child as mere beast, to be treated as kindly as human purposes permit but having no serious right to live (cf. section 15). Certainly inhibitions about killing a child so gravely retarded as never to gain the use of speech (even deaf-mute sign language) must rest on the institutional considerations and considerations of species solidarity which support the species principle, and these are not easily cashable in terms of intrinsic value. But, equally, we need have few qualms about behaving toward such a child as we would toward a person, since his sufferings will in any case be relatively slight, and since no stigma attaches to the use of a mere animal to attain an important human end, in this case the preservation of institutions designed to uphold human dignity, or the possibility of such institutions. Nor would morally sensitive parents (given appropriate assistance by the rest of us or perhaps even without it) suffer more from the lingering condition of their child than from taking part in a decision to kill him directly; indeed they might well suffer less.

In the absence of very severe mental retardation, one can affirm with some confidence, even apart from institutional considerations and considerations of solidarity, that such a life is not only an intrinsic good but one of very great moral importance. From none of this does it follow that every possible effort should be made to prolong such a child's life, nor even (directly) that his life should not be terminated. For all that has been said so far, there might be other considerations that outweigh the important value his life is. But it turns out that one must be (at least) extremely careful about acting on any such premises.

The opponent of euthanasia can maintain that, since the life of a human being is a basic good incommensurable with other such goods, it either ought never be directly attacked, or else that this should be done only when it proves to be necessary to the saving of other, equally valuable, human lives. Short of this, he can maintain that those who would engage in such attacks bear a very heavy burden of justification, and that advocates of mercy killing in such cases have not carried their burden with success.

On the other hand, the benefits in terms of length and richness of life may not be such as to warrant the expense, effort, and agony involved in trying to prolong such a child's life, so that he might be allowed to die peacefully without the invocation of medical heroics. The added suffering, if any, entailed by proceeding in this way rather

178

than by direct killing would not be pointless, since it would flow from and contribute to a recognition of the worth of human beings.

Second, euthanasia of animals is of course routine, but it ought not to be assumed that the animal's interest is what is at stake. Even when we are not concerned, say, to limit the number of cats by killing unwanted kittens, we might be killing incurably diseased, or defective, animals to spare ourselves what Hobbes would call the "pains of compassion." Failure to feel these pains might indicate a lack of sensitivity, of course, so that we still have on this hypothesis, some basis for thinking less of those who let animals suffer. But would we really think less—or be warranted in thinking less—of someone who, coming upon a cat torn by dogs,[20] refrained from killing it, not because he was indifferent to an animal's suffering, but because he felt that one must respect, where the interests of human beings permit, an animal's right (so to speak) to die in its own way? Such an attitude might open the charge that it treats animals as if they were human, but surely less so than the attitude that produces pet cemeteries. In any case, the chief lesson is that appeals to actions in the supposed interests of animals must be treated with extreme caution. Remember that the same animal shelters which provide for the painless killing of nonhumans sometimes also provide for their mutilation.

Third, we must consider the difficult concept of human dignity. One use of this concept is in the expression "death with dignity," a use that raises a number of knotty problems. Sometimes the expression means simply death without pain and suffering, in which case the concept raises no new issues. On the other hand, the concept is sometimes invoked to justify the killing of those who are in no pain, indeed of those who also do not or cannot give their consent. The underlying idea seems to be that the continued existence of such a creature is an indignity to the human race or to the individual the mercy killer wishes to kill.

But this view is unacceptable. The morally relevant sense of "human dignity" is not (1) a dignity inherent in all human beings or persons, no matter what may befall them, nor (2) (simply) control over the major aspects of one's life (or a good of the same level of ethical generality), lack of which might be thought a justification for killing. It is rather (3) acting and being treated as the concept of man expressed in

(1) requires. That is to say, the morally relevant sense of human dignity is the principle that we should act in accordance with the dignity which attaches to ourselves and other human beings but not to other animals. The implication of this idea for the present issue seems to be that death with dignity does not mean only—or even primarily—freedom from pain, suffering, or bowel incontinence. A martyr, even a mistaken one, may die with dignity, however gruesome his death. Death with dignity means dying in a way appropriate to a human being and not, say, dying like a dog. It follows that involuntary euthanasia (including "noninvoluntary euthanasia" à la Kohl), is not permissible from the standpoint of an ethics of human dignity. It is dogs, after all, who are put to sleep without their consent.

It is certainly intelligible that the principle of human dignity might require human beings to undergo sufferings which animals are spared. Certainly an aristocratic ethic (and it is the best model we have for man's relationship with the beasts, at least as it is conventionally understood) might require a lord to suffer what a peasant would be permitted to escape. And so the additional suffering implied by the rejection of involuntary euthanasia (whether or not voluntary euthanasia is allowed) is not a decisive objection to abstaining from the practice. But, appealing as such lines of thought may be in our Nietzschean moments, they do not represent the ultimate thrust of my argument, which is not that human beings should be treated less compassionately than other animals, but that they should be treated with a compassion more adequate to their complex reality.

But perhaps human dignity requires that a human being be free to dispose of his own life as he wishes, so that voluntary euthanasia, or rather all forms of consensual killing, are permissible or obligatory. To this contention I now turn.

24. Consensual Homicide

A STRAIN of liberal argument often heard in other contexts would seem to imply that if death is privately administered to a consenting adult, the killer should be immune from sanction whatever the reasons motivating the consent. And one defense of voluntary euthanasia—that advanced by Baruch Brody—explicitly accepts this implication.²¹ Briefly, Brody's argument goes like this: if the reason killing is wrong is that it is a violation of the victim's right to life, and if the only concern of the law and morality in this area is the protection of human rights, then law and morality have no reason to intervene to prevent killing of any sort when the decedent gives his consent, or at least his explicit consent at the time of the killing. For if *A* takes something to which *B* has a right, *B* is not wronged if he consents to its being taken. Thus we have an argument not only for voluntary euthanasia but also for human sacrifice with consenting victims. There have been also cases where one might consent to an attempt on one's life, while intending to resist the attempt—in a duel, for instance. Fraternity initiations and other consensual activities dangerous to life— though not, it seems, mountain-climbing—also seem to belong here.

As the examples above show, many of us would regard the consent of the decedent as not by itself sufficient justification for homicide. One way of explaining and supporting this belief is to argue that when a serious and irrevocable decision such as that to die is in question, adequate deliberation and the sheltering of the prospective decedent from pressure exerted by those who may want to rid themselves of him for selfish reasons needs to be provided for. In rights language, we may be concerned to make sure that the right to live is knowingly and intelligently waived. This line of thought would seem to warrant the state's reserving to itself the right to kill with the decedent's consent (as it generally reserves to itself the right to use deadly force), and the establishment of procedures guarantees that the person requesting death has given the matter adequate consideration, although not a scrutiny of his grounds.

But such a proposal quite frankly seems to me ghoulish. Qualms about suicide apart, there are two reasons for this reaction. (1) To require someone who is likely to be in considerable distress to go through a procedure—imagine forms, to be filled out in quintuplicate—determining whether he should live or die shows no very high degree of human sensitivity. (2) It is far from clear what *would* constitute adequate deliberation for consent to homicide. If someone is contemplating a sex-change operation, he can interview those who have gone through the experience and determine, on the basis of these interviews, whether that is what he wants. No such interviews are possible in the case of the dead. And since death is (as we are assuming) the annihilation of the personality, it cannot correspond to anything previously experienced by the person himself. Deliberation about whether one really wants to be killed is limited to waiting and seeing whether one's mood of depression or religious zeal passes, and as such is of little utility. If the mood does pass, it does not show that one did not really want to die, and that one's change of mind is anything but a loss of nerve. I conclude that there is no way of ascertaining the validity of consent which provides an adequate basis for treating consent as a justification of homicide.

Another argument to the same conclusion works from the example of voluntary slavery. We should think it wrong—we might even consider it a violation of a person's right to freedom—to enslave him, even if he consents to being a slave. If so, killing someone may also be a violation of his rights, even if he consents to being killed. To this argument Brody makes two replies:

> That it is wrong for A to enslave B does not entail that A has wrongfully deprived B of that freedom to which he has a right. It may be wrong for other, independent reasons, most notably because it may be wrong for us to treat another person as a thing to be used. Moreover, even if one insist that A has wrongfully deprived B of his freedom, the case is not like the case of euthanasia, because, unlike the case of euthanasia, the person deprived of the right goes on existing without that right. [22]

The first of these replies undercuts Brody's assumptions. If it is wrong, consent or no consent, to treat another as a thing to be used, it seems plausible that it is also wrong, consent or no consent, to reduce another to the status of a thing or to annihilate him in favor of one. So that either the right to life is not generally waivable or morality, and perhaps even the law, has a legitimate interest in restraining killing as such, independent of protecting the victim's right to live. The second reply is very perplexing, since, while it does serve to distinguish killing from deprivation of freedom, it serves equally well to distinguish killing from the model with which Brody seems to be working—deprivation of property. That killing deprives the decedent not of something he has, but of his very existence, means that it must be treated separately from all other kinds of dealings between people. Hence there are no good grounds for treating the right to live as a right like any other, or for defending consensual killing on this basis.

One might still want to hold that it is permissible to do *anything* to someone so long as his consent is obtained and the rights of third parties are not violated. On this view duels, human sacrifice with consenting victims, and voluntary enslavement (including, say, psychological conditioning, assisted perhaps by drugs or surgery, designed to prevent the slave from ever coming to desire freedom) would, contrary to most of our intuitions, be permissible. The core issue may well go as deep as our concept of the self, for instance, whether injuries to human persons can always adequately be conceptualized in terms of "boundary crossings."[23] If this is not the case, if for instance it is possible to injure someone by inducing him to injure himself or by denying him aid in his difficulties, then the strong libertarian claim will not be so plausible.

While commending the libertarian position to those who can believe it, I should remark that it at least avoids the most frightening aspects of defenses of euthanasia. For what is most disturbing about proposals to establish euthanasia as an institution is that it should somehow be officially determined that a given person would be better off dead, and the libertarian manages to avoid such a determination.

But perhaps the language of rights and their waiver does not reach the central intuition of those who defend consensual killing. If death is in any case inevitable—such people would argue—it is more consistent with human dignity that its time and manner be freely chosen, than that we should, like animals, await its coming passively. In pictorial terms, it is said that human dignity requires that we not insist that Death capture us, but rather go forth willingly to meet him.

One has to agree that human dignity includes the making of one's own choices concerning the major aspects of one's life, including the way one is going to die. A patient should for example decide, so far as possible, what ways of prolonging his life are ordinary and necessary and which can be dispensed with as, in his circumstances, extraordinary. (It is not so clear that a legal system accomplishes anything by way of furthering human dignity by offering those condemned to death a choice of methods of execution.) But to speak of choice in this kind of context does not entail that someone will choose any particular result— to be killed, for example, rather than to await his end patiently. Nor does it entail that, should he do so, we are obliged or even permitted to give effect to his choice. There are journeys, perhaps, that have to be taken alone.

I have so far considered consent to homicide unsupported by any strengthening moral consideration. But whatever grounds may be adduced to justify homicide, may be adduced also to strengthen consent to being killed. One might ask for instance whether John Harris's "survival lottery" (see section 21) could be made acceptable by limiting participation as donor or recipient to volunteers. Or a father might decide to give up his heart to save his son's life (his son having a longer life expectancy than he).[24] Or else someone might, out of pure altruism, decide to sacrifice all of his transplantable organs in order to save the lives of a large number of others. In all such cases physicians and nurses would have to decide whether to cooperate. Finally, a suicidally inclined or repentant murderer might well consent to being executed. I shall limit myself, however, to the case where the patient's consent is strengthened by the judgment of the physician (or whoever else is asked to end the patient's life) that the patient would indeed be better off dead.

25. Voluntary Euthanasia

I HAVE ARGUED in the last two sections that neither a judgment that the decedent is better off dead nor the decedent's consent, taken alone, suffices to warrant homicide. The question now is whether the two elements taken together will suffice where either one alone does not. My subject, that is to say, will be voluntary euthanasia.

1. One argument against voluntary euthanasia is that, once law and conventional morality, particularly that of the medical profession, admit the practice, it will be difficult or impossible to prevent the extension of its principle to involuntary euthanasia as well. This argument has been forcefully presented and documented by Yale Kamisar.[25] Kamisar does not seem, however, to accept the full case. He seems to be maintaining that the legislature which fails to legalize euthanasia, the physician who performs it, and the jury which acquits the physician contrary to law, may all be acting rightly. A legislator might (if Kamisar is correct) in good conscience vote against euthanasia in the morning

and put his grandfather to sleep in the evening. At first at least, it seems better to follow out the argument to the end and accept the moral rule against homicide without exceptions for euthanasia as a norm of action.

Defenders of euthanasia have attacked the slippery-slope argument with some heat. Marvin Kohl writes of "pernicious nonsense,"[26] Anthony Flew of "obscurantist flim-flam."[27] And Glanville Williams seems to think that he can answer those who are disposed sympathetically to entertain proposals for the painless and voluntary killing of those suffering from incurable cancer, but are convinced that geronticide or involuntary euthanasia for the insane would be seriously wrong, by endorsing C. M. Cornford's remark, "The wedge argument means this: that you should not act justly today, for fear that you may be asked to act still more justly tomorrow."[28] But the slippery-slope argument, being an appeal to the probable consequences of accepting a proposed exception to our moral rules, would seem to demand a hearing from any prudent moral agent.

The slippery-slope argument has often been hysterically overstated, so that it is important to distinguish its legitimate from its illegitimate applications. At this point we have the benefit of a careful discussion by Sissela Bok.[29] Bok enunciates three tests for such arguments: (1) the existence of a clear line between permissible and impermissible conduct, already drawn by law and tradition; (2) a danger that the contemplated change would produce very undesirable results, or alternatively the existence of a very important value which is protected by the presently existing line; (3) the existence of forces sufficient to cause the process initiated by the change of lines to continue, once it has been set in motion, and to make reversal of the trend difficult or impossible.

As far as test 1 is concerned, the presently existing line is the immunity of innocent human beings from direct lethal attack. It seems clear enough. Test 2 is an important qualification on the use of slippery-slope arguments. The quickest way of evading such arguments is to accept the threatened result. Opponents of racism are probably committed to not having very strong objections to marriages between their female relatives and members of other races, and the best reply to talk about creeping socialism is that one has no particular objections to socialism. Or the end of the slope may be considered bad, but not very bad. Someone might concede that old people ought not to be killed as a way of dealing with demographic problems, but consider their killing only a minor evil.

Light on this aspect of the slippery-slope issue may be had from the use of the argument in civil liberties contexts. Judicial protection is accorded even trivial and offensive modes of discourse in order to secure the safety of serious contributions to the public dialogue.[30] And George Orwell argues that if we "make a habit of imprisoning Fascists without trial, . . . perhaps the process won't stop at Fascists."[31] If free speech and personal liberty are precious enough to call the argument into play, the same must also be said of the right to live. One effective way of silencing a political opponent is to kill him.

The central question for the slippery-slope argument from voluntary to involuntary euthanasia is test 3: in trying to determine whether the slope in question is in fact slippery, it is worthwhile examining a dispute which, while the issues at stake are rather different, has nonetheless attracted on both sides a constellation of sentiments similar to those attracted by the question of euthanasia. The case of abortion provides us with an excellent illustration of the workings of the slippery slope—not only from abortion on somewhat-wider-than-traditional indications to abortion on demand, but also, more disturbingly to someone of my predispositions, from contraception to abortion, for instance, from *Griswold* v. *Connecticut* to *Roe* v. *Wade*. In view of this experience, it seems reasonable to fear the extension of euthanasia from a narrow class of patients to an ever-widening range of socially unwanted persons.

A point at which abortion and euthanasia converge is the killing of—perhaps only slightly defective—newborn babies, say where pre-natal diagnosis has failed to disclose the defects in question. Given present attitudes toward abortion, and supposing voluntary euthanasia to be the established practice, one has difficulty seeing how the force of Dr. Foster Kennedy's remark could in practice be evaded: "If the law sought to restrict euthanasia to those who could speak out for it, and thus overlooked these creatures who cannot speak, then, I say as Dickens did, 'The law's an ass.'"[32] But what is being advocated here is of course a form of involuntary euthanasia, and a crucial ethical divide has therefore been crossed.

There is also the question of reversibility. It remains to be seen whether pro-abortion trends will prove reversible, but there are in any case reasons to believe that euthanasia, once established, would be very difficult to dislodge from the structure of our institutions. If someone is wrongfully sterilized, say, [33] he remains in existence to complain of his treatment, sue for damages, and so on. If someone is wrongly killed, he is effectively excluded from the realm of moral discourse. To be sure, his relatives might still complain, but the kind of abuse one is most worried about in connection with euthanasia might well have the connivance of the victim's relatives. There is no need to speak, in making this argument, of a conspiracy to subvert our institutions or anything of the sort. All we need postulate is a temptation, experienced even by some of the best of us when dealing with some intractable human problem, to resolve it by removing from our environment the people who pose it. What is seductive is not so much killing as such, as the notion that we can kill in his own interests someone whose existence we find burdensome, thus avoiding the question of justice, which would arise if we killed him to gratify our desire to be free of him.

If it is asked why the line between voluntary and involuntary mercy killing is harder to hold than the line between combatants and noncombatants in the ethics of warfare, the answer is that the latter line has been notoriously difficult to hold, and that this is so represents a powerful argument for pacifism as the only effective way of avoiding the killing of the innocent. If, despite this argument, we find that we are unable to get along without warfare, our inability to do so gives us no reason for getting ourselves into a position where we will be unable to get along without euthanasia.

Slippery slopes of various sorts are of course a common debating maneuver, as common as is the converse strategy of proceeding step by step against opposition to a desired goal. That the fears of conservatives and the hopes of radical reformers have been frequently, though by no means always, fulfilled is clear, although we now are more likely to sympathize with the radical reformers of the past than with the conservatives. But it does not follow that the moral opinions of those who exist later in time are necessarily better than those who exist earlier, or that we should cease to fear a given social result just because our descendants (the inhabitants of *Brave New World* or *1984*, say) might welcome it or find it at least acceptable. The same, after all, might well be true if we molded a future more in accord with our hopes.

One still might have qualms about the slippery-slope argument, given the often dubious uses to which it has been put. I suggest, therefore, the following limitation on its legitimate employment. A slippery-slope argument can be used to defend a threatened moral principle only when the principle itself has some plausibility in its own right. (If its denial did not also have some plausibility, the slippery-slope argument would not have to be employed in the first place.) Now *any* kind of killing of human beings is at least subject to moral questions: indeed many persons express a repugnance to taking human life without attending to the exceptions they have been forced to concede in practice. And the position on which many people fall back, "do not kill the innocent except in cases of extreme necessity" (or "it is very strongly prima facie wrong to kill the innocent") also has, I think, a plausibility which can be set against any other proposed exceptions to the rule against killing. It is therefore quite admissible, when the principle of voluntary euthanasia is under consideration, to employ a slippery-slope argument to defend a conservative position.

2. Flew, in his defense of euthanasia, proposes to treat as irrelevant to the principle of euthanasia "particular and practical questions" concerning its administration.[34] This, I think, is unfortunate. If philosophers have something to say to the law, so also has the law something to say to philosophers. Attention to the working, or the possible working, of any institution or principle may well give us insight into weaknesses which remain concealed so long as it is posed in sufficiently abstract terms. In the case at hand, there is within the principle a three-way internal tension: between the desire for certainty of diagnosis, the desire to respect and further the autonomy of the sick person, and finally the desire to spare the patient pain.

The need for certainty in diagnosis is in conflict with both the desire to spare the patient pain and the desire to respect and further his autonomy. For certainty of diagnosis may require delay, and such delay will both be the occasion of great suffering on the part of the sick person and reduce his capacity to make intelligent choices. Likewise, the libertarian and humanitarian components of the case for euthanasia are in conflict: if it is desired to guarantee that euthanasia be founded on something clearer than the depressed phase of the alternating moods of the sick person, formalities will be necessary, and such formalities are not conducive to the reduction of suffering. Dr. Harry Roberts puts it: "We all realize the intensified horror attached to the death-penalty by its accompanying formalities—from the phraseology of the judge's sentence, and his black cap, to the weight-gauging visit of the hangman to the cell and the correct attendance at the final scene of the surpliced chaplain, the doctor and the prison governor. This is not irrelevant to the problem of legalized euthanasia."[35] If one supposes capital punishment to be sometimes justified, at least some of these formalities may be necessary—both to guarantee adequate deliberation and to mark off legitimate execution from other possible kinds of killing. But if one wants to spare a sick person as much pain as possible, the rational thing to do is to kill him while he is unconscious and yet unaware that his complaint is incurable. But that would be involuntary euthanasia.

When to the above considerations is added the difficulty of ascertaining the real will of someone who is either suffering from intense pain or who has been drugged to relieve it, the chances of securing valid consent *at the time of the administration of euthanasia* are severely reduced. There remains, however, the possibility of grounding a claim that the proposed euthanasia is consented to by the patient on a document—the so-called "Living Will"—drawn up before the sickness occurs, and confirmed, or in any case not revoked, at the time when euthanasia is supposed to be administered. It is evident that some opportunity at least must be given for revocation, since the approach of death is a significant occurrence in a human being's life, in the light of which someone might well alter his judgments. And the only way of being sure that a prior declaration has been brought to mind and not revoked is to remind the patient of it and to ask him if it remains his will. And so we are back with all the difficulties invoked in consent at the time of killing.

By the way of contrast, the alternative to direct euthanasia—the giving of as much pain reliever as is necessary, and the cessation of extraordinary means to prolong life—fits much better into existing institutions. No will-of-the-wisp of consent need be pursued to justify the giving of pain relievers: while the wishes of the sick person are to be followed where possible, it is safe to presume that anyone in great pain wants that pain relieved. As for the cessation of extraordinary means, the issues here are two: (1) whether, when the will to live (imputed to the patient on the basis of his maintaining himself as an organism) can no longer be said to be at work, there is any requirement that it be replaced by artificial devices; and (2) whether the patient, even if he should wish it, has the *right* to demand that medical resources be expended in an essentially futile attempt to prolong his life. (I should emphasize here that indirect euthanasia, while it meets some of the motivating concerns that underlie demands for direct euthanasia— desire to spare people suffering and repugnance at the practice of not letting those who are plainly dying die—it cannot satisfy the claims of an overt desire that the patient should die. If it could, it would not be indirect. It is not for instance indirect euthanasia to ordain as a general rule that certain classes of people are not to be treated for possibly lethal diseases.) Another virtue of indirect euthanasia is that it is at any rate more difficult to extend to the socially inconvenient, for instance, old persons requiring constant care. [36] It permits only measures whose principal point is the patient's well-being, and excludes only medical procedures to which objection can be taken for reasons other than their tendency to prolong life.

I have argued that the case for voluntary euthanasia exhibits serious internal tensions. But the relevance of these tensions might still be questioned. For such tensions are exhibited by many ideas that have won widespread acceptance. The religion clauses of the First Amendment do not always work in harmony (although sometimes they do), since the desire to protect government from religion, and the desire to protect religion from government, do not always point in the same direction. As government tends to penetrate society more and more, a strict application of a principle of no aid to religion will tend to reduce religion to pariah status within society. And critics of capitalism stress, among other things, both the undemocratic nature (and antidemocratic implications) of concentrations of economic power in the hands of a few and the economic irrationality resulting from the pursuit of private profit. But the desire to promote democracy in economic affairs and the desire to promote rationality through planning do not always work in harmony. But these considerations do not warrant a rejection of the religion clauses or of anticapitalist arguments.

One must distinguish, however, broad programs from concrete proposals. Broad programs quite legitimately contain conflicting strains. There is no cause for quarrel with the call for "death with dignity," so long as the expression is meant literally and is not a euphemism, although it contains many of the tensions heretofore exposed. But when one is dealing with a narrow and particular proposal, whose purposes can be in large measure met in other ways, and whose instability is much to be feared, the situation is something else again. In the one kind of case we are contemplating (perhaps far-reaching) changes in our institutions, most of the details of which are best left to those who will come after us. In the other we are worried about whether a particular concession may not *bring about* a far-reaching change in our institutions, whose implications our collective experience gives us every reason to fear.

3. Even when the case for considering death as in someone's best interests is at its apogee—when the patient's view of the matter is shared by a physician or other observer—troubling ambiguities remain in its grounds. For what is lacking is knowledge, not of the decedent's present state, but of the implications of the choice of death being made. So long as his heart continues to beat of its own accord, a source of ambivalence toward death will remain which cannot by its nature be rationally assuaged, since the knowledge which will assuage it is not to be obtained. And, somewhat paradoxically, even the most urgent request for death conceals within it the germs of ambivalence. For it would be silly to suppose that the sufferings of the dying, even those dying in great pain, are merely physical. And it is by no means beyond the range of human possibility to ask to be killed in order to be delivered from the fear of death.

At this point one may expect a vehement protest. The objector will say, in ordinary medical contexts direct euthanasia is unnecessary (if one is prepared to give the patient all the pain relievers he needs). But there are occasions where pain relievers are not available, say when a soldier is mortally wounded in the jungle and there is no one to care for him, or when (as in Malraux's *Man's Fate*) someone is about to be tortured to death, and one of his comrades has an opportunity to slip him poison.[37] And there may be medical cases (however rare) where no amount of pain reliever will make existence bearable. Or consider the following case: "Some years ago, in a railroad wreck, a man was inextricably entangled in the wreckage, which was burning. In great pain, he begged a policeman to shoot him. This the policeman refused to do, since it was against the law. As a result, the man suffered death by burning."[38]

On the version of the principle of double effect advocated by Germain Grisez (section 17 [1]), it might be possible in such cases to use whatever means are available to stop the sufferer's pain without directly intending his death (although shooting him, for example, might be wrong on other grounds, for instance, because it is illegal). Unfortunately, I am not persuaded that one can shoot someone in the head without intending to kill him, however appealing the case for so doing might be.

Surely, one might say, in these cases the sheer force of human agony is sufficient to warrant neglect of the conceptual ambiguities inherent in killing as benefit, and to override the institutional considerations advanced in this section. One might well oppose domesticating euthanasia within our institutions, while believing that it is or might be warranted at their fringes.[39] In such contexts, it might be argued, one is entitled to act, not on the basis of a utilitarian calculus, but on that of an overwhelming intuition that death or rather killing in such cases is right.

Arguments are available which meet this kind of intuition part of the way. If someone is sentenced to be hanged, drawn, and quartered, for example, the executioner clearly ought to kill as quickly and painlessly as he can, for reasons that perhaps have more to do with the nature of the act itself than with a judgment that life under torture is not worth living. It is for this reason that "I shot her in the soft white belly, so that it would take her longer to die" represents a specially immoral resolution. And there is perhaps some way one of the victim's comrades might be able to take upon himself the duty the executioner failed to perform. This line of reasoning would not be available if the victim was to be tortured *until* death rather than to death, however, since what the torturer would be doing then would not be killing directly but only inflicting prolonged pain. Moreover, my argument presupposes that the execution (although not its torture aspects) is in some minimal sense legitimate, since it is upon this legitimacy that the justification for *killing* rests.

Where such arguments are not available, four points need to be taken into account. First, the argument from overwhelming emergency might be advanced in favor of involuntary euthanasia as well as voluntary (where the patient is too crazed by pain to formulate a request).

Second, the ethics of indirect and passive euthanasia is *itself* an accommodation to extreme circumstances. (One would hardly wish doctors generally to let their patients die, or to be indifferent to the possible life-shortening effects of their therapies.) Third, it is harder to act in an uninstitutionalized manner than might be supposed: surely what soldiers do to or for their comrades, or police to or for citizens, involves the structure of our institutions as much as what physicians do to or for their patients. Even ordinary friendship is an institution of sorts whose conventions vary from culture to culture, and whether assisting a suicide is an "office for a friend" (*Julius Caesar*) is a question of some importance for its structure. If anyone can act upon a person without thereby conforming to, interpreting, breaching, or changing the norms of some institution, it is that person himself. Institutional considerations of this sort would not apply in a situation—Nevil Shute's *On the Beach*, for example—when all human institutions were doomed to destruction shortly. What becomes of ethics, not only the ethics of homicide, in such a situation is a very difficult question.

Finally, it is difficult in extreme situations to keep separate the question of justification (which alone is in the least doubt) from that of excuse and respect for the compassionate motive even when it leads the agent to possibly misguided action. Consider for instance G. R. Dunstan's observation that there are situations in which "no moralist, from the comfort of his chair, would condemn the bullet fired as mercy's sole available resort."[40] Bullets are of course not the primary objects of moral assessment, and by speaking of bullets Dunstan has avoided stating clearly whether it is the act or the agent that no moralist could condemn. The expression "from the comfort of his chair" suggests that it is the agent, but it is difficult to be sure of the correctness of this interpretation. Turning from the moralist to the agent himself, there are situations where a sensitive person will feel unhappiness no matter what he does, and where it will be difficult or impossible to distinguish a feeling of guilt from one of sorrow.

26. Suicide

WE THUS COME to the subject of suicide. Suicide is an act to which contemporary thought finds itself inadequate: we tend to agree with Wittgenstein when he suggests that it is "the elementary sin" and when he suggests that it is "in itself neither good nor evil."[41] We are tempted to regard suicide as constituting an anomaly in the logic of obligation the opposite of that which more often haunts moral reflection—the moral blind alley where all possible acts are forbidden. We are tempted, that is, to see suicide as an act not susceptible of moral evaluation of any kind, as neither morally required, nor morally permitted, nor morally forbidden. Such a temptation is reinforced by a tendency to make conclusive presumption of mental imbalance on the part of the suicide, or by treating suicide as a cause of death rather than a human act, or as a problem for the human sciences only and not for morality. This procedure has been forcefully criticized on the grounds that it isolates the suicide from the bonds of common humanity.[42] Nor is it sufficient to treat suicide as a special case of homicide (i.e., homicide with consent, where killer and consenting decedent are the same), since that they are the same makes a crucial difference in our intuitions.[43] It is even unclear whether suicide ought to be regarded as a species of homicide at all, whether homicide is to be defined as any killing of a human being by a human being, or as any killing of a human being by another human being. On the other hand, to urge suicide upon someone, and to provide him the means, or perhaps to do either one of these things, seems very little different from outright homicide, and even, at least without special justifications, in some respects worse.[44] And the attempt to justify assisting a suicide by the claim that death is in his best interests seems to be at bottom no stronger than the corresponding claim in cases of outright killing. Perhaps the matter is best summed up with the observation that, when a suicide takes place among a group of acquaintances, their reaction is both very different from that occasioned by an ordinary killing and very different from that occasioned by death by disease or accident.

One form these difficulties take is an unclarity in the distinction between our moral and our nonmoral responses to suicide. Consider some kinds of conduct I find distasteful, but to which I might be said not to have a genuinely moral negative response. If I want to know whether my repugnance to the vomitorium, to the prolonged kiss Paul Goodman once gave a dog,[45] or to joining clubs for men and women of high IQ, constitutes moral disapproval, I can ask myself three questions: (1) Do I myself consider abstention from kinds of conduct I find distasteful a principle of the highest priority? (2) Would I wish social sanctions, formal or informal, to be invoked against those who engage in such conduct? (3) Does a moral objection to these kinds of conduct fit in with my other admittedly moral judgments, say about promise-keeping and murder? None of these tests is infallible: I might be lax about moral matters but scrupulous about showing good taste, I might selfishly wish that activity I merely dislike be repressed, and my moral consciousness might be too complex for my powers of analysis. And of course any moral judgment I do make is both fallible and corrigible.

But the difficulties are compounded in the case of suicide. Since suicide is an act which can be successfully performed only once in a lifetime, one's access to his principles concerning the act is of necessity limited, and moreover any principles he has are likely to be confused with his instinct of self-preservation. The dead cannot be punished, the symbolic substitutes for such punishment are not acceptable to the contemporary moral consciousness, and there are obvious limitations on the advisability of sanctioning failed attempts when one cannot sanction successes. (The denial of Christian burial to one who, on philosophical grounds, kills himself is probably acceptable, but all this means is that a community's rites are not to be given one who in an emphatic way has repudiated its values, and thus must be presumed, to the extent that he is in the least clear-headed, not to desire them.) Finally, although, considered as an objection to homicide, an objection to suicide would seem to fit in as well as can be expected with our other moral judgments, many philosophers are prepared to deny that one can treat oneself in a morally wrongful fashion,[46] so that suicide cannot in general be wrong if such philosophers are right.

The denial of duties to oneself, in the sense explained, is at least open to doubt. Parents often instruct their children to avoid activities they consider to be destructive of the children themselves, and it seems arbitrary to refuse to call this activity moral education, or to regard it as in all cases objectionable.[47] Considerations of my own survival certainly can override other obligations (I am not bound to risk my life in order to fulfill a minor promise), which suggests that my survival is itself a matter of obligation. On the other hand, this feature of the ethics of promises may only mean that any obligation may sometimes be overridden by the interests of the person under the obligation, or that a reasonable promisee is presumed not to want the promisor to fulfill his promise at the cost of his life. Still further, although it may be possible in any given case to injure myself without injuring someone else, it is difficult for people who persist in self-harming activities to avoid injuring others. Hence we have a rule-consequentialist argument for regarding self-injuring conduct as wrongful. Finally, if one's act produces a bad result, does it matter so much that the injured party is oneself? (Utilitarians ought not to think so.) In any case, it is quite plausible to hold that a person can be wronged, even though he might have consented to what was done to him. Homicide and mutilation apart, I should hope that if the Louds should come to understand that they had been exploited by the publicizing of their familial difficulties in an American television series, their complaint would be understood and honored.

On the other hand, the existence of duties to oneself would not resolve the question either. For one might hold a half-Kantian half-utilitarian view which required one to respect the integrity of others while permitting or requiring one to use oneself as a means to one's own happiness.

Before proceeding further, I should like to distinguish, and set to one side, two kinds of acts which do not, in my view, form part of the problem of suicide. One such kind of act is indirect suicide, in which someone for a proportionate reason does what will shorten his life, although he chooses death neither as an end nor as a means. Samson's killing of the Philistines at the cost of his own life is perhaps an example, as is the refusal of medical treatments which are burdensome, degrading, or painful and will extend life for only a short, painful while.

Another such case is altruistic suicide—for instance by someone who is about to be tortured into revealing information which will destroy his comrades, or (to block the claim that he cannot know whether he will yield) who has been drugged for the same purpose and has an opportunity to kill himself before the drug deprives him of control over his tongue. Other forms of betrayal of a community might also be averted in this way. (So one might interpret the Jewish sources which countenance suicide to avoid baptism.) Self-execution also belongs here: Socrates, who (according to the *Phaedo*) condemns suicide and then takes the hemlock is not a hypocrite.[48] The least problematic kind of "suicide" is an act, like that of Captain Oates, which both is altruistic and produces death only indirectly. (If Captain Oates had been rescued by another Antarctic expedition, the aim of his act—sparing the members of his expedition the burden of caring for him—would not have been frustrated.)

It is, however, important to insist that the cause prompting an altruistic suicide be such as to confer upon others a tolerable claim to do the act themselves if that suicide is to be morally unproblematic. (Only a tolerable claim is necessary, since we need not worry about the agent's possible bias against his own interests.) It is not completely clear that the principle of self-defense extends so far as to permit soldiers to kill a comrade who is about to destroy them by giving the enemy information under torture, but it is not completely clear that it does not extend so far either, so that the demand for a tolerable claim is met in this case. But suicide by an old person to relieve his relatives of the burden of caring for him, or prevent the depletion of his estate, falls very much within the problem area.

Suicides of political protest present a difficult kind of case, since while they are altruistic and (in all interesting cases) devoted to a very important end, the connection between the death of the protestor and the good he is seeking is both indirect and problematic. It seems that hunger-striking is easily justifiable, since the protestor will not directly intend his own death (ideally he would linger until the authority in question relented). But, apart from a general defense of suicide, self-immolation is quite dubious, since it seems to manifest a kind of moral terrorism about which it is difficult not to feel scruples.

Suicides of honor present a particularly difficult kind of case, since they may be understood in more than one way. The suicide of honor may be interested in sparing himself or others the distress of his humiliation, or he may view his honor in a disinterested way, as something, like a great painting or a beautiful landscape, worth preserving in its own right. In any case the unclarity of the notion of honor places such suicides within the problem area. The same is true of a kind of suicide which is very similar to the suicide of honor, suicide prompted by an unwillingness to be the kind of thing which sickness produces.[49]

Lastly, the relationship between the (prudential) rationality and the morality of suicide needs to be illuminated. In general, an act may be both rational and moral, rational and immoral, irrational and moral, or

197

irrational and immoral for most accounts of what makes an action rational. So that my argument (section 3) that suicide cannot be rational in a particular sense does not itself settle the question of the ethics of suicide. Moreover, the decision to go on living is not rational in the sense of prudential calculation either.

I now turn to the question of suicide in one's own interest. I have argued (section 3) that the rational suicide defended by utilitarians is impossible. But the decision to go on living is irrational (or nonrational) in that sense, too, since it is based on calculation no more than the decision to kill oneself. It does have, however, among its credentials conformity with what can be usefully called the "natural desire" of a living being to persist as a living being, in other words a desire rooted in our very structure as human animals (sections 2, 3).

There are, it seems, two views of (direct, egoistic) suicide consistent with our (or my) intuitions and with what has been said so far.

1. In the absence of very strong obligations to others, which will often not be present when suicide is under consideration, suicide is morally permissible. It is, however, a privilege or liberty, not a right; that is to say, no other person is under an obligation either not to interfere with, or to assist, the prospective suicide. Rather, other people are under an obligation not to assist him, and under many circumstances at least to attempt to dissuade him or even to interfere with his actions, by pumping out his stomach for instance. It is difficult, however strong one's libertarian inclinations, to find fault with the New York taxi driver who locked a passenger in the back seat of his car in an attempt to avert a suicide; most of us indeed would find his actions praiseworthy, particularly since they took place in an environment where indifference to the lives and welfare of others is too often the rule. [50]

But the point of these obligations might not be to prevent wrongdoing on the suicide's part or even, directly, to save his life (although this is how the intervenor will think of his actions at the time). Its point might be rather to guarantee that he leaves life only when he has resolved to do so after the most careful consideration. On this view, if someone tries to starve himself to death, he should not be force-fed, although food should be made available, and it should be made clear that the prospective suicide can change his mind and eat without cause for shame.

Liberal writers tend to explain the duty to restrain a suicide in somewhat different terms, as based on a rebuttable presumption that suicide is irrational.[51] Quite apart from my difficulties about the basis for the presumption itself or its possible overruling, it seems that a follower of Mill ought rather to presume that an adult knows what he is doing. Even if we assume that it would be irrational for most of us to kill ourselves, when we deal with an attempt at suicide we are not dealing with a randomly chosen member of the population but with one of the minority which chooses to die.

One point of asserting a mere liberty to kill oneself is that this formulation precludes the assertion of a right to suicide in a context of agitation. A troublesome ambiguity arises when a right to suicide is asserted on behalf of other people, as is presumably the case when the claim is made by a living writer. Some of the literature provokes the question, whether straightforwardly involuntary euthanasia might not be a more honorable course than persuading a burdensome person to kill himself or consent to his being killed by another.[52] If a suicide is going to take place, it is better that the decedent take full responsibility for his own death, including the raising of the issue and the actual use of the lethal measures involved. There seems to be no legitimate place for the argument which would place the responsibility for execution in hands other than those of the decedent, on the grounds that suicide is messy or lonely.[53] Death always has messy aspects, and I should think that self-chosen death (or rather dying) would be very lonely, even if one's whole society were there cheering one on. The state of someone on the ledge of a building, urged to jump by a crowd gathered below, is hardly enviable.

The advocate of suicide is presumably interested only in the sick and the old (or at least the unhappy). But suicide is a phenomenon of youth as well as of age, and there are many examples of sick or otherwise miserable people who cling passionately to life. To argue that suicide is rational to escape physical pain, but not suicide for any other reason, is to show oneself out of touch with the depth and complexity of human motives. Perhaps those who so argue think that pain (in contrast to, say,

199

the loss of a loved one) is an evil completely independent of the sufferer's attitude. But in fact there are circumstances—admittedly highly special ones—in which the sensations we call "pain" (or would call "pain" if they were unpleasant) can be felt with relative indifference or even enjoyed.[54]

Suicide is one kind of act which cannot be performed for frivolous reasons, since to do so would be to show that one took "frivolity" with deadly seriousness. Even a suicide for very strange reasons—for instance, to avoid having to defile oneself with food[55]—cannot be easily dismissed as unreasonable, since to act in this way is to show what one considers supremely important. The difference between this and more ordinary suicides lies not in their lack of rationality, but in our lack of understanding. It is even rational on some premises—for instance, that what matters is to make sure that one lives the good life to the very end—for two lovers to kill themselves at the height of their happiness, before time and circumstance have a chance to spoil it. (Those who find this a perverse reading of the idea of a good life might prefer Spinoza's remarks that in order to live well, one must live.) It follows that if one wishes to defend suicide, one is forced, with Hume, to take the suicide's own evaluation of his situation as self-certifying. In Hume's words, "No man ever threw away life while it was worth keeping."[56] Something like this premise may underlie Glanville Williams's otherwise quite astounding suggestion, that a mentally ill person may be competent to decide to commit suicide, although he may be competent to make no other decision.[57]

I ought finally to consider the duties to others which may, on this hypothesis, limit one's liberty to kill oneself. It may seem fatuous to address such considerations to a suicide, but there are clearly moral limitations on the way one kills oneself, even granting that the act of suicide itself is blameless. One ought not for instance place a bomb on an airplane in which other people are going to travel. Nor ought one make one's dependents penniless, or defeat the legitimate expectations of other people. And if the stigma on suicide is likely to be the cause of great unhappiness on the part of others, the act should be disguised as an accident. But beyond these requirements it is not possible to go, since as far as one's effect on the world is concerned, if one kills oneself one is only ceasing to do good. And someone who kills himself is likely to be persuaded that the good he is able to do is very limited indeed.

And as far as the grief of others is concerned, a determined defender of suicide might argue that those who really care for a person's welfare should be glad rather than sorrowful that he has found the courage to free himself of his wretched existence. And that he has so freed himself is the sole and sufficient grounds for saying that it was, in the relevant sense, wretched—not that I expect the families and friends of suicides generally to feel this way, of course; and the propaganda in favor of the right to suicide which (if anything) could bring them to feel this way is not permitted by the thesis I am now developing. So that, even on the view which holds that there is a liberty to commit suicide, the grief that one's family might experience will remain a consideration. But it will be entitled to no more consideration than the sorrow they might feel because of their disapproval of, say, one's politics.

2. Alternatively, one might hold that (direct, egoistic) suicide is never right. The underlying moral premise here is that each person should live the best life of which he is capable, and that this principle governs not only our dealings with others, but also our dealings with ourselves. One has, it would seem to follow, an obligation to realize whatever value one can in his life, however wretched his circumstances might be. And the same complexity which makes it impossible to second-guess a suicide once the liberty to kill oneself is conceded, makes it impossible to place limits on what a person must endure. So long as the capacity for choice remains, there remains a possibility of achieving something of value through courageous acceptance of one's situation. And once the capacity for choice is lost, there are no moral problems, for one has ceased to be an agent.

It seems to me that the characteristic stoic attitude toward suicide is inconsistent. If one holds that one's freedom consists in his capacity to alter his attitude toward the world rather than the world itself, it would seem that the application of this principle to suicide would be an exhortation to be prepared to accept whatever suffering might befall one rather than to take action to eliminate that suffering, including action resulting in one's own death. The same attitude which produces submission to tyranny or suicide in preference to rebellion or flight would seem to indicate a preference for enduring whatever a tyrant or disease might do rather than killing oneself to escape it. Since I do not accept the underlying premises of such a stoic argument, however, I need pursue this line of thought no further. The case against suicide which I find most persuasive rests, not on a general interdiction on action to improve one's condition, but on a presumption against the taking of human life, and the impossibility of stably rebutting this presumption by showing that one's own life has nothing in it worth living for, or not enough to require enduring what one has to endure.

It should be added that it does not follow, from the supposition that suicide is wrong, that others are required, or even permitted, to take all possible measures to avert it. The concept of extraordinary means has a place even here. The wound to human dignity inherent in force-feeding, for instance, may well justify, or even require, our abstaining from such measures when someone undertakes to starve himself to death.

In any case, while most of us most of the time are followers neither of Unamuno nor of Richard Cory, there is no way of arriving, in a principled way, at a degree of unhappiness at which life ceases to be worth living. One must thus either license nearly all suicides (although with the restrictions I have indicated on the cooperation of others), or else forbid nearly all of them. Which is the proper course would seem to rest on considerations excluded by the constraints placed upon the arguments in this book. The observance of these constraints—avoidance of overtly religious or antireligious premises—accounts for the somewhat fragmentary and impressionistic character of some of the discussion in this chapter. Its *institutional* conclusions, however, stand fast for a wide range of perspectives.

VII /

CONCLUSION

THE UNDERLYING THEME of this book is a presumption against killing. Some such presumption is a necessity of social life, and, to the extent that a society becomes more just and more humane, to that extent will the presumption against homicide be given greater and greater force.

In this work, the presumption against the legitimacy of homicide has operated at three levels. First, each individual act of homicide, if it is not to be considered murder, must be justified, mitigated, or excused in some way. Second, kinds of justification offered for homicide must be subjected to careful scrutiny, more careful than is commonly the case in justifying what is prima facie wrong. The following justifications of homicide have for this reason been rejected: that homicide would in this case be good on the whole, that it would help deter other people from wrongdoing (say murder), or that it is in the interests of or consented to by the prospective decedent. Third, in determining who or what is protected by the moral rule against homicide, I have preferred expanding the protected class to contracting it. Thus fetuses are to be regarded as persons in preference to withdrawing the status of person from infants.

I would also argue—though I cannot do so in detail here—that if unborn children are persons there is no reason why the law should not accord them protection.[1] Even if their status is a matter of reasonable doubt, the law might well prefer to be on the safe side on this issue. Protecting unborn children against killing falls squarely within the scope of the principle permitting restrictions on liberty to avert harm to others. And the argument sometimes made against anti-abortion laws—that they forbid inconspicuous conduct not clearly condemned by the prevailing moral culture—is not of sufficient strength to require us to tolerate unjustified killing.

A woman's right to control the use made of her body might, in legal contexts at least, override the unborn child's right to life in cases of rape, where one can fairly say that the woman has been forced to become pregnant. But when the risk of conception has been voluntarily assumed, such an argument has considerably less force. And there ought to be ways of helping distressed pregnant women, and of improving the lot of the poor, which do not involve the taking of human life.

There is, moreover, no objection in principle to judicial intervention to protect the unborn (as has taken place in West Germany). But judicial intervention to withdraw such protection (as has happened in the United States) is in the highest degree objectionable both from a legal and from a moral standpoint. It is a matter for bitter irony that the Supreme Court should have deferred to the judgment of the elected representatives of the people when judicial homicide was in question, but have substituted its own judgment on the side of killing when the issue was one of the protection of life. [2]

On the other hand, the presumption against killing has not been pressed here as far as it conceivably might be—the author is neither a vegetarian nor a strict pacifist. Moreover, the presumption is not to be pressed equally far in all contexts: conceivably, a just constitution would limit itself to permitting anti-abortion laws, while a just code of laws would allow exceptions, which a conscientious woman or doctor would decline to make use of. And I would argue that the conscientious scruples of opponents of war or abortion (or of this war or this abortion), even when we would think them unreasonable, are to be respected, whether or not they have a religious basis. [3]

An argument often made against positions like the author's is that their evaluation of the fetus (to take just one example) rests on a religious foundation, and that this foundation is either just irrational, or at least has no legitimate place in the framing of law and social policy for a community that includes people of all religious beliefs and none. For example, a recent Report of the United States Commission on Civil

Rights contends that those who would outlaw abortion "should clearly understand that they would be compelling every woman to accept the view that a constitutionally protected person exists from the 'moment of conception'; even when such a view conflicts with an individual woman's religious views."[4] And, in a discussion of euthanasia, Marvin Kohl complains that "paradoxically, many men who do not believe in God nevertheless believe that all human life properly belongs to Him."[5]

One way of replying to such arguments is to deny their premise, and to maintain that religious belief can and should shape both individual moral conviction and the laws and policies of societies in which large numbers of religious people live. Whether religious belief is of necessity irrational is too large a question to discuss here. But, if some form of religious belief is rationally acceptable, it is foolish to suppose that those who hold it can be asked to ignore it in determining their moral and political convictions. Although the precise way in which religion bears on morality, and morality on politics and law, is a matter requiring considerable discussion, it is safe to say that someone who resolves not to let his religious beliefs influence his moral ones, or his moral beliefs influence his political ones, either is willfully perverse or does not know what it is to hold a moral or a religious conviction. And there are limits to how far one can go in accommodating those whose beliefs are different from one's own without wholly compromising one's adherence to one's position. To concede that forms of homicide one regards as seriously wrong may justly be made a matter of constitutional right is to go well beyond that kind of tolerance which is in any sense a virtue.

It remains the case, however, that a separation of religious and secular fields of concern, and the coexistence of a variety of religious and nonreligious modes of life within the same society, are important constitutional principles of our society. It will thus be necessary to give detailed attention to separationist arguments against the implementation of the views defended in this book.

Another way of replying to such criticisms is to point out that they are not consistent with the critics' own commitments. Against the Civil Rights Commission, it is worth pointing out that the civil rights movement was led by a minister, and directed against a social system which some believed to reflect the will of God. And the abolitionists, whose partial victory is reflected in the Thirteenth through Fifteenth Amendments, included among their ideas religious doctrines not, then or now, universally shared.[6] And someone who wishes to defend the Supreme Court's abortion decision on the grounds that prohibitions of abortion are "religiously entangled" needs to be reminded that, if this prohibition is religiously entangled, traditional ideas concerning marriage, family, and sexuality are even more so. And, far from rejecting all legislation enforcing traditional attitudes in these areas, the Court has upheld laws against pornography and homosexual activity, as well as zoning ordinances hostile to communes.

One can make the same argument without explicit mention of religion. Disagreements about abortion reflect deep differences in people's perception of life, death, the nature of sex and reproduction, and the relationship between the two biological sexes. Hence it is frequently argued that it is unjust to impose the perceptions of those who oppose abortion upon those who do not share them. But this argument proves too much. Similar remarks can be made about racial attitudes, or attitudes toward departures from traditional sex roles by women. But defenders of abortion do not characteristically hold that racial or sex-based discrimination may not be legally restricted.

The trouble with this kind of argument is that it is a demand for consistency, and thus will not be effective against a relentless critic. Someone who prefers the mores of classical antiquity to those of a civilization influenced by Christianity and Judaism will surely find this kind of argument unimpressive.

A third line of reply restates the chief arguments of this book, which do not appeal to the sovereignty of God over human life, notions about the soul, or even to quasi-religious notions such as the sanctity of life. Anyone who regards high infant mortality as a matter of secular concern in its own right (and not, say, only an index of poverty) cannot regard a defense of the fetus as an attempt to impose distinctively religious norms. At minimum, some of the arguments here should suffice to refute such claims as that the question of the beginning of human life cannot "be discussed in secular terms at all"[7] or that such discussion must always have a conclusion unfavorable to the fetus.

And while opposition to suicide, and hence to even voluntary euthanasia, can easily be portrayed as religiously based, institutional arguments such as those presented by Yale Kamisar have a powerful persuasive impact without appealing to any theological or religious premises. Whether my reflections on the opaqueness of death are religious or secular in character is a question I leave to those who understand the distinction better than I do. They cannot be dismissed, in any event, as mere irrational responses.

But no one who is prepared to explain opposition to some form of killing as resulting from a vestigial religious tenet is likely to be impressed by this kind of argument. Any moral argument, including mine, takes as its starting point a set of intuitions, and a determined defender of forms of killing against which I have argued can regard my intuitions as religious responses. The difficulty is our lack of a criterion for distinguishing religious from secular norms. Perhaps prohibitions on bribery are religious ones, for example: the practice is forbidden in the Torah (Deuteronomy 16:19) and is consistent with at least the minimum conditions of social life.

In any event, it is necessary to face the following questions: Why should we care so much about infants? Why should the status of those who are not able to bargain for their rights not be a matter of the convenience of those who are able to do so? Why should we object to the use of small children in cancer research, if their parents consent and any damaged subjects are painlessly killed?

One reason for placing a high value on the continued existence of human beings may be found in Kant's principle of personality: that human beings are always to be treated as ends and never as means merely. If this principle means anything at all, it implies that people may not be destroyed as a mere matter of social convenience, nor supposed people regarded as subhuman just because it suits the convenience of those making the distinction to do so.

The principle of personality has not lacked eloquent spokesmen. John Rawls affirms that "each person possesses an inviolability founded on justice that even the welfare of society as a whole cannot override."[8] And, since one argument sometimes urged upon us for neglecting considerations of human dignity is that we can thereby reduce human suffering, it is also worthwhile to quote Charles Fried: "We must reduce the suffering of men, not so much because suffering is bad, as because it is human beings who are suffering. Consequently it is more important that we retain respect for our own and each other's humanity as we relieve suffering, than that suffering be relieved."[9]

But neither Rawls nor Fried does more than set forth his formulation of the principle of respect for persons as expressive of an axiomatic intuition. Someone alert for attempts to smuggle religious tenets into the secular forum could easily interpret this principle as a vestige of the doctrine of the infinite worth of each human soul. Certainly it is not a feature of every moral code.

Attempts to find a further ground for the principle of respect for persons quickly lead to an impasse. W. G. Maclagan treats respect for persons as an aspect of agape (or unselfish benevolence), but concerning the grounds of agape itself finds himself driven to remark:

> What in this predicament *can* we say but that the recognition of the worth or importance of persons is actually integrated with the Agape-response itself, is a constitutive moment in it, response and recognition being only different facets of a single experience? On this view it is *in* Agape that we *see* the significance of persons, and we could say with equal truth, and so long as we attend carefully to our meaning, with equal safety, that Agape is warranted by the apprehended worth of its object or that Agape provides its own warrant. [10]

He might have been better advised to give this explanation for the principle of respect for persons directly, without picking up the additional problems presented by the notion of agape. Another group of writers makes the same point in more contemporary terms, speaking of respect for persons as a "form of life," or framework of attitudes and behavior, which neither requires nor is capable of getting a justification external to itself. [11]

Neither Maclagan's account nor its restatement in terms of forms of life is likely to make much impression on a determined critic. Such a critic will point out that erotic love or political enthusiasm can lead someone to see admirable qualities wholly lacking in the object of his devotion; and will argue that a form of life centered on respect for persons, like one centered on belief in witches, is subject to the corrosive impact of critical intelligence.

The principle of personality is both plausible in its own right and capable of making sense of many of our considered judgments about moral issues. The difficulty of arguing with those who do not share our intuitions on this point should not inhibit our acting upon our convictions, whether as individuals or as citizens. To allow philosophical skepticism concerning the first principles of ethics to paralyze action would be to surrender the practical sphere to immoralists and fanatics, neither of whom is likely to be troubled about such issues. So far as ethics proper is concerned, this kind of reply will have to suffice.

And for some of my readers it will no doubt prove sufficient. But others will not be content with it, and will find themselves led to press the ultimate question: why should we bother so much about a kind of creature subject, among other things, to hiccoughs? In the context of this kind of question, the contradiction alleged by Kohl—between disbelief in God and belief that all life belongs to Him—can pose a real problem. At any rate the contradiction is one that can be resolved in more than one way.

Notes

Chapter I. Introduction

1. There have been occasional attempts—most recently in connection with United States belligerency in Viet Nam—to treat the ordinary soldier in a war of aggression as a criminal in international law. See, e.g., Richard Wasserstrom, "The Relevance of Nuremburg," *Philosophy & Public Affairs*, 1 (1971), 28, 35ff.; Richard A. Falk, "The American POW's: Pawns in Power Politics," *Progressive*, March 1971. But the weight of both the authority and the reasoning clearly favors the contrary conclusion.

2. Cross references by section will be in this form throughout.

3. My argument will be consistent with Plato's claim that the worst harm inflicted by a wrongful act is the harm done the wrongdoer.

4. I use "friends" to include family members, lovers, and acquaintances as well as friends in the strict sense. The important differences among these different kinds of relationship will not affect my argument.

5. Joel Feinberg, "The Rights of Animals and Unborn Generations," in William T. Blackstone, ed., *Philosophy and Environmental Crisis* (Athens, Ga., 1974), pp. 51–55, and pp. 60–61 (on so-called human vegetables).

6. Sissela Bok, "Ethical Problems of Abortion," *Hastings Center Studies*, Jan. 1974, p. 43.

7. One can also lose something bad, of course, but this does not bear on our present discussion.

8. This example is taken from Bok. Bok's hermit-killer commits suicide: mine simplifies discussion by dying of natural causes.

9. The case of destroying the universe is also of interest in another connection, since this is an aspect under which human beings have often considered suicide and found it attractive.

10. Glanville Williams, *The Sanctity of Life and the Criminal Law* (New York, 1957), pp. ix–x.

11. *Nicomachean Ethics* 1115a 25 (tr. W. D. Ross).

12. Lucretius, *De Rerum Natura*, III, 870 ff.
13. Paul Edwards, "'My Death,'" in Paul Edwards, ed., *Encyclopedia of Philosophy* (New York, 1967), Vol. 5.
14. Richard B. Brandt, "The Morality and Rationality of Suicide," in James Rachels, ed., *Moral Problems*, 2d ed. (New York, 1975), p. 375.
15. Bernard Williams, *Problems of the Self* (Cambridge, Eng., 1973), pp. 84–88; excerpt pp. 85–86.
16. Thomas Nagel, "Death," *Moral Problems*, 2d ed., p. 406.
17. Mary Mothersill, "Death," in *Moral Problems*, 1st ed. (New York, 1971), pp. 371–383.
18. This contention seems to underlie much of the argumentation in Marvin Kohl, *The Morality of Killing* (New York, 1974).
19. G. E. M. Anscombe, "Two Kinds of Error in Action," in Judith Jarvis Thomson and Gerald Dworkin, eds., *Ethics* (New York, 1968), p. 287; criticized in Joel Feinberg, "On Being 'Morally Speaking a Murderer,'" in ibid., pp. 295–297. If "just" has the extended sense of "morally right or acceptable," we are back with our initial definition of "murder" as "wrongful homicide." If, on the other hand, we read "unjust" as "unjustified," the definition is essentially correct, although strictly speaking one should allow for the possibility of excuse or mitigation as well.
20. My intuitions on this point are strengthened by some remarks in Joel Feinberg, "Noncomparative Justice," *Philosophical Review*, 82 (1974), pp. 327 (on the Kent State murders) and 301 (not all cases of wrongful promise-breaking injustice). See also John Salmond, *Jurisprudence*, 12th ed., P. J. Fitzgerald, ed. (London, 1966), pp. 60–61: "Rape is an abhorrent act, but the last description to be applied to it is that of being unjust."
21. *Nicomachean Ethics*, V. 11.
22. It now becomes necessary to distinguish *human beings*, that is to say members of our species, from *persons*, that is to say those protected by the moral rule against homicide. For further discussion of this distinction, see sections 8, 15.
23. The ideal-regarding/want-regarding distinction is due to Brian Barry, *Political Argument* (London, 1965), ch. 3, sec. 3. See also his *Liberal Theory of Justice* (Oxford, 1973), pp. 20–21.
24. See Richard G. Henson, "Utilitarianism and the Wrongness of Killing," *Philosophical Review*, 80 (1971); excerpt p. 325. Cf. R. N. Smart, "Negative Utilitarianism," *Mind*, n.s., 67 (1958), 542–543 (utilitarianism as the mere elimination of suffering leads to the extermination of all life).
25. Jan Narveson, *Morality and Utility* (Baltimore, 1967); excerpt p. 196.
26. For Narveson's most recent thoughts on procreation, see his "Moral Problems of Population," *Monist*, 57 (1973), 162–186.

27. *Morality and Utility*, p. 255. Leibniz held a similar doctrine: that if there were no best of all possible worlds for God to create, He would create no world at all. See David Blumenfeld, "Is the Best Possible World Possible?" *Philosophical Review*, 84 (1975), esp. p. 166.

28. An exception is the kind of argument offered by Sissela Bok, in the context of a defense of abortion, against the killing of hermits in their sleep: "Whereas it is possible to frame a rule permitting abortion which causes no anxiety on the part of others covered by the rule—other embryos or fetuses—it is not possible to frame such a rule permitting the killing of hermits without threatening other *hermits*. All hermits would have to fear for their lives if there were a rule saying that hermits can be killed if they are alone and asleep and if the agent commits suicide" (p. 43). But this argument is not plausible, since so narrow a rule would hardly pose a real threat to hermits, and in any case there are not so many hermits that a degree of anxiety on their part is not, from a utilitarian point of view, socially tolerable. (The more fundamental objection to this kind of argument is, of course, that it makes anxiety over being killed the source of the badness of death rather than its result.)

29. J. J. C. Smart puts the matter this way: "I would argue that Moore's principle of organic unities destroys the essential utilitarianism of his doctrine. He need never disagree in practice, as a utilitarian ought to, with Sir David Ross. Every trick Ross can play with his *prima facie* duties, Moore can play, in a different way, with his organic unities" ("Outline of a System of Utilitarian Ethics," in J. J. C. Smart and Bernard Williams, *Utilitarianism, For and Against* [Cambridge, Eng., 1973], p. 27).

30. A recent social-contract treatment of the ethics of homicide is R. E. Ewin, "What Is Wrong with Killing People?" *Philosophical Quarterly*, 22 (1972), quotation p. 126.

31. John Rawls, *A Theory of Justice* (Cambridge, Mass., 1972), esp. pp. 62, 92.

32. Ewin, p. 137.

33. G. R. Grice, *The Grounds of Moral Judgement* (Cambridge, Eng., 1967).

34. Ronald Green, "Conferred Rights and the Fetus," *Journal of Religious Ethics*, Spring 1974, p. 61.

35. Grice, pp. 147–150 (children under ten have no rights beyond those derived from the interests of their parents). Cf. Thomas Hobbes, *Leviathan*, Michael Oakeshott, ed. (London, 1969), pp. 133, 152–153 (parental power arises from the ability of parents to destroy their children).

36. James Childress, "A Response to 'Conferred Rights and the Fetus,'" *Journal of Religious Ethics*, Spring 1974, p. 81.

37. *A Theory of Justice*, sec. 77.

A. Hart, *The Concept of Law* (Oxford, 1972), pp. 189–195.
kind of argument occurs in unexpected places. Glanville Williams
defends eugenic infanticide by citing the bitch who kills her mis-
shapꞈ.. pies (*The Sanctity of Life*, p. 20).

40. My discussion of St. Thomas's theory of natural law is based largely on
Germain Grisez, "The First Principle of Practical Reason," in Anthony Kenny,
ed., *Aquinas* (Garden City, N.Y., 1969), pp. 340–382; see also his *Contraception and the Natural Law* (Milwaukee, 1964), ch. 3.

41. Arthur C. Danto, "Human Nature and Natural Law," in Sidney Hook,
ed., *Law and Philosophy* (New York, 1964), pp. 187–199.

42. Aristotle, *Politics, Books III and IV*, Richard Robinson, ed. and tr.
(Oxford, 1962), p. xxiii. I am indebted to Alan Donagan ("The Scholastic
Theory of Moral Law in the Modern World," in Kenny, ed., *Aquinas*, p. 335)
for this reference.

43. Some natural-law moralists add to their descriptive premises the assumption that the universe is essentially moral. In view of both the vagueness of
this premise and its theological entanglements, it seems to me more appropriate
to rely on the intuitive point that there is some sort of connection between the
kind of creature a human being is and the sort of life that is good for him.

44. Kenneth Stern, "Either-Or or Neither-Nor?" in *Law and Philosophy*,
pp. 247–259.

45. This is of course a bit too quick; for detailed discussion see Chapters IV
and V.

46. A portion of this chapter was read to the American Philosophical Association (Pacific Division) March 1978.

CHAPTER II. SCOPE OF THE PROHIBITION:
Nonhumans, Robots, and Infants

1. R. M. Hare, "Abortion and the Golden Rule," *Philosophy & Public
Affairs*, 4 (1975), 201–222. Hare's strategy should be compared with that of
Glanville Williams, "Euthanasia and the Physician," in Marvin Kohl, ed.,
Beneficent Euthanasia (Buffalo, N.Y., 1975), pp. 156–157.

2. Sissela Bok, "Ethical Problems of Abortion," *Hastings Center Studies*,
Jan. 1974, pp. 40–41.

3. Or infanticide. See Michael Tooley, "A Defense of Abortion and Infanticide," in Joel Feinberg, ed., *The Problem of Abortion* (Belmont, Calif., 1973),
p. 91. This is a revised version of Tooley's "Abortion and Infanticide," *Philosophy & Public Affairs*, 2 (1972), 137–165.

Notes

4. Peter Singer's review of *Animals, Men and Morals*, in the *New York Review*, April 5, 1973, p. 19.

5. Similar replies are available to refute another *ad hominem* against the opponents of abortion, that they ought to be equally concerned for the possible or probable victims of famine as for these who are killed in the womb. For an example of this *ad hominem* in the scholarly literature, see Onora Nell, "Lifeboat Earth," *Philosophy & Public Affairs*, 4 (1975), 290, n. 9. More important, no one I know of celebrates starvation as a positive good, while there are many who are prepared to welcome easily available abortion as the latest triumph of human progress.

6. Indeed, it is possible to argue for vegetarianism without assuming that animals count for as much as people, as in Robert Nozick, *Anarchy, State and Utopia* (Oxford, 1974), pp. 36–38.

7. "Of Suicide," *Philosophical Works*, Thomas H. Green and Thomas H. Grose, eds. (Aalen, 1964), vol. 4, p. 410.

8. Nozick, pp. 39–41. As precise a statement of present conventional morality about animals as possible is the following: An animal is not to be caused or allowed to suffer, except where such suffering is necessary to some end other than sheer sadistic enjoyment of animal pain.

9. I have attempted a fuller discussion of the vegetarian argument in my "The Moral Basis of Vegetarianism Examined," *Philosophy*, Oct. 1978.

10. Roger Wertheimer, "Philosophy on Humanity," in Robert L. Perkins, ed., *Abortion* (Cambridge, Mass., 1974).

11. Letting *T* be the complex of traits we think of as distinctively human, these principles may be stated as follows. *Species principle:* All biological humans (or all members of species characterized by *T*) have a serious right to life. *Present enjoyment principle:* All creatures which presently enjoy the possession of *T* have a serious right to life. *Potentiality principle:* All creatures which potentially possess (now or will in due course possess) *T* have a serious right to life.

12. Joseph F. Fletcher, "Four Indicators of Humanhood—The Enquiry Matures," *Hastings Center Report*, Dec. 1974, p. 6.

13. In Bruce Hilton et al., eds., *Ethical Issues in Human Genetics* (New York, 1973), p. 113.

14. It is employed in Judith Jarvis Thomson, "A Defense of Abortion," *Philosophy & Public Affairs*, 1 (1971), 47–48, and in Marvin Kohl, *The Morality of Killing* (New York, 1974), p. 42. It also makes brief appearances in Roger Wertheimer, "Understanding the Abortion Argument," *Philosophy & Public Affairs*, 1 (1971), 74, 82.

15. Lawrence C. Becker, "Human Being: The Boundaries of the Concept," *Philosophy & Public Affairs*, 4 (1975), esp. pp. 337–345.

16. This kind of strategy turns out to be crucial in Vecors (pseud.), *You Shall Know Them*, Rita Barisse, tr. (Boston, 1953).

17. Michael Tooley thinks that adult polar bears for instance may be self-conscious ("A Defense of Abortion & Infanticide," p. 91). But the only workable criterion of self-consciousness that I can see is the use of a language involving something corresponding to the pronoun "I."

18. Paul Ziff, "The Feelings of Robots," in Alan R. Anderson, ed., *Minds and Machines* (Englewood Cliffs, N.J., 1964.)

19. Hubert L. Dreyfus, *What Computers Can't Do* (New York, 1972), esp. ch. 7.

20. Asimov's three laws of robotics are as follows: (1) A robot may not injure a human being or, through inaction, allow a human being to come to harm. (2) A robot must obey orders given it by human beings, except where such orders would conflict with the First Law. (3) A robot must protect its own existence, except where such protection conflicts with the First or Second Laws. See, e.g., Isaac Asimov, *I, Robot* (New York, 1950).

21. See Asimov, "That Thou Art Mindful of Him!" *Fantasy and Science Fiction*, May 1974; also in Edward L. Ferman and Barry N. Malzberg, eds., *Final Stage* (New York, 1974).

22. Despite Michael Scriven's suggestion ("The Compleat Robot," in Sidney Hook, ed., *Dimensions of Mind* [New York, 1960], p. 119) that a human mother might be thought of as manufacturing her offspring.

23. Lazlo Versényi, "Can Robots Be Moral?" *Ethics*, 84 (1974), esp. p. 251; cf. p. 255.

24. Fetal experimentation is an important issue in its own right, and someone's response to it will be closely linked to, although not I think uniquely determined by, his response to that of abortion. For recent discussion see LeRoy Walters, "Ethical Issues in Experimentation on the Human Fetus," *Journal of Religious Ethics*, Spring 1974; Paul Ramsey, *The Ethics of Fetal Research* (New Haven, 1975); "Fetal Research," *Hastings Center Report*, June 1975; David W. Louisell et al. "Fetal Research: Response to the Recommendations," *Hastings Center Report*, Oct. 1975; Peter Singer, "Bioethics: The Case of the Fetus," *New York Review*, Aug. 5, 1976.

25. Despite, e.g., Kohl, pp. 41–45 (arguing that a fetus is not a human being as a matter of ordinary English).

26. "A Defense of Abortion and Infanticide," pp. 54–55.

27. The expression "human persons" distinguishes the kinds of creatures we are from what may be called nonhuman persons: ghosts, angels, gods, and so forth. The ethics of our relations to such beings, should they exist, need not concern us here.

28. This argument is taken from Wertheimer, "Philosophy on Humanity," esp. pp. 110–113, where its conclusion is given the somewhat odd name of "Factunorm Principle."

29. The position I take in the text is, I think, consistent with the sophisticated form of relativism adopted by Gilbert Harman, "Moral Relativism Defended," *Philosophical Review*, 84 (1975), 3–22. According to Harman, one kind of moral judgment—what he calls an "inner judgment" makes sense only in terms of an implicit understanding or agreement to which the agent to whom the judgment is addressed is a party. Concerning nonparties there can only be external judgments: they are evil, savage, enemies, and the like. Harman's account includes the possibility of revising such agreements for the sake of coherence, and in this way he accounts for moral rules protecting those, such as animals, who are unable to bargain for their rights. His discussion of this point includes a provocative sentence asking us to "recall that infanticide used to be considered as acceptable as we consider abortion to be" (p. 21).

30. Scrutiny may reveal that those who practice infanticide in such contexts have some sense of wrongdoing, although they feel that they cannot help themselves. This is how the Eskimos seem to feel about killing their aged, though the old person to be killed consents. See Alexander H. Leighton and Charles C. Hughes, "Notes on Eskimo Patterns of Suicide," in Anthony Giddens, ed., *The Sociology of Suicide* (London, 1971), ch. 13, esp. p. 165.

31. I discuss moral blind alleys more fully in my "The Conscious Acceptance of Guilt in the Necessary Murder," *Ethics* (forthcoming).

32. "A Defense of Abortion and Infanticide," p. 165.

33. "Abortion and Infanticide," p. 44. Cf. "A Defense," pp. 59–60.

34. "A Defense," p. 60.

35. "Abortion and Infanticide," p. 49 n. 18.

36. Joel Feinberg, "The Rights of Animals and Unborn Generations," in William T. Blackstone, ed., *Philosophy & Environmental Crisis* (Athens, Ga., 1974), p. 62. Feinberg is talking about fetuses, but a fetus' property could also be so used, for instance, to pay the expenses of delivery.

37. "A Defense," p. 67.

38. Ibid.

39. And Joel Feinberg. See his "The Rights of Animals and Unborn Generations." Cf. also Richard B. Brandt, *Ethical Theory* (Englewood Cliffs, N.J., 1959), ch. 17.

40. See the various formulations of the self-consciousness requirement in "A Defense," pp. 59–60, esp. Requirement 3.

41. Mary Anne Warren, "On the Legal and Moral Status of Abortion," in Richard Wasserstorm, ed., *Today's Moral Problems* (New York, 1975), pp. 135, 136.

42. S. I. Benn, "Abortion, Infanticide, and Respect for Persons," in *The Problem of Abortion*; quotation p. 102.

43. Ronald Green, "Conferred Rights and the Fetus," *Journal of Religious Ethics*, Spring 1974; quotations pp. 62, 63, 68.

CHAPTER III. SCOPE OF THE PROHIBITION:
Fetuses and "Human Vegetables"

1. Joel Feinberg, ed., *The Problem of Abortion* (Belmont, Calif., 1973), p. 4.

2. "Individual:. . . An object which is determined by properties peculiar to itself and cannot be divided into others of the same kind" (OED). Thus bicycles, embryos of more than four weeks gestation, and infants are individuals, whereas water droplets, zygotes, and amoebas are not. Nor, by a natural extension of the same idea, are pairs of sperm and egg, since these can be split and rearranged to form other pairs.

3. Joel Feinberg, "The Rights of Animals and Unborn Generations," in William T. Blackstone, ed., *Philosophy and Environmental Crisis* (Athens, Ga., 1974), p. 55.

4. See Mortimer Adler, *The Difference of Man and the Difference It Makes* (New York, 1967). As Adler notices, the belief that man differs radically from brute animals would not be refuted by a discovery that dolphins (say) were not brute animals after all.

5. See Robert Morison, "Death: Process or Event?" and Leon R. Kass, "Death as an Event: A Commentary on Robert Morison," both in Richard W. Wertz, ed., *Readings on Ethical and Social Aspects of Bio-medicine* (Englewood Cliffs, N.J., 1973), pp. 105–109, 109–113.

6. Immanuel Kant, *Critique of Pure Reason*, A 650ff., B 678ff., Norman Kemp Smith, tr. (London, 1963).

7. The anomolous role of incest in the abortion discussion is pointed out by Roger Wertheimer, "Understanding the Abortion Argument," *Philosophy & Public Affairs*, 1 (1971), 90. One moderate writer goes so far as to sanction abortion against the woman's will where the pregnancy is incestuous in origin (George Huston Williams, "The Sacred Condominium," in John T. Noonan, Jr., ed., *The Morality of Abortion* [Cambridge, Mass., 1970], pp. 164-165). Cf. pp. 167-168 (compulsory abortion at the husband's option in cases of adulterous conception).

8. Marvin Kohl, *The Morality of Killing* (New York, 1974), p. 52, n. 4; p. 67. I discuss Judith Jarvis Thomson's superior feminist argument below, section 16 (2).

9. See Paul Ramsey, "Screening: An Ethicist's View," in Bruce Hilton et al., *Ethical Issues in Human Genetics* (New York, 1975), p. 154, citing Robert W. Stock, "Will the Baby Be Normal?" *New York Times Magazine*, March 2, 1969.

10. If the child were under ten, G. R. Grice would presumably think he could be (*Grounds of Moral Judgement* [Cambridge, Eng., 1967], pp. 147–150).

11. There does not appear to be any information on the sentencing of those, other than their parents, who kill children, since statistics on punishment are gathered according to the characteristics of the offender rather than those of the victim.

12. This is the argument made in Morison.

13. One of these rivals is "tutiorism," the view that one must not act unless one is sure beyond a reasonable doubt that one's action is right. There is also a range of intermediate positions.

14. Germain Grisez, *Abortion* (New York, 1970), pp. 306, 344. Both passages are in italics in the text.

15. So, following Hume, Derek Parfit, "Personal Identity," *Philosophical Review*, 80 (1971), 13–27.

16. These strategies are taken from John Perry, "Can the Self Divide?" *Journal of Philosophy*, 69 (1972), 463–488.

17. The move to which I am objecting is made by Lawrence C. Becker, "Human Being: The Boundaries of the Concept," *Philosophy & Public Affairs*, 4 (1975), esp. p. 340.

18. For a history of this distinction, see John T. Noonan, Jr., "An Almost Absolute Value in History," in *The Morality of Abortion*, pp. 6, 10, 15, 17, 20, 26–27.

19. Ludwig Wittgenstein, *Philosophical Investigations*, tr. G. E. M. Anscombe (New York, 1966), sec. 281. Cf. secs. 283, 420, p. 226.

20. John Rawls, A *Theory of Justice* (Cambridge, Mass., 1972), pp. 490–491.

21. John T. Noonan, Jr., *How to Argue about Abortion* (New York, 1974).

22. See Wertheimer, and Ronald Green, "Conferred Rights and the Fetus," *Journal of Religious Ethics*, Spring 1974 (contrasting the sympathy-arousing circumstances in which we view new-born infants). Green sees that the situation of doctors and nurses—who are asked actually to *perform* abortions—is rather different (pp. 7off.). His response to their problem seems to be to counsel self-deception.

23. Baruch Brody, *Abortion and the Sanctity of Human Life* (Cambridge, Mass., 1975), pp. 113-114.

24. H. Tristram Engelhardt, "Viability, Abortion, and the Difference between a Fetus and an Infant," *American Journal of Obstetrics and Gynecology*, 116 (1973), 432.

25. Ralph B. Potter, Jr., "The Abortion Debate," in Donald R. Cutler, ed., *Updating Life and Death* (Boston, 1969), p. 117.

26. *Jones v. Jones*, 114 N.Y.S. 2d 820 (1955).

27. See also the testimony from art and literature eloquently mustered by Noonan, *How to Argue Abortion*, pp. 17–19.

28. This suggestion is due to William T. Barker.

29. See for instance *Burns v. Alcala*, 95 S. Ct. 1180, 1187–1189 (Marshall, J. dissenting). Justice Marshall was part of the majority in the abortion decisions.

30. John Salmond, *Jurisprudence*, 11th ed., p. 355, quoted in *Problems of Abortion*, p. 7. Notice the pronouns, however.

31. *Keeler v. Superior Court*, 470 P. 2d 617 (Calif., 1970) (killing of unborn child by woman's estranged husband not murder), *State v. Dickinson*, 28 Ohio St. 65 (1970) (vehicular homicide). The *Keeler* holding has been reversed by statute, California Penal Code, sec. 187 (feticide under some circumstances murder).

32. Compare Kant's remarks on bastard infanticide in the *Metaphysical Elements of Justice*, John Ladd, tr. (New York, 1965), p. 106.

33. R. B. Brandt, "The Morality of Abortion," in Perkins, ed., *Abortion* pp. 166–168.

34. Cf. Michael Tooley, "A Defense of Abortion and Infanticide," *The Problem of Abortion*, pp. 60–62; and H. Tristram Engelhardt, Jr., "The Ontology of Abortion," *Ethics*, 84 (1974), 220–221.

35. "The Rights of Animals and Unborn Generations," p. 57. I speak here in a strictly secular context. To bring in such things as prayer for the repose of the dead man's soul would carry us outside the constraints I have imposed on the argument of this book.

36. This is the view Tooley ends up with. See "A Defense," p. 62, esp. Condition (2) (b).

37. Letter to the *New York Times*, March 9, 1967. Quoted, e.g., in Paul Ramsey, "Points in Deciding about Abortion," *The Morality of Abortion*, p. 79.

38. "A Defense of Abortion and Infanticide," pp. 63–64.

39. "Abortion and Infanticide" *Philosophy & Public Affairs*, 2 (1972), 60–61.

40. "A Defense," p. 84.

41. Ibid., p. 88.

42. By a pragmatic consideration I mean one that skirts a central divergence in perceptions, for instance the claim that slavery is economically inefficient.

43. "The Rights of Animals and Unborn Generations," p. 68.

44. Jérôme Lejeune reports receiving "a very badly written letter from [a mongol] girl, and the letter said in those bad letters that she could draw, 'I like you because you love the Mongol'" (*Ethical Issues in Human Genetics*, p. 213).

45. Becker, p. 353. Becker accepts the paradox (pp. 357–358).

46. Cf. "A Definition of Irreversible Coma," *Journal of the American Medical Association*, 205 (1968), 337–340; also in *Updating Life and Death*, ch. 3.

47. See Alexander Morgan Capron and Leon R. Kass, "A Statutory Definition of the Standards for Determining Human Death," *University of Pennsylvania Law Review*, 121 (1972), esp. pp. 104–108.

48. Hans Jonas, *Philosophical Essays* (Englewood Cliffs, N.J., 1974), p. 137.

49. Anthony Boucher's "Wolf-Wolf" is a person while in the wolf phase of his existence, without regard to his possible resumption of human form, since he retains the mental capacities of a human being. See *The Compleat Werewolf* (New York, 1972).

50. Portions of this and Chapter II are derived from my paper "Tooley on Infanticide," American Philosophical Association (Eastern Division), Dec. 1973.

CHAPTER IV. THE PRINCIPLE OF DOUBLE EFFECT

1. For the traditional formulations, see Francis Connell, *Outlines of Moral Theology* (Milwaukee, 1953), pp. 22–24. Recent discussions include Germain G. Grisez, "Toward a Consistent Natural Law Ethics of Killing," *American Journal of Jurisprudence*, 15 (1970), esp. p. 78; Grisez, *Abortion* (New York, 1970), pp. 321ff.; John Finnis, "The Rights and Wrongs of Abortion," *Philosophy & Public Affairs*, 2 (1973), 125–144.

2. In Judith Jarvis Thomson and Gerald Dworkin, eds., *Ethics* (New York, 1968). Views like Bennett's are quite common; see for instance R. M. Hare, "Reasons of State," *Applications of Moral Philosophy* (Berkeley, Calif., 1972), pp. 13–16, and Michael Tooley, discussed above, section 14.

3. Outside the ethics of homicide, the principle of double effect seems also to be employed in the doctrine of "equivocation." According to this doctrine, under circumstances where a direct untruth is not permissible, it may be permissible to use ambiguous expressions with the intention of leaving one's questioner in as much doubt after one's answer as before it. A useful discussion is Christopher Devlin, *The Life of Robert Southwell* (London, 1967), App. 'C.'

4. T. Lincoln Bouscaren, *The Ethics of Ectopic Operations* (Milwaukee, 1944). See the case cited by Bernard Häring, "A Theological Evaluation," in

John T. Noonan, Jr., ed., *The Morality of Abortion* (Cambridge, Mass., 1970), pp. 136–137 (removal of bleeding uterus vs. removal of fetus to contract the uterus and thus stop a hemorrhage).

5. *Philosophy & Public Affairs*, 1 (1971); quotations from p. 66.

6. See ibid., pp. 55–57.

7. Ibid., p. 66.

8. For an attempt to employ Thomson's line of reasoning in order to justify abortion to prevent the birth of a defective child, see Harry H. Wellington, "Common Law Rules and Constitutional Double Standards," *Yale Law Journal*, 83 (1973), 304ff.

9. Cf. Michael Tooley, "Abortion and Infanticide," *Philosophy & Public Affairs*, 2 (1972), 52–53 and n. 22.

10. Wellington, p. 308. Cf. Thomson's analogy between sexual intercourse followed by pregnancy and opening a window and letting a burglar (or people seeds) in ("A Defense of Abortion," pp. 58ff.).

11. John T. Noonan, Jr., *How to Argue about Abortion* (New York, 1974), pp. 2ff; quotation from p. 6.

12. *Depue v. Flateau*, 100 Minn. 299, 111 N.W. 1 (1907). Perhaps a more suitable example for Noonan's purposes is the following (taken from Robert Nozick, *Anarchy, State and Utopia* [Oxford, 1974], p. 180): the owner of an island may not drive a castaway back into the sea as a trespasser.

13. Thomson moves away from her position as I have described it in "Rights and Deaths," *Philosophy & Public Affairs*, 2 (1973), 146–159, and back toward it in "Killing, Letting Die, and the Trolley Problem," *Monist*, 59 (1976), 204–217.

14. See Thomas Nagel, "War and Massacre," *Philosophy & Public Affairs*, 1 (1972), 123–144, and articles following for a recent exploration of this set of problems.

15. Paul Ramsey, *The Just War* (New York, 1968).

16. Arthur C. Danto, "Basic Actions," in Alan R. White, ed., *The Philosophy of Action* (Oxford, 1968), ch. 2; "Freedom and Forebearance," in Keith Lehrer, ed., *Freedom and Determinism* (New York, 1966); "What We Can Do," *Journal of Philosophy*, 60 (1963), 435–445; *Analytical Philosophy of Action* (Cambridge, Eng., 1973).

17. This and the two previous points are taken from Eric D'Arcy, *Human Acts* (Oxford, 1963), pp. 10ff.

18. Cf. John E. Atwell, "The Accordion-Effect Thesis," *Philosophical Quarterly*, 19 (1969), 337–342.

19. Thomson, "Killing, Letting Die, and the Trolley Problem," Cases (5) and (6).

20. K. W. Rankin, *Choice and Chance* (Oxford, 1961), ch. 2, sec. 2. And see H. L. A. Hart, "The Ascription of Responsibility and Rights," in Anthony Flew, ed., *Logic and Language,* 1st and 2d series (Garden City, N.Y., 1965).

21. Glanville Williams, *Criminal Law: The General Part* (London, 1953), p. 13. On the vicissitudes of this rule of law, see The Law Commission, *Imputed Criminal Intent* (London, 1967). The Criminal Justice Act 1967 (U.K.), sec. 8, relieves the severity of this doctrine, but not by distinguishing foresight and intention.

22. *D. P. P.* v. *Smith.* (1961) A.C. 290, 302 (U.K.), quoted in Glanville Williams, *The Mental Element in Crime* (Jerusalem, 1965), p. 33, n. 2.

23. For further defense and exploration, see Anthony Kenny, "Intention and Purpose," *Journal of Philosophy,* 63 (1966), 642–651. A revised version of this article is published as "Intention and Purpose in Law," in Robert S. Summers, ed., *Essays in Legal Philosophy* (Berkeley, Calif., 1968).

24. *The Mental Element in Crime,* p. 15.

25. Jeremy Bentham, *Principles of Morals and Legislation,* J. H. Burns and H. L. A. Hart, eds. (London, 1970), ch. 8, secs. 6, 11.

26. John Austin, *Lectures on Jurisprudence,* I, 3d ed., Robert Campbell, ed. (London, 1869), p. 436.

27. Jack W. Meiland, *The Nature of Intention* (London, 1970), ch. 1.

28. Finnis, pp. 137–144.

29. "Rights and Deaths," p. 157.

30. Finnis, pp. 143–144.

31. "Toward a Consistent Natural Law Ethics of Killing," p. 66.

32. Ibid., p. 91; *Abortion,* pp. 335f. Grisez is strictly speaking not entitled to this result, since execution to prevent future crimes by the criminal himself is indirect on his analysis (Paul Ramsey). The difference between such a case and the killing of someone who has a loaded gun and is about to fire is not the structure of the killer's intention, but the fact that it will nearly always be possible to prevent such crimes without killing, even if we are sure that the criminal will commit them if given a chance. Of course, where nonlethal means for defending the community are available, Grisez is entitled to argue that such killing violates due proportion.

33. "Toward a Consistent Natural Law Ethics," pp. 89–90.

34. Cf. ibid., p. 90 (sacrificial adultery).

35. Ibid., p. 95.

36. Ibid., p. 94.

37. I owe this pair of examples, but not their analysis, to James G. Hanink; see his "Some Light on Double Effect," *Analysis,* 35 (1975), 151.

38. This paragraph is a response to Joseph M. Boyle, Jr., "The Double Effect Principle and the Crainiotomy Case," *Michigan Academy* (Philosophy Section), April 10, 1975. I wish to thank Dr. Boyle for a copy of this paper. See now his "Double Effect and a Certain Type of Embryotomy," *Irish Theological Quarterly*, 44 (1977), 303–318.

39. Cf. Bennett, p. 220.

40. G. E. M. Anscombe, "War and Murder," in Richard A. Wasserstrom, ed., *War and Morality* (Belmont, Calif., 1970), p. 50. But compare Peter Geach's suggestion that the providence of God can be relied upon to avoid moral blind alleys, though these are consistently conceivable (*God and the Soul* [London, 1969], p. 128). Geach can hardly claim that God's providence has always prevented refusal to do a wicked act from resulting in the death of the innocent, however.

41. Cited in Nagel, p. 131.

42. "We may plead that we trod on the snail inadvertently; but not on a baby.... Of course it *was* (*really*), if you like, inadvertence: but that word constitutes a plea, which is not going to be allowed, because of standards" (J. L. Austin, "A Plea for Excuses," *Philosophical Papers* [Oxford, 1971], pp. 142-143).

43. Bennett, p. 213.

44. D. H. Hodgson, *Consequences of Utilitarianism* (Oxford, 1967).

45. Defended in Harry S. Silverstein, "Simple and General Utilitarianism," *Philosophical Review*, 83 (1974), 339-363.

46. J. J. C. Smart, "Extreme and Restricted Utilitarianism," in Thomson and Dorkin, eds., *Ethics*, pp. 145–146. For a subtler, though no less devious, development of this same idea see Rolf Sartorius, *Individual Conduct and Social Norms* (Encino, Calif., 1975), ch. 4, esp. sec. 3.

47. Marvin Kohl seems to think that all rule-utilitarian arguments are like this; see his *Morality of Killing* (New York, 1974).

48. Bennett, pp. 227–228.

49. "Abortion and Infanticide Revisited," American Philosophical Association (Eastern Division), Dec. 1973. Cf. the example of the two patients needing each other's organs discussed by Daniel Dinello, "On Killing and Letting Die," *Analysis*, 31 (1971), 85–86.

50. P. J. Fitzgerald, "Acting and Refraining," *Analysis*, 27 (1967), 133–139.

51. For an attempt to treat the feeding of the starving as a duty of perfect obligation, see Peter Singer, "Famine, Affluence, and Morality," *Philosophy & Public Affairs*, 1 (1972), 229–243.

52. "A difference in intention can relate identical behavior in quite different ways to our moral attitude, and to the self being created through our moral attitude. If one intends to kill another, he accepts the identity of killer as

an aspect of his moral self. If he is to be a killer through his own self-determination, he must regard himself in any situation as the lord of life and of death" (Grisez, "Toward a Consistent Natural Law Ethics," p. 76).

CHAPTER V. JUSTIFICATIONS OF HOMICIDE:
Other Persons

1. G. E. M. Anscombe, "Does Oxford Moral Philosophy Corrupt the Youth?" *The Listener*, Feb. 14, 1957, p. 157.

2. Some of these are discussed in Judith Jarvis Thomson, "Killing, Letting Die, and the Trolley Problem," *Monist*, 59 (1976), 204–217.

3. G. E. M. Anscombe, "War and Murder," in Richard A. Wasserstrom, ed., *War and Morality* (Belmont, Calif., 1970), pp. 46–50.

4. Jan Narveson's claim that pacifism is inconsistent has been adequately answered by other writers. For the claim see Jan Narveson, "Pacifism: A Philosophical Analysis," in James Rachels, ed., *Moral Problems*, 2d ed. (New York, 1975), pp. 346–360. For replies, see Tom Regan, "A Defense of Pacifism," in Richard Wasserstrom, ed., *Today's Moral Problems* (New York, 1975), pp. 452–465, and Michael Martin, "On an Argument against Pacifism," *Philosophical Studies*, 26 (1974), 437–442.

5. Consider Anscombe's remark: "It is equally the case that the life of a ruler is usually a vicious life: but this does not show that ruling is as such vicious activity" ("War and Murder," p. 44).

6. Yale Kamisar, "Euthanasia Legislation: Some Non-Religious Objections," in A. B. Downing, ed., *Euthanasia and the Right to Death* (Los Angeles, 1970), p. 104.

7. Glanville Williams, "Euthanasia Legislation: Rejoinder to Non-Religious Objections," in ibid., p. 134, n. 1.

8. Mill's essay on Bentham, quoted in Anthony Flew, "The Principle of Euthanasia," in ibid., p. 48; emphasis mine. See Mill, *On Bentham and Coleridge*, F. R. Leavis, ed. (New York, 1962), p. 92.

9. Richard G. Henson, "Utilitarianism and the Wrongness of Killing," *Philosophical Review*, 80 (1971), 335–336.

10. Alan Donagan, "Is There a Credible Form of Utilitarianism?" in Michael D. Bayles, ed., *Contemporary Utilitarianism* (Garden City, N.Y., 1968), p. 188. "Murdering" should be "killing" here, since the question at issue is whether this sort of killing is justified.

11. This line of thought is suggested by Rolf Sartorius, *Individual Conduct and Social Norms* (Encino, Calif., 1975), ch. 4, esp. secs. 2,3.

12. In addition to Grisez's published writings, I have consulted an article in manuscript entitled "Against Consequentialism," now available in the *American Journal of Jurisprudence*, 23 (1978). I wish to thank Professor Grisez for sending me a typescript of this article.

13. Grisez could of course avoid the following argument by withdrawing his contention that skill in play is a basic human good. But it is not this premise which makes his view implausible: so far he has given an excellent explanation for our feeling that there is something distinctly low about throwing sports contests for money.

14. Consider Roger Wertheimer's use of the overpopulation argument in "Understanding the Abortion Argument," *Philosophy & Public Affairs*, 1 (1971), 94, n. 19.

15. Examples of arguments for euthanasia which emphasize the interests of those other than the patient include Williams, "Rejoinder to Non-Religious Objections," pp. 134ff., and Avral A. Morris, "Voluntary Euthanasia," in Jay Katz, ed., *Experimentation with Human Beings* (New York, 1972), pp. 717–718.

16. This case is due to Joseph Fletcher, *Situation Ethics* (Philadelphia, 1966), p. 133.

17. *Regina* v. *Dudley & Stephens*, 14 Q.B.D. 273 (1814). Lon Fuller, "The Case of the Speluncean Explorers," *Harvard Law Review*, 62 (1949), 616–645.

18. *United States* v. *Holmes*, 26 F. Cas. No. 15, 283 (1842).

19. Cf. James G. Hanink, "Persons, Rights, and the Problem of Abortion" (Michigan State University, Ph.D. diss., 1975), p. 315; also his "Some Light on Double Effect," *Analysis*, 35 (1975), 148–149.

20. Baruch A. Brody, "Abortion and the Sanctity of Life," in Joel Feinberg, ed., *The Problem of Abortion* (Belmont, Calif., 1973), pp. 104–120.

21. Cf. David Daube, *Collaboration with Tyranny in Jewish Law* (London, 1965). Hanink has argued ("Persons, Rights," p. 241) that, since the intended scapegoat has the right to defend himself against the villagers (even, it would seem, when they come to hand him over—this way of putting the issue does not seem to make possible a distinction between killing and handing over) they have no right to assault him. But first, this way of putting the issue seems to beg the important question, whether the villagers in this situation would be unjust aggressors. And, second, it is unclear that the scapegoat does have such a right in a situation where, as I am supposing, his resistance will do great damage and no good.

22. Cf. Hans Jonas, "Philosophical Reflections on Experimenting with Human Subjects," in Paul A. Freund, ed., *Experimentation with Human Subjects* (New York, 1970), esp. sec. XIV.

23. Cf. John Harris, "The Survival Lottery," *Philosophy*, 50 (1975), 81–87. The defense of this lottery in terms of intention is made on p. 86. For another reply, see James G. Hanink, "On the Survival Lottery," *Philosophy*, 51 (1976), 223–225.

24. G. E. M. Anscombe, "Modern Moral Philosophy," in Judith Jarvis Thomson and Gerald Dworkin, eds., *Ethics* (New York, 1968), pp. 206–207, n. 7.

25. This is the kind of situation where pastoral considerations enter in. See James F. Gustafson, "A Protestant Ethical Approach," and Bernard Häring, "A Theological Evaluation," both in John T. Noonan, Jr., ed., *The Morality of Abortion* (Cambridge, Mass., 1970), pp. 101–145.

26. Michael Walzer, "World War II: Why Was This War Different?" *Philosophy & Public Affairs*, 1 (1971), esp. p. 21. Cf. his "Political Action," *Philosophy & Public Affairs*, 2 (1973), 160–180.

27. Paul Ramsey, *The Just War* (New York, 1968), and "The Morality of Abortion," in *Moral Problems*, pp. 37–58.

28. Cf. Robert Nozick, *Anarchy, State, and Utopia* (Oxford, 1974), pp. 34–35.

29. Remoteness is perhaps not the crucial consideration (cf. ibid., pp. 126ff.), but for innocent threats it would have to be.

30. Thus Anscombe is vaguely—but only vaguely—right in the way she distinguishes private persons and rulers in "War and Murder," pp. 45–46.

31. This practice was formalized as a matter of law. See Halil Inalcik, *The Ottoman Empire*, Norman Itzkowitz and Colin Imber, trs. (New York, 1973), p. 59.

32. But cf. Jonathan Bennett, "Whatever the Consequences," in *Ethics*, p. 211, appearing to suggest that sometimes the woman's life should be sacrificed.

33. Albert Blumenthal, in Robert E. Cooke et al., *The Terrible Choice* (New York, 1968), p. 14. The necessity of answering this contention was pointed out to me by Hans Sluga.

34. Thomas Hobbes, *Leviathan*, Michael Oakeshott, ed. (London, 1962), p. 105.

35. John Locke, *Of Civil Government*, Second Essay, sec. 17 (Everyman's Library, London, 1936), p. 125.

36. Marvin Kohl, *The Morality of Killing* (New York, 1974), pp. 103–104.

37. Ibid., p. 62.

38. Ibid., pp. 27–28, citing John Hersey, *The Wall*. For some reason, Kohl has changed the baby's name. In the novel it is "Israel."

39. Page 179 n.

40. Thanks are here due to David Wieck, "The Negativity of Anarchism," *Interrogations*, Dec., 1975. Cf. also Giovanni Baldelli, *Social Anarchism*

(Chicago, 1971). In contrast with the idealized portrait of the anarchist drawn in the text, some professed anarchists (e.g., Baldelli)—and the "anarchist" Nozick uses as a foil—admit what looks very much like a state, albeit a somewhat rudimentary one. On the contrast between statelike protective associations and the state itself, and the slippage from one to the other, see Nozick, Pt. I.

41. Charles L. Black, Jr., *Capital Punishment* (New York, 1974), p. 96. Black is arguing within the context of present institutions; moreover, he does not consider the limited and special class of cases in which I have argued that capital punishment might be justified.

42. One opponent of capital punishment would be prepared to sanction the practice given even a strong possibility that such punishment would be an effective deterrent. See David A. Conway, "Capital Punishment and Deterrence," *Philosophy & Public Affairs*, 3 (1974), 431-443.

43. Cf. Anscombe, "War and Murder," p. 43.

44. For a conventionalist approach to noncombatant immunity, see George I. Mavrodoes, "Conventions and the Morality of War," *Philosophy & Public Affairs*, 4 (1975), 117–131.

45. See, e.g., Newton Garver, "What Violence Is," in *Today's Moral Problems*, pp. 410–423; John Harris, "The Marxist Conception of Violence," *Philosophy & Public Affairs*, 3 (1974), 192–220.

46. Ibn-Jamā'ah (1241-1333), quoted by Guenter Lewy, "Changing Conceptions of Political Legitimacy," in David Spitz, ed., *Political Theory and Social Change* (New York, 1967), 96.

47. *The Just War*, Pt. V.

48. "Moral Judgment in Time of War," in *War and Morality*, pp. 54–62.

49. French proverb, quoted from Julian Pitt-Rivers in Kohl, p. 33 and n. 6.

50. Ibid., p. 35 *et passim*.

51. I am here indebted to a discussion with E. S. Daigle.

CHAPTER VI. JUSTIFICATIONS OF HOMICIDE:
The Decedent Himself

1. See the Voluntary Euthanasia Bill, 1969, sec. 1 (2), in Marvin Kohl, ed., *Beneficent Euthanasia* (Buffalo, N.Y., 1975), p. 242.

2. Marvin Kohl, "Voluntary Beneficent Euthanasia," in ibid., p. 131.

3. Marvin Kohl, *The Morality of Killing* (New York, 1974), p. 81.

4. A subsidiary issue is whether it is proper to speak in this context of "mercy." Setting issues of substance to one side for the moment, one can use the word "mercy" as a synonym for kindness if one wishes, but it is on the whole

better not to, since its judicial overtones can only confuse discussion. The expression "mercy killing" is too well established to abandon, however.

5. For *reductio ad absurdum* of the attempt to further the cause of euthanasia through deftly chosen euphemisms, see Mary Rose Barrington, "New Words for New Ideas," in *Beneficent Euthanasia*, App. 2.

6. Richard Brandt, "A Moral Principle about Killing," in ibid., p. 114.

7. An extraordinary remedy is a remedy the agent has a proportionate reason to omit. The only means of prolonging life which are ordinary whatever the circumstances are not remedies but such things as food, water, and air ingested in the usual way.

8. For an argument to the conclusion that what looks like an act ending life (e.g., turning off a respirator) may in fact be better analyzed as an omission, see George P. Fletcher, "Prolonging Life," *Washington Law Review*, 42 (1967), 71–84; reprinted in A. B. Downing, ed., *Euthanasia and the Right to Death* (Los Angeles, 1970). See also Joseph V. Sullivan, *The Morality of Mercy Killing* (Westminister, Md., 1950), p. 72, Case (R).

9. For practical discussion, see the ethics of "pre-mortem care" (Paul Ramsey) outlined in Arthur Dyck, "Beneficent Euthanasia and Benemortasia," in *Beneficent Euthanasia*, pp. 124ff. See also R. G. Tycross, "A Plea for 'Eu Thanatos,'" *Month*, 136 (1975), 36–41, an essay that won a competition organized by the (English) Voluntary Euthanasia Society, even though it did not advocate (direct) mercy killing.

10. See his "Euthanasia," in Jay Katz, ed., *Experimentation with Human Beings* (New York, 1972), p. 74; also "Euthanasia and the Physician," in *Beneficent Euthanasia*, p. 147.

11. "Euthanasia and the Physician," p. 154.

12. *Experimentation with Human Beings*, ch. 1.

13. Ibid., p. 47.

14. Kohl, "Voluntary Beneficent Euthanasia," p. 134. Later on, Kohl drops the clumsy "noninvoluntary" in favor of the confusing "voluntary" as a way of expressing this concept. But this is clearly a case where clumsiness is to be preferred to confusion.

15. This is the *Paight* case (1950), cited in Yale Kamisar, "Euthanasia Legislation: Some Non-Religious Objections," *Euthanasia and the Right to Death*, pp. 108–109. Carol Ann Paight insisted that "Daddy must never know he had cancer" (p. 129, n. 91) and so killed him, in part to keep him from finding out.

16. T. Goodrich, "The Morality of Killing," *Philosophy*, 44 (1969), 136.

17. *The Morality of Killing*, p. 82.

18. "Voluntary Beneficent Euthanasia," p. 132.

19. Ibid., p. 131.
20. This is Brandt's example ("A Moral Principle," p. 109).
21. Brody, "Voluntary Euthanasia and the Law," in *Beneficent Euthanasia*. For a very different discussion of the same problem by the same author, see his "Morality and Religion Reconsidered," in Baruch Brody, ed., *Philosophy of Religion* (Englewood Cliffs, N.J., 1974), sec. 5.10.
22. "Voluntary Euthanasia and the Law," p. 222.
23. Cf. Robert Nozick, *Anarchy, State, and Utopia* (Oxford, 1974), esp. p. 341, n. 12.
24. This example is taken from Paul Ramsey, *The Patient as Person* (New Haven, 1975), pp. 188–190.
25. Kamisar, esp. pp. 106–116.
26. *The Morality of Killing*, p. 50.
27. Anthony Flew, "The Principle of Euthanasia," in *Euthanasia and the Right to Death*, p. 47, n. 14.
28. Glanville Williams, "Euthanasia Legislation: Reply to Non-Religious Objections," in *Euthanasia and the Right to Death*, p. 143.
29. Sissela Bok, "The Leading Edge of the Wedge," *Hastings Center Report*, Dec. 1971.
30. See, e.g., *Cohen v. California*, 403 U.S. 15, 24–25 (a jacket inscribed "Fuck the Draft").
31. George Orwell, "Freedom of the Press," *New York Times Magazine*, Oct. 8, 1972, p. 74.
32. *New York Times*, Feb. 14, 1939; quoted in Kamisar, p. 108. The reasoning here is spelled out more fully in Kohl, "Voluntary Beneficent Euthanasia," pp. 135–136.
33. Sterilization is Glanville Williams's example. See his "Reply to Non-Religious Objections," pp. 144–145.
34. Page 31.
35. Harry Roberts, *Euthanasia and Other Aspects of Life and Death* (London, 1936), pp. 14–15; quoted in Kamisar, p. 91.
36. Cf: "Most of the literature discussing voluntary euthanasia has concerned the 'merciful release' of those who are painfully diseased. Yet this is only part of the wider problem of easing the passage of all those who are burdened with the ills associated with age" (Glanville Williams, "Euthanasia and Abortion," *University of Colorado Law Review*, 38 [1966], 184).
37. The case from *Man's Fate* is cited somewhat out of context. For one of the recurring themes of the novel is that the characters are unable to express love or friendship except by hurting one another. So that when Katow gives Souen poison, his act is a deeply ambiguous, although to be sure self-sacrificial, one.

38. Richard B. Brandt, *Ethical Theory* (Englewood Cliffs, N.J., 1959), p. 449, n. 3.

39. This appears to be the position taken in *On Dying Well* (London, 1975).

40. G. R. Dunstan, *The Artifice of Ethics* (London, 1974), p. 89.

41. Ludwig Wittgenstein, *Notebooks 1914–1916*, G. H. von Wright and G. E. M. Anscombe, eds., G. E. M. Anscombe, tr. (New York, 1969), p. 91.

42. A. Alvarez, *The Savage God* (New York, 1972).

43. In Scripture, the suicide of Saul is not blamed. But the reluctance of his armor-bearer to assist is reported, I think with approval, and the man who claims to have killed Saul at his own request is punished by David (I Sam. 31: 4; II Sam. 1:16).

44. Consider R. v. *Nbakwa* (1956) 2 S. A. 557 (Southern Rhodesia), cited in H. L. A. Hart and A. M. Honoré, *Causation in the Law* (Oxford, 1962), pp. 294–295. In this case the accused "had lost his daughter and accused his mother of killing her. His mother did not deny the charge but promised to commit suicide. Eight days later, his mother still not having committed suicide, he fetched a rope, tied a noose to the end and said to her: 'I have already fixed the rope. Get up and hang yourself', which she did." Whether such a man is legally guilty of murder—the Southern Rhodesian Court held that he was not—he is surely morally so guilty, or would be in this culture. Cf. *Commonwealth* v. *Bowen* 13 Mass. 356 (1816).

45. George Denison, "In Memory of Paul Goodman," *New York Review*, Dec. 13, 1973, p. 51.

46. See Kurt Baier, *The Moral Point of View* (Ithaca, N.Y., 1969), ch. 9; Marcus G. Singer, *Generalization in Ethics* (New York, 1961), pp. 311–318.

47. The matter is pursued further in W. D. Falk, "Morality, Self, and Others," in Judith Thomson and Gerald Dworkin, eds., *Ethics* (New York, 1968), pp. 349–390. See Thomas E. Hill, Jr., "Servility and Self-Respect," *Monist*, 57 (1973), 87-104, for a defense of duties to oneself from another angle.

48. Cf. Sullivan, p. 71, Case (O).

49. Consider the suicide of Charles Wertenbaker, cited and discussed in R. F. Holland, "Suicide," in James Rachels, ed., *Moral Problems*, 2d ed. (New York, 1975), pp. 398–400.

50. See *New York Times*, Feb. 10, 1975.

51. Richard Brandt, "The Morality and Rationality of Suicide," *Moral Problems*, p. 386; Joel Feinberg, *Social Philosophy* (Englewood Cliffs, N.J., 1973), p. 51.

52. Consider, e.g., Walter C. Alvarez, "The Right to Die," in Maurice Visscher, ed., *Humanistic Perspectives in Medical Ethics* (Buffalo, N.Y., 1972), pp. 67–68: "Right now I know of a woman who is not insane enough to be put in a hospital. Instead, she will live for some months with a married sister, and as a result her brother-in-law generally must leave the house and go to his club, where he remains until the half-insane woman is transferred to the home of another sister. If this psychotic person were to ask for voluntary suicide, I would be for granting her the right, because she is mildly insane and for no useful reason she is almost ruining the lives of others."

53. Cf. Williams, "Reply to Non-Religious Objections," p. 143.

54. For further discussion see R. M. Hare, "Pain and Evil," in Joel Feinberg, ed., *Moral Concepts* (Oxford, 1969), ch. 2.

55. This example is due to Hans Sluga.

56. David Hume, "Of Suicide," in *Philosophical Works*, Thomas H. Green and Thomas H. Grose, eds. (Aalen, 1964), vol. 4, p. 414. Seneca says: "Not only the prudent or the brave or the unhappy man may wish to die, but also the one who is surfeited" (*Ad Lucillium Epistulae Morales*, LXVII, Loeb Classical Library ed., vol. 2 [London, 1920], p. 173; my translation).

57. "Euthanasia and the Physician," p. 161.

CHAPTER VII. CONCLUSION

1. Next to abortion, the forms of private homicide whose legal aspects have received the most attention are suicide and euthanasia. I have said what I have to say about their legal aspects in Chapter VI.

2. On abortion and the law, see Baruch Brody, *Abortion and the Sanctity of Human Life* (Cambridge, Mass., 1975), chs. 3, 10; and John Finnis, "Three Schemes of Regulation," in John T. Noonan, Jr., ed., *The Morality of Abortion* (Cambridge, Mass., 1970). On the constitutional aspects, see John Hart Ely, "The Wages of Crying Wolf," *Yale Law Journal*, 82 (1973), 923–947.

3. Selective conscientious objection is discussed in detail in David Malle-ment, "Selective Conscientious Objection and the *Gillette* Decision," *Philosophy & Public Affairs*, 1 (1972), 363–386.

4. United States Commission on Civil Rights, *Constitutional Aspects of the Right to Limit Childbearing* (Washington, D.C., 1975), p. 27. A similar argument is made at length in Laurence H. Tribe, "Toward a Model of Roles in the Due Process of Life and Law," *Harvard Law Review*, 87 (1973), 1–53. No anti-abortion law requires anyone to *believe* anything, of course.

5. Marvin Kohl, *The Morality of Killing* (New York, 1974), p. 102.

6. See Lewis Perry, *Radical Abolitionism* (Ithaca, 1973), esp. pp. 33–54.

7. Tribe, p. 20.

8. John Rawls, A *Theory of Justice* (Cambridge, Mass., 1972), p. 3.

9. Charles Fried, *Medical Experimentation* (Amsterdam, 1974), p. 140.

10. W. G. Maclagan, "Respect for Persons as a Moral Principle," *Philosophy*, 35 (1960), 208–209.

11. P. F. Strawson, "Freedom and Resentment," *Proceedings of the British Academy* (1962), esp. pp. 205–211; Michael S. Pritchard, "Human Dignity and Justice," *Ethics*, 82 (1972), esp. pp. 311–313; and Joel Feinberg, *Social Philosophy* (Englewood Cliffs, N.J., 1973), pp. 88–94.

Selected Bibliography

GENERAL

Abelson, Raziel, ed. *Ethics and Meta-ethics.* New York, 1966.

Aristotle. *Nicomachean Ethics.* W. D. Ross, tr.

D'Arcy, Eric. *Human Acts.* Oxford, 1963.

Daube, David. *Collaboration with Tyranny in Jewish Law.* Oxford, 1965.

Dunstan, G. R. *The Artifice of Ethics.* London, 1974.

Feinberg, Joel, ed. *Moral Concepts.* Oxford, 1969.

Grice, G. R. *The Grounds of Moral Judgement.* Cambridge, Eng., 1967.

Grisez, Germain. "Against Consequentialism," *American Journal of Jurisprudence,* 23 (1978).

———. "The First Principle of the Practical Reason." In Anthony Kenny, ed., *Aquinas.* Garden City, N.Y., 1969.

Harman, Gilbert. "Moral Relativism Defended." *Philosophical Review,* 84 (1975), 3–22.

Hobbes, Thomas. *Leviathan.* Michael Oakeshott, ed. London, 1969.

Hodgson, D. H. *Consequences of Utilitarianism.* Oxford, 1967.

Holmes, Oliver Wendell, Jr. *The Common Law.* Boston, 1926. Esp. ch. 2.

Locke, John. *Of Civil Government.* Everyman's Library ed. London, 1936.

McCormick, Richard A., S.J. "Ambiguity in Moral Choice." Père Marquette Theology Lecture, 1973.

Melden, A. I., ed. *Human Rights.* Belmont, Calif., 1970.

Narveson, Jan. *Morality and Utility.* Baltimore, 1967.

Nozick, Robert. *Anarchy, State, and Utopia.* Oxford, 1974.

Philosophy & Public Affairs. Princeton, 1971ff.

Rachels, James. *Moral Problems.* New York, 1971; 2d ed., 1975. Both editions should be consulted.

Rawls, John. *A Theory of Justice.* Cambridge, Mass., 1972.

Sartorius, Rolf E. *Individual Conduct and Social Norms.* Encino, Calif., 1975.

Thomas Aquinas. *Treatise on Law.* Chicago, 1970.

Thomson, Judith J., and Gerald Dworkin, eds. *Ethics.* New York, 1968.

Wasserstrom, Richard, ed. *Today's Moral Problems.* New York, 1975.

Williams, Glanville. *The Mental Element in Crime.* Jerusalem, 1965.

LIFE, DEATH, AND KILLING

American Law Institute. *Model Penal Code*. Art. 210, sec. 207.11.

Barth, Karl. *Church Dogmatics*. Ch. 12, sec. 55(2). G. W. Bromiley and T. F. Torrance, eds. and trs. Vol. III/4. Edinburgh, 1961.

British Broadcasting Corporation. *Morals and Medicine*. London, 1970.

Capron, Alexander Morgan, and Leon R. Kass. "A Statutory Definition of the Standards for Determining Human Death." *University of Pennsylvania Law Review*, 121′ (1972), 87ff.

Culter, Donald R., ed. *Updating Life and Death*. Boston, 1969.

Edwards, Paul. "'My Death.'" In Paul Edwards, ed., *The Encyclopedia of Philosophy*. New York, 1967. Vol. 5.

Ewin, R. E. "What Is Wrong with Killing People?" *Philosophical Quarterly*, 22 (1972), 126–139.

Glover, Jonathan. *Causing Death and Saving Lives*. Harmondsworth, 1977.

Goodrich, T. "The Morality of Killing." *Philosophy*, 41 (1969), 127–139.

Grisez, Germain. "Toward a Consistent Natural Law Ethics of Killing." *American Journal of Jurisprudence*, 15 (1970), 64–96.

Hall, Elizabeth, with Paul Cameron. "Our Failing Reverence for Life." *Psychology Today*, April 1976.

Hastings Center Institute. *Report. Studies*. Bibliographies. Reprint Series. Hastings-On-Hudson. N.Y., 1970ff.

Henson, Richard G. "Utilitarianism and the Ethics of Killing." *Philosophical Review*, 80 (1971), 320–337.

Hilton, Bruce, et al., eds. *Ethical Issues in Human Genetics*. New York, 1973.

Human Life Review. Published by the Human Life Foundation, Washington, D.C., 1975ff.

Kadish, Sanford H. "Respect for Life and Regard for Persons in the Criminal Law." *California Law Review*, 64 (1976), 871–901.

Katz, Jay. *Experimentation with Human Beings*. New York, 1972.

Kluge, Eike-Henner W. *The Practice of Death*. New Haven, 1975.

Kohl, Marvin. *The Morality of Killing*. New York, 1974.

Lucretius. *De Rerum Natura*.

McCloskey, H. J. "The Right to Life." *Mind*, 84 (1975), 403–425.

Meyers, David. *The Human Body and the Law*. Chicago, 1972.

Morison, Robert. "Death: Process or Event?" and Leon R. Kass, "Death as an Event: A Commentary on Robert Morison." Both in Richard W. Wertz, ed. *Readings on Ethical and Social Aspects of Biomedicine*. Englewood Cliffs, N.J., 1973. Pp. 105–113.

"Philosophical Problems of Death." *Monist*, April 1976.

Ramsey, Paul. *The Patient as Person*. New Haven, 1975.

235

"Selected Issues in Medical Ethics." *Journal of Religious Ethics,* Spring 1974.

Shils, Edward, et al. *Life or Death: Ethics and Options.* Seattle, 1968.

Sumner, L. W. "A Matter of Life and Death." *Noûs,* 10 (1976), 145–171.

Suter, Ronald. "Moore's Defense of the Rule 'Do No Murder.'" *Personalist,* 54 (1973), 361–375.

Thomas Aquinas. *Summa Theologiae.* II IIae Q 64. In Blackfriars *Summa,* vol. 38. New York, 1975.

Unamuno, Miguel de. *The Tragic Sense of Life.* Anthony Kerrigan, tr.; Anthony Kerrigan and Martin Nozick, eds. Princeton, 1972.

Van Evra, James. "On Death as a Limit." *Analysis,* 31 (1971), 170–176.

Williams, Glanville. "Euthanasia and Abortion." *University of Colorado Law Review,* 38 (1966), 178ff.

——. *The Sanctity of Life and the Criminal Law.* New York, 1957.

CASES: *D.P.P.* v. *Smith* (1961) A.C. 290 (U.K.).

Matter of Quinlan, 355 A. 2d. 647 (New Jersey, 1976).

Parker v. *The Queen,* 111 C.L.R. 610 (Australia, 1965).

Regina v. *Dudley and Stephens,* 14 Q.B.D. 273 (1814).

United States v. *Holmes,* 26 F. Cas. No. 15,283 (1842).

ABORTION

Brody, Baruch. *Abortion and the Sanctity of Human Life.* Cambridge, Mass., 1975.

Cohen, Marshall, Thomas Nagel, and Thomas Scanlon, eds. *The Rights and Wrongs of Abortion.* Princeton, 1974. Contains articles from *Philosophy & Public Affairs.*

Denes, Magda. "Performing Abortions." *Commentary,* Oct. 1976.

Ely, John Hart. "The Wages of Crying Wolf." *Yale Law Journal,* 82 (1973), 923–947.

Feinberg, Joel, ed. *The Problem of Abortion.* Belmont, Calif., 1973.

Grisez, Germain. *Abortion.* New York, 1970.

Hanink, James G. "Persons, Rights and the Problem of Abortion." Ph.D. diss., Michigan State University, 1975.

Hellegers, André. "Fetal Development." *Theological Studies,* 30 (1970), 3–9.

Newton, Lisa. "Abortion in the Law." *Ethics,* 87 (1977), 244–250.

——. "Humans and Persons." *Ethics,* 85 (1975), 332–336.

Noonan, John T., Jr. *How to Argue about Abortion.* New York, 1974.

——, ed. *The Morality of Abortion.* Cambridge, Mass., 1970.

Perkins, Robert L., ed. *Abortion.* Cambridge, Mass., 1974.

Pluhar, Werner. "Abortion and Simple Consciousness." *Journal of Philosophy,* 24 (1977), 159–172.

Ramsey, Paul. *The Ethics of Fetal Research*. New Haven, 1975.

Sartre, Jean-Paul. *The Age of Reason*. Eric Sutton, tr. London, 1970.

Warren, Mary Anne. "On the Moral and Legal Status of Abortion." *Monist*, 57 (1973), 43–61. Reprinted with a postscript in *Today's Moral Problems*.

CASES: *Beal* v. *Doe*, 15 U.S.L.W. 4781 (1977), and companion cases.

Commonwealth v. *Edelin*, 359 N.E. 4 (Massachusetts, 1976).

Doe v. *Bolton*, 410 U.S. 179 (1973).

Judgment, Constitutional Court, German Federal Republic, February 25, 1975; Robert E. Jonas and John D. Gorby, trs. *John Marshall Journal*, 9 (1976), 605–684.

Morgentaler v. *The Queen*, 53 D.L.R. 3d 161 (Canada, 1975).

Planned Parenthood v. *Danforth*, 428 U.S. 52 (1976), and companion cases.

Roe v. *Wade*, 410 U.S. 113 (1973).

STATUS OF NONHUMANS

Adler, Mortimer. *The Difference of Man and the Difference It Makes*. New York, 1967.

Anderson, Alan R., ed. *Minds and Machines*. Englewood Cliffs, N. J., 1964.

Asimov, Isaac. *I, Robot*. New York, 1950.

Barkas, Janet. *The Vegetable Passion*. London, 1975.

Devine, Philip E. "The Moral Basis of Vegetarianism Examined." *Philosophy*, Oct. 1978.

Donaghy, Kevin. "Singer on Speciesism." *Philosophic Exchange*, Summer 1974. Pp. 125–127.

Dreyfus, Hubert. *What Computers Can't Do*. New York, 1972.

Feinberg, Joel. "The Rights of Animals and Unborn Generations." In William T. Blackstone, ed., *Philosophy and Environmental Crisis*. Athens, Ga., 1974.

Godlovitch, Stanley and Roslind, and John Harris, eds. *Animals, Men and Morals*. New York, 1971.

Hook, Sidney, ed. *Dimensions of Mind*. New York, 1960.

Maincas, Peter T. "Men, Machines, Materialism, and Morality." *Philosophy and Phenomenological Research*, 27 (1966), 238–246.

Passmore, John. "The Treatment of Animals." *Journal of the History of Ideas*, 36 (1975), 195–218.

Putnam, Hilary. "Robots: Machines or Artificially Created Life?" In Stuart Hampshire, ed., *Philosophy of Mind*. New York, 1966.

Regan, Tom. "The Moral Basis of Vegetarianism." *Canadian Journal of Philosophy*, 5 (1975), 181–214.

SELECTED BIBLIOGRAPHY

——, and Peter Singer, eds. *Animal Rights and Human Obligations.* Englewood Cliffs, N.J., 1976.

Singer, Peter. *Animal Liberation.* New York, 1975.

——. Review of *Animals, Men and Morals. New York Review of Books,* April 5, 1973. Reprinted with a postscript in Rachels, 2d ed.

Steinbock, Bonnie. "Speciesism and the Idea of Equality." *Philosophy,* 53 (1978), 247–256.

Stone, Christopher D. "Should Trees Have Standing?" *Southern California Law Review,* 45 (1972), 450ff.

Vecors (pseud.). *You Shall Know Them.* Rita Barisse, tr. Boston, 1953.

Versényi, Lazlo. "Can Robots Be Moral?" *Ethics,* 84 (1974), 248–259.

CASE: *Sierra Club* v. *Morton,* 405 U.S. 727 (1972).

WAR, CAPITAL PUNISHMENT, AND POLITICAL VIOLENCE

Barzun, Jacques. "In Favor of Capital Punishment." *American Scholar,* 32 (1962), 181–191.

Beduau, Hugo Adam. *The Death Penalty in America.* Rev. ed. Chicago, 1976.

Black, Charles L., Jr. *Capital Punishment.* New York, 1974.

Cohen, Marshall, Thomas Nagel, and Thomas Scanlon. *War and Moral Responsibility.* Princeton, 1974. Contains articles from *Philosophy & Public Affairs.*

Conway, David. "Capital Punishment and Deterrence." *Philosophy & Public Affairs,* 3 (1974), 431–443.

Gross, Feliks. *Violence in Politics.* The Hague, 1972.

Howe, Irving. "The Return of Terror." *Dissent,* 22 (1975), 227–237.

Joll, James. *The Anarchists.* Boston, 1964. Esp. ch. 5.

Laqueur, Walter. "The Futility of Terrorism." *Harper's Magazine,* March 1976. Pp. 99ff.

McWilliams, W. Carey. "The Politics of Assassination." *Commonweal,* 102 (1975).

Ramsey, Paul. *The Just War.* New York, 1968.

——. *War and the Christian Conscience.* Durham, N.C., 1961.

Sullivan, Shaun J., O.F.M. *Killing in Defence of Private Property.* Missoula, Mont., 1976.

Taylor, Telford. *Nuremburg and Vietnam.* Chicago, 1970.

Walzer, Michael. *Just and Unjust Wars,* New York, 1977.

——, ed. *Regicide and Revolution.* Cambridge, Eng., 1974.

Wasserstrom, Richard, ed. *War and Morality.* Belmont, Calif., 1970.

Woods, Martin T., and Robert Buckenmeyer. *The Morality of Peace and War.* Santa Barbara, Calif., 1974.

Zellner, Harold N., ed. *Assassination.* Cambridge, Mass., 1974.

CASES: *Coker* v. *Georgia,* 45 U.S.L.W. 4961 (1977).

Furman v. *Georgia,* 408 U.S. 238 (1972).

Gilmore v. *Utah,* 97 S.Ct. 436 (1976).

Goering et al., Judgment of the International Military Tribunal (1946).

Gregg v. *Georgia,* 96 S. Ct. 2909 (1976), and companion cases.

SUICIDE AND EUTHANASIA

Alvarez, A. *The Savage God.* New York, 1972.

Beauchamp, Tom L. "Analysis of Hume's 'Essay on Suicide.'" *Review of Metaphysics,* 30 (1976), 73–95.

Behnke, John A., and Sissela Bok, eds. *The Dilemmas of Euthanasia.* Garden City, N.Y., 1975.

Daube, David. "The Linguistics of Suicide." *Philosophy & Public Affairs,* 1 (1972), 387–437.

Downing, A. B., ed. *Euthanasia and the Right to Death.* Los Angeles, 1970.

Grisez, Germain. "Suicide and Euthanasia." Forthcoming.

Hogan, Michael, S.J. *The Ecclesiastical Review on Morality of Hunger-Strike.* Jersey City, N.J., ca. 1933.

Hume, David. "Of Suicide." In *Philosophical Works.* Thomas H. Green and Thomas H. Grose, eds. Aalen, 1964. Vol. 4.

Kohl, Marvin, ed. *Beneficent Euthanasia.* Buffalo, N.Y., 1975.

On Dying Well. London, 1975.

Plato. *Phaedo.*

Seneca. *Ad Lucillium Epistulae Morales.* Loeb Classical Library ed. London, 1920.

Sprott, S. E. *The English Debate on Suicide from Donne to Hume.* La Salle, Ill., 1961.

Sullivan, Joseph V. *The Morality of Mercy Killing.* Westminister, Md., 1950.

CASES: *Commonwealth* v. *Bowen,* 13 Mass. 353 (1816).

Paight (1950) in Kamisar, "Euthanasia Legislation: Some Non-Religious Objections" in *Euthanasia and the Right to Death.*

People v. *Werner,* Crim. No. 58-3636, Cook Co. Ct., Ill. (1958), in Meyers, *The Human Body and the Law.*

R. v. *Nbakwa* (1956) 2 S.A. 557 (Southern Rhodesia).

Repouille v. *United States,* 165 F 2d. 153 (1947).

Index

241